Chesapeake Rumrunners
of the
Roaring Twenties

The steam yacht *Istar* was called "queen of the rumrunners."

CHESAPEAKE RUMRUNNERS

OF THE
ROARING TWENTIES

ERIC MILLS

TIDEWATER PUBLISHERS
CENTREVILLE, MARYLAND

Library of Congress Cataloging-in-Publication Data

Mills, Eric, 1959–
      Chesapeake rumrunners of the Roaring Twenties / Eric Mills.—1st ed.
          p. cm.
      Includes bibliographical references and index.
      ISBN 0-87033-518-9 (hc)
      1. Smuggling—Chesapeake Bay (Md. and Va.)   2. Prohibition—Chesapeake Bay (Md. and Va.)   I. Title.

HJ6690 .M55 1999
364.1'33—dc21   99-048511

Manufactured in the United States of America
First edition

To
George Howard Gillelan (1917-1998)
archer, author, mentor, friend—and above all, father of the bride

CONTENTS

PREFACE

With its long, nook-and-cranny coastline and its optimally situated mid-Atlantic location, Chesapeake Bay is naturally conducive to the practice of the smugglers' art. Of this reality I was made continually aware while writing *Chesapeake Bay in the Civil War*. During the great conflict, smuggling was rampant upon the Bay, this border-zone water highway linking North and South. Leap ahead to modern times, and innuendo still gives smugglers their currency, for there are frequent, hushed mentions of slick vessels, high-end drug shipments, and clandestine Chesapeake landings. Between the years of log canoes sneaking musket-caps and oysters to old Richmond, and the days of speedboats and pleasure yachts supplying cocaine and marijuana to the East Coast corridor, there was, in the Bay country, a golden age of smugglers and smuggling, an epoch when the hard-knuckle "go-through guys" on the water were joined in their efforts by a reckless new breed of automobile confreres on land. In this age the prevailing contraband was neither war necessities nor narcotics, but that wide family of potables collectively known as "demon rum" to detractors and "the liquid that cheers" to law-ignoring consumers. The contraband was hooch.

Chesapeake Bay and Prohibition-era rumrunners were ideally mated. I was drawn by the marriage of place (the Bay) and time (the Roaring Twenties), and it led me to a fascinating research project. I first tumbled to the idea via indigenous lore, tales still told among locals about so-and-so's daddy who ran moonshine, or so-and-so's grand-daddy who was a big bootlegger in these parts. I wanted to follow the smoke trail to the fire. I wanted to find the facts that fed the folklore and learn what I could about the dimly remembered lawbreakers, the forgot-ten wild ones of regional history. I found Chesapeake watermen and New York syndicate toughs, English aristocrats and crooked cops, holdup men and moonshine artists, and a fleet of vessels big and small, all involved in punching through the product, all engaged in the life. Be-cause of them, the Twenties roared in the Bay country. Compared to these enterprising hellions of yore, we are, most of us, tame souls.

The fruition of this book was achieved through the support and co-operation of the following people, to whom I am grateful:

- Richard Peuser, archivist with the Old Navy Maritime Records at the National Archives, who steered me ably through the volumi-nous material in the Records of the United States Coast Guard;
- Dr. Robert Browning, chief historian of the U.S. Coast Guard, for advice and the supplying of cartography;
- the helpful staffs of the Library of Congress, the National Ar-chives Still Pictures Branch, the Maryland State Archives, and the Maryland Historical Society;
- photographer Christopher Tyree for his superlative lens work; likewise Thomas Miller for his photographic expertise;
- Geneva Hall, a charming lady who graciously welcomed me for an interview session;
- Milford Elliott, a gentleman of the Chesapeake, a rugged veteran of the water and a celebrated boatbuilder, who was willing to share his memories of yesterday;
- Joseph Norris, Warren Parker, Ty Pruitt, Bruce Scheible, and all others who agreed to reminisce for me, both on and off the re-cord;
- my former colleagues at the Chesapeake Bay Maritime Museum for their encouragement early on in the project—particularly

Mark Adams, who introduced me to Milford Elliott, and Pete Lesher, who made me aware of, and availed me of, a pertinent bit of rare old photography;

- Terry and Barbara Mullikin, who introduced me to Geneva Hall; Neil Keddie, who introduced me to Warren Parker, whose insights to the lower Eastern Shore were illuminating;

- Jerry Keiser, Maryland Room librarian at the Talbot County Free Library in Easton, Maryland, for bringing to my attention a long-lost, rarely seen newspaper clipping;

- sundry family members on both sides, who offered encouragement and, in several cases, hospitality as well;

- and above all, my wife Harriet, for living through another book creation, for believing in my work, and for making life a joy even when I was chin-deep in the labors of research and writing.

CHESAPEAKE RUMRUNNERS

OF THE
ROARING TWENTIES

CHAPTER ONE

"I LOVE TO HATE YOU"

Satan walked through Norfolk, Virginia. It was a wet, gray Friday in January, and the lord of all evil was here for a funeral. He led the procession tramping through crowded thoroughfares to the tabernacle. The coffin was twenty feet long. Satan wept. John Barleycorn was dead.

The funeral meant victory to the great orator now railing: Billy Sunday, the charismatic evangelist, one of the most powerful preachers in America and thus one of the most influential men in America. Thanks to an exhaustive touring schedule and to the modern miracle called radio, Sunday's fiery condemnations reached far and wide, solidifying heartland Christian opinion, rallying grassroots piety. Iowa-born, a former professional baseball player, Billy Sunday had the common touch and a silver-tongued oratorical talent that could make crowds cry, laugh, and repent, all within the course of one revival meeting. Billy Sunday was magnetic, hypnotic, a brilliant, eloquent speaker, and he had chosen to appear in this bustling port city of the lower Chesapeake Bay on this most profound of days. For twenty-six years he had devoted his far-famed talent for stentorian zealotry to the age's foremost holy crusade: the death of King Alcohol and the birth of a sober, moral nation. Friday, January 16, 1920, spelled jubilation for Billy Sunday and all others who had crusaded with ardor and grim certitude for so long. At exactly one minute past midnight, it would be real: Prohibition in the Constitution. John Barleycorn was dead.

To celebrate, Billy Sunday had arranged this bombastic show, this symbol-steeped ceremony attended by an overflow crowd of nearly fifteen thousand souls. The mock funeral procession through Norfolk began at one in the afternoon at Union Station, where the dead alcohol-god's "corpse" had arrived via "special train from Milwaukee." It took twenty freakishly costumed pallbearers to get the frighteningly huge casket on the carriage. The parade, the popping flashbulbs, the bawling actor in horns portraying His Satanic Majesty in defeat—all were part of Billy Sunday's impassioned victory theatrics. Police were needed for crowd control when the procession reached Sunday's tabernacle. The officers cleared the surging throng from the doorway, and the procession made its way down the aisle as thousands cheered. Satan wept. The absurdly garbed pallbearers set the coffin down on the platform and sang "John Barleycorn's Body Lies A-Moulding in the Clay." Three young girls came forward with roses and carnations from women's temperance organizations and gave them to Billy Sunday. The great preacher sermonized on into the night. People cried, shouted, sang. The great preacher stood over the giant coffin, and he said: "Good-bye, John. You were God's worst enemy. You were Hell's best friend. I hate you with a perfect hatred. I love to hate you."

America always drank. We brought it over on the boat and deemed it providential to have it, this elixir amid a harsh life. The musket, the Bible, the jug—they were all standard equipment. The colonial settlers perceived "ardent spirits" as healthful tonic for a panoply of ailments and woes. No less stern a personage than Puritan patriarch Increase Mather stated in 1673, "Drink is in itself a creature of God, and to be received with thankfulness." Alcoholic beverages were thought to have sublime restorative powers for those at hard labor, more healthy, even, than water itself. In the Chesapeake Bay country, at the Jamestown settlement in Virginia, the settlers griped when they requested beer and got only water; it was, they cried, "contrary to the nature of the English." In

Maryland, the colonial lifestyle-observer John Hammond noted that a clear distinction between the ideal wife and a bad one was whether she served up beer or water to the household; a Maryland husband subjected to mere water, noted Hammond, was the sign of a "sloathful and careless" housewife. Benjamin Franklin quipped, "If God had intended man to drink water, He would not have made him with an elbow capable of raising a wine glass." Farmers, doctors, clergymen, lawyers—men, women, blacks, native tribes—all drank in early America, and drank heavily by the standards of future, tamer generations. It is emblematic that the father of our country was a whiskey distiller. "The benefits arising from the moderate use of strong liquor . . . are not to be disputed," said George Washington, one of the more eminent pioneers of liquor trafficking in the Chesapeake watershed.

White men led the pack. Among white men it was cultural, traditional—as close to universal as a habit, or vice, can be. White men encouraged their young sons to drink, and to learn to drink early. It was a proud day when a father could bring his son along for the daily tavern sojourn, to bring him along as a mug-for-mug drinking equal. Indoctrination might begin in infancy; parents would rouse a slumbering one-year-old and dose him down with rum, whiskey, or brandy. Toddlers were induced to kill off the tail-end of a parent's glass. By the age of twelve a lad might be a swaggering tavern regular. Innocence corrupted? Not intentionally. The belief was that an early introduction to alcohol would make the youngster better able to hold his liquor as an adult.

Every social occasion had its drinking component. The muster and drill of the local militia served as pretense for drunken revelry on the village green. Weddings, funerals, pig roasts, turkey shoots, barn raisings, barn dances, livestock auctions, town meetings, sewing circles, quilting bees, hangings, harvest festivals, elections—all were generally well-lubricated occasions.

An early American's day began with a bracing, prebreakfast "eye opener" of bitters combined with gin, whiskey, or rum. In parts of the Chesapeake country, the morning snort was known by various names: "phlegm-cutter," "fog-cutter," or "antifogmatic." It was a fortifier against the dawn's fog upon the river and therefore a boon to embarking oystermen. At eleven in the morning, it was time for "the elevens," when men of business recessed in order to quaff a few slings (gin with hot water and sugar) or toddies (rum or whiskey with hot water and sugar). Eleven also was time for New World yeomen working the farm fields to break for an invigorating swig off the rum jug, kindly placed by the overseer beneath a tree alongside the pasture. At one in the afternoon in old Virginia, it was time for juleps—whiskey (or peach brandy) with sugar and ice. Crushed mint was a popular julep enhancement. Dinner was at two in the afternoon, and throughout the colonies that meant time to break out the hard cider. More liquor was consumed throughout the afternoon, at supper, and on into the night, at public house or home hearth.

Women drank. Like their menfolk, they drank from passed-around jugs at country dances. Well-heeled ladies of the cities drank juleps and other sweet strong drinks whenever they gathered socially. The tavern wasn't a proper place for a woman to drink, unless she was emerging road-weary from a cross-country carriage and needed something to wash down the dust before taking a room for the night. Most of all, women drank at home; even those who counted themselves among the ranks of the temperate wouldn't hesitate to hurl back a generous dose of some crude medicine that had a mule-kick alcohol content.

Indians drank. Maryland and Virginia settlers along the Potomac discovered that the indigenous residents made a mind-altering brew from maple sap and fermented birch. Throughout the eastern seaboard, liquor trade with the Indians was brisk. Various colonies sought to abolish this traffic, including Maryland, which in 1715 voted to forbid the selling of more than a gallon of liquor a day to any Indian. The penalty: a steep 3,000 pounds of tobacco. Stopping the Indian liquor trade became a federal effort when Congress passed a law in 1802 giving the president power to fight the traffic.

Slaves drank. The master would throw them a three-day bender at Yuletide, and watered-down whiskey helped to fuel the extra work at harvest. Through the underground barter economy, blacks managed to indulge in inebriation other times as well, even though the prevailing legalities were against their savoring drink except when prescribed.

The colonists were adept at squeezing spirits out of just about anything not made of stone. They made fermented beverages from cherries, blackberries, elderberries, plums, potatoes, pumpkins, pawpaw, persimmons, carrots, turnips, parsnips, and honey. Peach brandy, also known as "Virginia drams," was prevalent. That most American of fruits—the apple—provided the omnipresent hard cider as well as something more distilled and more brain-scrambling: apple whiskey, or applejack, as it was called. A Maryland tobacco factor, writing to a friend in England about 1740, mentioned apple spirits as he versified about what later would be referred to as "the land of pleasant living":

> Our fires are wood,
> Our Houses are good;
> Our diet is Hawg & Hominie
> Drink juice of the Apple,
> Tobacco's our staple,
> *Gloria tibi Domine.*

By the eighteenth century, rum (originally "rumbullion") ruled in America; by the eve of the nineteenth century, whiskey had gained the top spot. Before the Revolutionary War, rum distillation from imported molasses was the number-one manufacturing process from Philadelphia northward. Along with the homemade product, imported rum was dumped here in great quantities, often at a loss to a distributor who was eager to load his ship with more valuable cargo. Rum became ubiquitous in the colonies; it was a vital commodity in the import-export barter system of a shipping economy that found colonial entrepreneurs lacking in currency but long on valuable trade goods. Early on, prohibitive English trade restrictions engendered in the Americans a pragmatic penchant for smuggling. Such restrictions fostered a revolutionary attitude in the colonists and taught them something about business: when laws are not conducive to profit-earning, there's nothing like a good ship and a dark night to circumvent the problem. A nocturnal black-market philosophy became ingrained in the American spirit. And a later century's rumrunners would look back to their storied colonial past for the man they considered their patron saint: signer of the Declaration of Independence, the richest man in New England, the spiritual granddaddy of American rum smuggling, John Hancock, himself a successful dabbler in the illicit enterprise.

In 1770, with America on the threshold of revolution, 4 million gallons of rum were imported to the colonies on top of the 5 million gallons that were bottled there. It was a veritable rumbullion inundation. Rum had become so cheap that a common laborer, it was said, could earn enough in a day to stay besotted for a week. In Virginia, William Byrd II inveighed against the overuse of cheap, readily available rum and the effect it was having on his colony's lower classes. They "are fonder of it than they are of their Wives and Children," observed Byrd, "for they often sell the Bread out of their mouths, to buy Rumm to put in their own."

While the unwashed masses were ruining themselves with cheap rum, Byrd and other gentlemen of his social standing were enjoying such costly potables as fine imported Madeira and Canary wines. Wine, expensive and elitist, was the province of the affluent. Drinking clubs, formed in emulation of English gentlemen's clubs, had the finest of the ruling class as members. The Tuesday Club in Annapolis, Maryland, was one such celebrated organization for inebriation. Its members gathered to sample the best bottles of wine, then sample more and still more, chasing after what might be regarded as an excessive amount of good cheer. And in Virginia, a traveler noted that any man considered a true gentleman not only would encourage his guests to drink, but would be sure to send them on their way nothing short of stinking drunk.

Many factors led to the passing of rum from the forefront of American imbibing and to the rise of whiskey in its stead: the disruption of molasses imports during the Revolution and the resultant fluctuation in price and quality; the mass arrival of distillation-savvy Scotch-Irish, who spilled into western Pennsylvania and the mountains of Virginia; and the invention in Kentucky of an ingenious new corn-based liquor called bourbon. In the earliest days of American whiskey-making, before corn took over, the predominant indigenous grain spirit had been rye whiskey, thanks largely to distillers in Maryland and Virginia, the two Chesapeake colonies being the original headquarters of whiskey-production in America.

The popularity of whiskey drinking in the early nineteenth century coincided with the unfortunate rise of American alcoholism. The formative years of the young United States were saturated with liquor; between 1790 and 1840, per capita alcohol consumption rose to the highest rate ever in the nation's history. Between 1800 and 1830, average annual intake was more than five gallons of hard stuff per American, a drinking level nearly three times higher than that of late twentieth-century America. Foreigners visiting the United States in the early nineteenth century noted with disdain that the whole country seemed to be on a national binge.

The habit was getting out of hand, and it called for some sort of counteraction, some reining-in. Actually, since early times there had been laws against this sort of thing—not against drinking, of course, but against blatantly exuberant inebriation. The Maryland colony weighed in early, enacting in 1642 a law that penalized public drunkenness by a fine of 100 pounds of tobacco. In 1658 Maryland initiated a new enforcement. Anyone caught out and about in a drunken state (the required number of witnesses was two) would be locked in the stocks for six hours or fined 100 pounds of tobacco. A whipping was the sentence for a second offense. A third offense branded the drinker a "person infamous," unable to vote or hold office for three years. The Virginia colony, meanwhile, defined a "common drunkard" as anyone who had been found intoxicated three times. In 1668 Virginia passed a law limiting "tippling-houses" to one per county. It proved unenforceable.

Whiskey, the raw frontier, and a young country feeling its oats made the early 1800s a rowdy, raucous, rakish era. "The thing has arrived to such a height that we are actually threatened with becoming a nation of drunkards," a moralizing Delaware pamphleteer warned in 1815. And therein lay the gist: even in a world where drinking was universally accepted, the inability to hold one's liquor was most unacceptable. Drinking, even steady, daily drinking, may have been perfectly fine; obvious drunkenness was certainly not. The influential men had long recognized this distinction, and while George Washington the whiskey distiller may have praised strong drink's beneficial qualities, that same patriarch condemned excessive liquor use as "the ruin of half the workmen in this Country." And while Puritan leader Increase Mather may have praised wine as God's gift, he was quick to qualify: "The wine is from God, but the Drunkard is from the Devil."

At first, the antialcohol movement arose intelligently, from a standpoint of sensible restraint. Alcohol was not the ill; too much alcohol was. A warming campfire is a blessing, but not if it ends up burning down the forest. Dr. Benjamin Rush, the great eighteenth-century American physician, launched the movement with the publication in 1784 of "An Inquiry into the Effects of Spiritous Liquors." Rush's seminal essay pointed out what subsequent generations would come to accept as the obvious: that daily consumption of huge amounts of alcohol can be very bad. Alcohol abuse led to a variety of ill effects, the doctor had observed. But Rush argued for moderation, not absolute abstinence from drink. Beer, wine, even mildly mixed rum punch were put forth as acceptable substitutes to harder stuff. At first Rush was a lone voice crying in the grog-steeped wilderness, but gradually his views began to gain adherents. His essay, reprinted again and again, became one of the primary tracts of a growing crusade.

Quakers and Methodists were among the first on board. By the mid-1700s, Quakers already had begun to exercise restraint, passing the jug around only twice at a funeral, as opposed to the debauchery that often characterized such occasions then. Led by Anthony Benezet, the Quaker leader who attacked both distilled spirits and slavery in his pamphlet "The Potent Enemies of America," the Quakers gradually aspired to greater and greater restriction in their drinking habits; by the 1780s, total abstinence was their dominant creed. The Methodists, likewise, came to dryness in stages. Early on, a quart of peach brandy a day was deemed acceptably "temperate" for a Southern Methodist, but as did the

Quakers, the Methodists ultimately came to preach total abstinence well before the other denominations.

The movement grew, and it was a much-needed antidote, perhaps the best hope for an alcoholic society. It began with medical men citing empirical data. It was taken up and furthered by religious people, and as the movement grew, it changed. Begun by scientists, it was popularized by moralists; begun as science, it metamorphosed into religion. What started as an argument for sensible moderation evolved into a holy war demanding absolute elimination of alcohol from American life.

At Chase's Tavern in Baltimore, Maryland, six friends routinely gathered to toast and swallow until they were as drunk as lords. One night, two of them went to a temperance speech given by the Reverend Matthew Hale Smith, down from New York to spread the word. The two tipplers may have gone to the lecture out of bemused curiosity, but the reverend's impassioned rhetoric worked magic upon them. They saw the light. They not only swore off alcohol, they went back to Chase's Tavern and convinced the other four to change their ways as well. The six Baltimore drinking chums had become avid converts, and they formed one of the most influential antialcohol organizations in America, the Washington Temperance Society. In just half a year's time, the group had more than a thousand members—all former drinkers—and before long one hundred times that number had joined. Thus was born the Washingtonian movement. One of its leading lights was John H. W. Hawkins, the Baltimore hat-seller who toured America railing against demon drink as only an erstwhile rummy could. The reformed drunkard gave more than five thousand speeches nationwide, appealing to people's emotions with gut-wrenching anecdotes of melodramatic sorrow. The best was the one about his sweet little daughter Hannah, who came to him one day with tears on her cheeks and begged, "Papa, please don't send me for whiskey today!" The moment, as Hawkins recounted it, was his epiphany, and he ditched his fifteen-year drinking habit there and then.

The Washingtonian Movement was launched in 1840; it claimed a hundred thousand members signed its abstinence pledge within one year. A significant supporter was Abraham Lincoln, who in an 1842 address to the Washingtonian Society of Springfield, Illinois, called for a "temperance revolution."

The revolution grew stronger and more vociferous with the founding of the Woman's Christian Temperance Union (WCTU) in 1874. Once the religious movement became a women's movement as well, there was no stopping it. Carry Nation, the imperious WCTU warrior-queen, became a turn-of-the-century icon with her hatchet-wielding, saloon-busting methodology. Accompanied by the crusading reporter Anne Royall, Nation toured the Potomac approaches to Washington and observed, appalled, "the too free use of spiritous liquors." The women watched the boats hauling stone for the Capitol Building and lamented that there "was no one there sober enough to unload the vessels." There were about two hundred men at work on the structure and, noted Nation, "there are perhaps not a half dozen sober men here." Even worse, all about the work area, "abandoned females" were hawking "whiskey . . . fresh off the river boats." On a lecture tour through the Delmarva Peninsula, Nation brandished her hatchet, bellowed, "This is the hole!" and smashed up a booze-and-billiards parlor in Parksley, on the Virginia Eastern Shore. A big brawl ensued.

The movement won by degrees. Counties went dry by "local option," and each county won over to temperance was one step closer to a dry state and, ultimately, a dry nation. "Woman! You have placed the star of Maryland in the galaxy of States and territories that guard as doth a sentinel the safety of the children," said Edwin Higgins, president of the Maryland State Temperance Alliance, praising the cooperative efforts of the WCTU at an 1886 convention. The Maryland Temperance Alliance, founded in 1873, had plenty to feel heady about by that thirteenth annual convention held at Baltimore's Oratorio Hall on April 20 and 21, 1886. Higgins joyfully spoke to the six hundred delegates assembled: "When the Alliance was organized, there was neither an election precinct nor county in the State where liquor was not sold. Now, Prohibition prevails in Kent, Garrett, Harford, Caroline, Cecil, Calvert, Howard and Montgomery counties; and in all of Somerset,

Queen Anne's and Talbot counties, except one district in each; Dorchester, two districts; in Anne Arundel, except Annapolis and one precinct; ten districts in Frederick county; five towns and two districts in Baltimore county; two towns in Worcester county; and one school district in Wicomico county."

The cause was conquering Maryland, chunk by chunk. In the crowded Baltimore hall, the Reverend S. M. Hartsock of the Eutaw Street Methodist Episcopal Church offered an opening prayer. After the "amen," President Higgins rose and addressed the throng: "The historian is ever busy recording the conflict between RIGHT and WRONG. . . . We draw inspiration from the prosecution of our cause and feel the assurance of its final triumph. . . . Thirteen years ago, when the Maryland State Temperance Alliance was organized, there was neither an election district nor county under Local Option or Prohibition. Today that which is equivalent to thirteen counties, more than one-half the State, enjoy the blessings incident to the enforcement of these laws. These events . . . have all transpired within the memory of the living. They show how, step by step, the Right has won its way in spite of opposition through years of prejudice and self-interest."

Even more progress was made in Virginia, which, like so many states, was brought inexorably to a turning point: the question of statewide prohibition by constitutional amendment. On Saturday, September 19, 1914, Virginians prepared to decide by referendum vote their state's dry-or-wet fate. As the World War heated up an ocean away, a Prohibition parade wended its way through the streets of Norfolk. The pageantry stretched for a mile: Boy Scouts marching, bands playing, children singing as they waved banners that begged, "Save Us and Our Fathers" and "We Ask for Your Protection." Men's Bible-study groups marched in formation. The county chapter of the WCTU went by on a float called the Old Ship of Zion, its proud flag declaring, "We're Sailing to Victory." The nautical theme continued with a float paid for by the Hampton Roads Paper Company. It was a ship named *Booze Fighter;* its crew was made up of members of the Baptist Sunday school, the head of which was the manager of the Hampton Roads Paper

Company. A carrot-and-stick sexual stratagem underlay another float, bedecked with beautiful young maidens flaunting flags that admonished all the ogling fellows, "The Lips That Touch Liquor Shall Never Touch Mine."

Some Virginians who liked their whiskey had begun stockpiling. Those who did were glad they had by the following Tuesday, for the drys won Virginia impressively. Led by the formidable Reverend James Cannon, Jr., of the Methodist Episcopal Church, the Virginia temperance movement had been destined for victory. The dour Cannon—a fellow dry crusader called him "cold as a snake"—was one of the key figures in the movement nationwide. As a boy growing up in Salisbury, Maryland, Cannon had lived next door to a bar. Cannon liked to recount how one day, a drunkard emerged from the bar and let go of his dog's leash. The big, slobbering mastiff bit Cannon's uncle, who subsequently died of blood poisoning. Cannon's mother had founded a WCTU chapter, and she used to take the boy with her on antisaloon prayer demonstrations. The boy grew up to be a shrewd, religiously driven Virginia political powerhouse. And as Virginia went dry, a drinking man remarked bitterly that the alliance of preachers and housewives had been an unbeatable one.

Other states were falling in line. The logical extreme of a dry America seemed ever more feasible. While America was distracted by the First World War, an increasingly dry-controlled U.S. Congress made historic moves. On August 1, 1917, the U.S. Senate adopted the fateful resolution to submit the idea of a Constitutional Prohibition amendment to the states. The House followed suit on December 18, and on January 29, 1919, the Eighteenth Amendment was ratified, prohibiting the manufacture or sale of alcoholic beverages. It was to go into effect in one year's time. The enforcement arm of the Eighteenth Amendment—the National Prohibition Act, or Volstead Act— was passed by Congress on October 28, 1919. The movement had won.

For more than a quarter of a century, one of the movement's most effective voices had been a former drunkard. He took the abstinence pledge and never touched another drop. He became an impassioned preacher. "Twenty-six years ago, John, I drew the sword against your infamous business," Billy Sunday shouted at the giant coffin. "I pledged God to fight you as long as I could stand up, that I would kick you as long as I had a kick left in me; that I would bite you as long as I had a tooth left in my head; and that I would gum you to the doors of Hell. Like Hamilcar of old, who swore young Hannibal eternal enmity against Rome, I have perpetuated this feud against your business until, thank God, I have lived long enough to see the white-winged dove of national Prohibition build her nest on the dome of the Capitol at Washington and spread her bright pinions of sobriety and peace over our fair and glorious land."

When Prohibition arrived it felt like a fait accompli, for America had staggered toward dryness in stages. As has been said of the fall of the Roman Empire, it was a process, not an event. Great portions of the land already had been dry for years. On the national level, wartime prohibition measures had made people grudgingly accustomed to the idea of liquor laws. The gradual move toward Prohibition had an interesting side effect: it allowed criminals gradually to get used to the idea of the killing they were about to make. Dry-state trafficking and wartime prohibition were rehearsals for outlaws; for them it was a preview of the imminent bonanza.

Baltimore had held out on dryness. As other parts of the state had fallen in line with temperance momentum, Baltimore had killed the prospect of Baltimore Prohibition by a three-to-one vote. Naturally, the wet town became a major export center for neighboring dry territory. Washington Boulevard became a hazardous route as the reckless "rumrunners of the road," often quite seriously blotto on the product they were transporting, went barreling toward dry Washington, D.C., with carloads of liquor. A pair of wounded soldiers, survivors of the nightmare warfare in Europe, almost didn't survive the ride from Washington to Baltimore, as the car in which they were being driven was run off the road and wrecked by drunken Baltimore rumrunners speeding to D.C. Such accidents were occuring daily on the Washington Boulevard in 1919. A brisk maritime trade likewise was developing in the Prohibition preview period. Several police officers were implicated in a smuggling ring that was supplying dry Norfolk from wet Baltimore by way of the Chesapeake Bay. Smugglers were making thrice-weekly runs, using steamboat staterooms to stash loads of liquor bound for Norfolk wharves. Several Norfolk policemen were caught in the roundup, as were employees of the Bay Line steamer *Florida*. It was described in the press as "a whiskey business almost as great as that done when the city was wet." Independent operators were afloat as well in 1919, such as Captain S. J. Lindsley, "known in Norfolk and Baltimore shipping circles," convicted for running twelve hundred bottles of whiskey from Baltimore to Norfolk. He was captured while transporting the cargo from a scow to a waiting automobile. Other men who were helping him unload escaped to make mischief another day.

"We have passed through the most momentous epoch in the history of our nation," Billy Sunday said. "The English language does not contain words sufficient for us to express our admiration for the achievement of our boys, on the land and on the sea, who helped to overthrow one of the greatest menaces to liberty and freedom the world has ever known—Prussian military autocracy. And now we have overthrown booze autocracy at home, and life has a new meaning."

For those not in Billy Sunday's tent, the victory of the temperance movement served as a cold awakening slap. "Never in the whole history of politics, economics or morals has there been a more insolent, impudent set of men than the cranks and fanatics who had had their way in cramming Prohibition down the throats of the people," wrote one F. A. R. of Washington, D.C., in a 1919 letter to the *Baltimore Sun*. "It is true, and no one can pretend to deny it, that the march of Prohibition is rushing and resistless. It is going into the Constitution, but it is not going in by the edict of the people of the United States. It is going in because the cowardly politicians and legislators have succumbed to the brutal driving of self-constituted guardians of public morals and habits.

". . . The people have been asleep, but they will be heard from in due time. The colossal impudence and aggression of politicians may put

Prohibition in the Constitution, but it will be a dead letter. It will be a fizzle after all this worked up hysteria has passed away, as it inevitably will. Mark the prediction."

"The Puritanical fanatics have had full sway and have ruled with an iron hand," wrote William Washam of Baltimore as Prohibition loomed closer. "But in this 1920 we the people are awakening from our lethargy. . . . Don't think, Mr. Fanatic, that because you, through all manner of deceit, succeeded in having inserted in our Constitution the offensive Eighteenth Amendment, you have won the fight! You haven't. Your troubles have only begun.

"Our day of revenge is coming, slowly, maybe, but surely. We lovers of liberty are going to show you before the close of this year that the National Prohibition Amendment is but a synonym of treachery and crooked policy and that it surely is contrary to the will of the people. It was born and bred while real Americans shed their blood in Flanders to make the world fit to live in.

"When Uncle Sam's soldiers returned, what did they find? First of all, they found their personal liberty gone, a measly $60 bonus awaiting them, without hope of more compensation. At the same time, they find that our Government, by coercion of a set of despots in the persons of the drys, can pay millions of dollars for the enforcement of a law which they detest. Men of America, is this a square deal?"

Squarely or not, the movement owned the day. "No earnest, intelligent man or woman can deny but that the saloon and drunkenness was the curse of the United States; and those who loved their country most and were most interested in the welfare of our nation mourned this terrible blight," said Billy Sunday. "And we arose in our indignation and smote the saloon serpent."

One week before national Prohibition took effect, the eminent Baltimorean General William B. Warfield held court over somber proceedings at the Maryland Club. Members gathered and drew lots for the remaining liquor stock of the club's once-proud cellar. It was a time for morose ceremonies and last-minute transport of goods. On Calvert Street, a sad crowd had crammed against mahogany walls to mourn the passing of Dick Goodwin's saloon, once dubbed "the handsomest barroom in the South." In Baltimore Harbor, the rush was on to load ships with "wet cargo" to get the product of the distilleries out to sea before the Prohibition deadline. Out there beyond the shore there was a great big world where liquor was still marketable. The freighters *Maumee, Lake Ellerslie,* and *Adelheid* were laden with 42,000 cases of whiskey, gin, and sundry spirits, in addition to 8,200 barrels of whiskey. They were cleared on the day before Prohibition began, bound for the Bahamas with a cargo that would prove to have boomerang characteristics.

The departing barrels and bottles needed export stamps that cost a dime each, earning the federal government about $3,000. Regular taxes on the same cargoes would have made the government about $2 million. Already it was evident that Prohibition meant more than giving up vice; it meant giving up profits for American distilleries, and it meant giving up huge tax revenues for the government. Any money made from liquor sales now would go somewhere else.

The liquor that shipped out in time was fractional compared to that which was left behind. An estimated 4 million gallons remained in bonded warehouses in Maryland; the owners' only hope of recouping their investment was to distribute the product on the still-legitimate medicinal-alcohol prescription market. Large wholesale outfits such as the Baltimore-based Triaca Company, one of the largest liquor distributors in the East, hastened to register with Internal Revenue for the drug trade. Private citizens, meanwhile, clamored for private stock in the final days before Prohibition took effect. Whiskey in Baltimore was going for $125 a case, and buyers were glad to pay it, because in a matter of days, the only legal imbibing would be that which took place in the privacy of home.

"Good-bye John, old top, the people of America are fit for self-government at last," said Billy Sunday. "The people are free from the chains you riveted about them at last. The wrath of an outraged public has been quenched and your putrid corpse is hanging from the gibbet of public shame."

In Baltimore, at a Monument Street garage on the last Sunday before national Prohibition, the watchman heard a knock. It was just past midnight. He went to the door. He shouldn't have opened it: four men, pistols drawn. They shoved him against the wall. There were two cars, motors running, and more men, seven total. The guarded garage was storage for a large private liquor stash. The robbers loaded up their cars. They ran out of space and there was plenty more liquor. They stole a car in the garage and started loading it up, too. Someone came in. The robbers turned. Two men had walked in to get their car. The gunmen lined them up against the wall alongside the guard. The criminals got away with forty-three cases of whiskey and a case of brandy, in all a haul worth five thousand dollars.

"Good-bye, John, old top, we don't need to guess twice where you are," said Billy Sunday. "During your life you never caused one smile. Over your carcass no one sheds a tear. Heaven rejoices; the devil is your only mourner. You never made anyone prosperous; you never benefited any human being; you never made any man happier; you never made any home brighter. You have left behind you broken-hearted wives, mourning for the husbands you robbed them of; you have left behind you broken-hearted mothers, shedding tears and wringing their hands over the grave where you buried their boy, a drunkard; you have left behind you ragged, hungry children; you have left behind you jails, penitentiaries, scaffolds and electric chairs; you have left behind you insane asylums and orphans."

On Friday, January 16, Prohibition Eve, policemen surrounded a waterfront bungalow along Bear Creek in Baltimore County. The sergeant who had received the tip was heading up the ambush, backed by two city sergeants and three plainclothesmen. The order came down from the marshal: do the raid whether it's city or county. It was nightfall when they got to the bungalow belonging to Henry "Heinie" Hulseman, thirty-six, divorced, and described in the press as "widely known in East Baltimore and on the Chesapeake Bay because of his yachting proclivities." As for

Heinie's waterfront retreat, it was reported that "for months the place has had the reputation as being the center of gay celebrations and midnight parties."

Patrolmen surrounded the bungalow. The officers went in. Women screamed. The officers lined up the men. The place was swank, two fireplaces blazing, one at each end. The large living room was bedecked with sailing trophies, big silver cups from Chesapeake regattas. A fox-trot blared on the radio. Dozens of empty whiskey bottles were scattered about, some unlabeled, others with labels tying them to the Monument Street garage heist. In addition to the empties, there was an unopened bottle of rare eighteen-year-old stuff. The lawmen also found pistols and, most damning, an additional full case of whiskey with the labels and identification mark of the garage cache. Another squad car pulled up.

The officers arrested the men and told the women to "keep each other company." The ladies gave their final fast kisses to the men being hauled off.

Downtown, Hulseman admitted to acquiring some of the stuff but asserted he wasn't a bandit. The garage watchman picked out the holdup men. Hulseman and party cohort Herman Skinner became witnesses for the state. The other six bungalow boys were charged for the Monument Street job. The judge set their bail at twenty thousand dollars aggregate. One of them, Harry Sellman, twenty-one, ponied up his twenty-five hundred and was released. The other five were locked up. All were in their twenties. Each gave his occupation as "chauffeur."

The police were skeptical about the names, particularly the alleged Joseph McGrath and the alleged O'Brien boys. The law had pegged them as New Yorkers who'd come down to set up a hooch-moving operation working out of the vicinity of Franklin and Paca streets. As for the whereabouts of the rest of the whiskey—the great majority of the whiskey—lifted from the Monument Street garage, the police said they had "no clue."

Members of the Baltimore chapter of the Woman's Christian Temperance Union were celebrating their success on Prohibition Eve. It was a time to rejoice, to reflect on the great victory won, and to ponder with enthusiasm the bright years ahead. They gathered in their headquarters at 516 Park Avenue, and Mary Haslup delivered an address on "The Jubilee and What It Means." Dr. Bourdeau Sisco discussed "The New Program for the WCTU." And the Reverend John W. Laird gave an optimistic speech titled "Looking Toward the Future."

At around two in the morning on Saturday, January 17, with National Prohibition about one hour and fifty-nine minutes old, five men stole four trucks from a Gay Street garage in Baltimore and drove out to the Gwynnbrook Distilling Company warehouse near Owings Mills. John Whiten and John Clark, black watchmen, heard a knock. They opened the door: five white men, saying they were government inspectors. They lingered in the warehouse office for almost half an hour. Whiten looked at the time and announced he was due to make his rounds. He tried to leave. Two pistols were aimed at his brain. The gunmen told him to stick up his hands. The watchman whipped his brass clock around and whacked the attacker in the head, introducing him to the floor. The other gunman let fly; the bullet ripped through Whiten's shoulder. His partner Clark moved to help, but they had him covered. Nearby farm dogs were barking up a storm. The whiskey thieves got worrisome and tore off. Clark got hold of the county marshal. Whiten was taken to University Hospital for surgery. The police later found the stolen trucks, abandoned. The marshal praised Whiten for thwarting the robbery of thousands of dollars worth of liquor. Police headquarters issued a general alarm.

Baltimore's Lyric Theatre was packed to the rafters as the Maryland chapter of the Anti-Saloon League gathered to celebrate the great "victory over booze" and to cheer the dawning of "a dry world." It was Sunday, January 25, the Noble Experiment a week young. The rally drew a huge, boisterous crowd, which filled the Lyric's main floor and almost filled the boxes and gallery seats as well as additional seating set up right on the stage. The men of the Monument Street Methodist

Episcopal Church bible class, hundreds of them, sang a stirring rendition of "Good-bye Forever, Saloon!" Strident orator Dr. George W. Crabbe, the league's state superintendent, derided "backsliders in the Maryland State Legislature" who were against Prohibition; their mere mention was met with shouts of "No! No!" and "Put 'em out!" And those who had opposed Prohibition were derided as "poor losers." Soon came the main attraction, a special appearance by none other than America's "chief booze cop," United States Prohibition Commissioner John F. Kramer. He was a small, frail, pasty-looking figure, a disappointing contrast to the beefy, red-faced Dr. Crabbe whose burly voice had just resounded through the Lyric. But John F. Kramer was a long-time fighter in the movement, a crusader stirred more by religion than by politics, and his speech soon swayed the initially dismayed throng. As had Crabbe, he invoked "church spirit" as he beseeched the audience to "wade into the fight" to help enforce the new law of the land. He said it was "a great thing to be permitted to live in this twentieth century. It is great to be a Christian—a member of the church and a citizen. But of the two it is greater to be a Christian and a member of the church—to carry on the work of God!"

There was talk among some people in those heady days that perhaps Prohibition could be repealed, that perhaps America would never really go dry. Commissioner Kramer said, "Men might as well talk of flying without a flying machine as to think that the nation will ever go in the other direction on this question!"

Burglars rolled up in trucks, broke into the Wineke-Arey Company warehouse on Eastern Avenue and Sixteenth Street in Baltimore, and stole sixty-four thousand dollars worth of whiskey early Sunday morning, February 1, 1920. They broke the lock, laid down skids, and rolled out sixty-four barrels into the waiting vehicles. They pulled off the job between watchmen's shifts and made no attempt to be quiet about it. The booze crooks were out in force now, brazen and creative. A Baltimore and Ohio Railroad detective got wise to a new style of larceny that February on a train car laden with eighty barrels of grain alcohol. The car was off on a siding at Stone House Cove. Inventive thieves drilled a hole through the floor and drained grain. The detective found evidence of their handiwork, but he never found them. Also never found: the criminals who busted into Luke P. McGuire's home at 735 East Twenty-first Street in Baltimore and made off with several barrels of private whiskey stock one Friday night. Neighbors watched as the home invaders noisily loaded up their truck, so blatant in their activity that the neighbors figured McGuire must have sent them. He hadn't.

The robbery happened while McGuire was at church. Now, even a church itself could become criminals' prey, for sacramental wine was exempted from the restrictions of Volstead. The wife of the Reverend H. P. Almon Abbott, rector of Grace and St. Peter's Protestant Episcopal Church in Baltimore, woke up when she heard a cough at three in the morning on Sunday, February 22, 1920. Mrs. Abbott headed down the rectory hallway to the bedroom of young Osler Abbott, figuring the tyke was sick. Then she heard noises downstairs. She yelled for her husband and switched on the hall light. Downstairs: two men, running. They dashed out the front door.

They had broken in through a cellar window. They had taken the church's entire stock of communion wine and transferred it from bottles into jam jars. Apparently they had been inside for quite a while, for it looked like the plunder was ready for the hauling when Mrs. Abbott spooked them and sent them running. The Reverend Abbott told the press that "this was all the wine Grace and St. Peter's Church had on hand . . . its loss would have been a serious one to the church, as there appears to be no present possibility of getting any more." The rector pegged the thieves as "men who knew something about the house."

Suddenly, whether you were McGuire or the Lord, your private hoard was a bandit magnet. The 1920 Prohibition kickoff crime wave engulfed the Chesapeake country, from Norfolk (where discriminating robbers made off with a huge private hoard of fine brandy) to the Maryland Eastern Shore (where burglars broke into the historic waterfront manor home Readbourne in Queen Anne's County and made a clean getaway with the whiskey) to western Maryland (where the Fairchance distillery was hit by crooks thirteen times in four months). According to the *Baltimore Sun,* "Revenue officers declare no other distillery in the country has been visited by burglars as often as the one in the mountains near Fairchance." The thirteenth heist, a truckload of whiskey barrels worth $11,500, was reported on February 17, 1920, the same day that western Maryland resident Joseph Frost looked down and saw that his dog had a human foot in its mouth.

The dog led Frost to a dismembered corpse. The parts were scattered: the rotting skull here, the still-clothed torso frozen in ice there, other parts missing. In the corpse's clothing were a watch and a thermometer that helped investigators identify the remains as those of Dr. Joseph Gilder, fifty-five, medical man for the Taylor Coal and Coke Company. The *Sun* reported that Dr. Gilder had been missing since November, "after being threatened, it is said, by Italians whom he had said he would expose for selling whisky." The doctor had gone out on a house call; he never made it. On the same day that Joseph Frost's dog brought home the physician's foot, coincidentally, it was reported in nearby Hagerstown that C. J. Davison's dog had dragged home a severed human head.

"It is up to us Christians . . . to save the world," said U.S. Prohibition Commissioner John F. Kramer. "God has put it up to us to save it. If He had wanted to save it all by Himself, He would have done it 2,000 years ago.

". . . Everyone is bound to fall into two groups. There is no middle group. Either they are barnacles on the ship of state, impeding its progress, else they are like unto steam in her boilers, driving her ahead through the seas. Either they are parasites on the body politic, sucking its blood, or they are red corpuscles, giving the blood of the nation strength and vigor."

The smugglers' lair was at Harvest Moon Shore along a creek off Middle River, which feeds into the Chesapeake northeast of Baltimore. It was known as a good place to fish for pike and bass. Secret agents of the United States Internal Revenue Bureau had been on the case for two weeks, and they weren't fishing for pike and bass. They were onto their biggest booze case yet, a case with long tentacles, with a syndicate up to its elbows in liquor heists worth an estimated two hundred thousand dollars.

It was Saturday, February 21, 1920. A light snow fell. A federal agent playing bootlegger flashed cash and suckered the Harvest Moon Shore boys. As they bought the play, a U.S. Army truck was turning off Eastern Avenue onto Back River Neck Road. The deal was made: the fed pretended he was on a buying mission for "New York cabarets" and engineered a transaction. The truck spilled feds; guns drawn, they surrounded the shore shack. They handcuffed the outlaws, seven of them, and rolled evidence up into the truck. The prisoners, six Marylanders and an Englishman, were suspected of being part of an outfit responsible for a string of U.S. bonded warehouse jobs. Two more arrests quickly followed. Nine barrels worth fifteen thousand dollars were seized. The Harvest Moon Shore case was described as "the biggest yet undertaken by the Prohibition agents" and "of such magnitude that it was difficult to estimate where it would end." Controversy would arise over how the raid was played; no search warrants were issued and the sting smacked of entrapment. Field operative Charles W. Hand explained, "We will get the warrants later. In a case where quick action is necessary we get the prisoners, and the warrants come next."

"You were a thief, John," said Billy Sunday. "You stripped us of manhood and womanhood; you clothed us in rags. You took away our friends and our health and our occupation. You robbed us of our families; you impoverished our children; you took the shirt from off the backs of shivering men; you took the milk from the breast of nursing mothers; you took the last crust of bread from starving children; you took the virtue from our daughters; you were the blood-sucker of the universe."

A mother, two sons, and a police sergeant were among those nabbed and charged for the St. Patrick's Day 1920 robbery of forty-nine cases of whiskey from the Legum Company warehouse at 314–316 Light Street in Baltimore. All sorts of citizens were getting in on the action now.

John Maggid, a Baltimore storekeeper, was arrested in February when police saw a truck unload a barrel of whiskey right at the front door of his Eutaw Street store. Grilled about the barrel, Maggid told the lawmen it was "only vinegar." It was whiskey, suspected to have come from a prominent warehouse-robbing ring, and Maggid soon confessed he'd paid $1,750 for it. The warehouse heists continued. Thieves tried to hit the Monticello Distilling Company warehouse at 408 Holliday Street in April. They broke down a door and got half a block away with nine cases of whiskey; they were stashing it in a sandpile when the job got scotched by watchman Frank Schirmer. The thieves shot at Schirmer; he got a call in to Central Police Station. When the law arrived, all but one of the burglars had fled; they found the last one in the alley with a half-empty whiskey bottle and a drawn pistol, standing over the half-buried booze haul.

The flow of illegal drink was leading to the rise of places to drink illegally. It looked like William Madson's old saloon at 1918 Gough Street was being revived that April when Baltimore patrolmen noticed twenty-two cases of whiskey being unloaded from a truck parked out back in the wee small hours. The policemen approached. The truck tore off. Thomas Ray was in the yard with the whiskey. He had his gun drawn as he charged past the policemen. He didn't get far. Madson's was nailed, but it was just one spot on a large map; drinking joints already were cropping up all over town in those opening months of the drinkless era. After a week's surveillance, internal revenue inspectors raided a party house at 816 East Pratt Street in March. They arrested the customers and found wine, vermouth, and whiskey. As they made the raid, the inspectors had to do battle with a pack of angry bulldogs.

"John Barleycorn," said Billy Sunday, "we bury you because you destroyed our health; you disfigured our bodies; you ruined our nervous system; you dethroned our reason; you caused idiocy and insanity; you destroyed every principle of manhood and womanhood; you squandered our property; you produced pauperism; you crowded our poorhouses, and jails, and penitentiaries; you corrupted our courts; you defied our laws; you destroyed both soul and body; you darkened our homes; you broke our hearts; you beggared our wives and children; you led men to commit every conceivable crime."

In Baltimore's Highlandtown district, twelve masked bandits invaded the Mount Vernon Distillery warehouse, tied up the guards, and trucked off with fifty-four barrels of whiskey at half past two on the morning on March 11. Internal Revenue Agent Henry C. Wheatley was there with watchmen Gus Frank and Frank Mohn. They heard motors in the warehouse yard. They opened the inner office door. Four masked men pointed pistols at them and told them to put their hands up. Eight more bandits crowded into the room. They bound and gagged the federal man and the two security guards. The bandanna-faced robbers couldn't find the keys to the storage area; they busted the big lock on the storeroom door and got to where the whiskey was. They loaded their trucks and scooted. Watchman Mohn had a small pocketknife. He got it out and fumbled it open and started sawing awkwardly on the thick ropes that held him. It took him three hours to get free. He grabbed the phone. The line had been cut.

The stolen whiskey was officially worth $25,000; its bootleg street value was more like $80,000. Adding insult to injury, the Mount Vernon Distillery technically had to pay tax on the whiskey "removed from the warehouse." Heist or no heist, the booze had been "removed," and that meant the company owed taxes to the tune of $6.40 a gallon; the additional gouge totaled $17,280.

The masked men had said, "We don't stop at killing." The internal revenue agent refused to go back to his post. He was transferred.

Joined by his equally evangelical wife, the wildly popular "Ma" Sunday, Billy Sunday sang:

John was a murderer,
Last night he died;
Toll the bells for John is dead—
Darn his drunken, filthy hide.

Baltimore detectives received a tip after midnight on March 26: wild champagne party in progress, Hotel Kernan, second floor. The informant tagged the revelers as the bootleggers who two days earlier had robbed the country home of Howard Bruce at Lawyer's Hill in Howard County, making off with nearly a thousand dollars' worth of whiskey, champagne, and assorted wines. The detectives got to the Kernan before one in the morning and barged in on the party: two men, two women, a whole lot of bottles. One of the men jumped out the window. Detective Freeman popped off two shots to alert the beat patrolman down the street, but the bootlegger got away. The other three got a ride to headquarters. The party girls were questioned and released. The man said he was Daniel Dougherty of Richmond, Virginia. Howard Bruce of Howard County was called in to identify his property. The five unopened bottles of champagne in the hotel room were indeed his. So was the Portuguese white wine. So were those eleven empty champagne bottles strewn about; so was the empty two-gallon whiskey jug.

The night before Bruce was robbed, another home had been targeted: the Catonsville farm of Antonio T. Carozza. Four soldiers from Fort McHenry took part in the botched attempt to make off with Carozza's sizable private whiskey stock. The scheme was hatched in Highlandtown. The soldiers and their coconspirators headed out in a pair of trucks. They rolled up to Carozza's place and rousted the caretaker. While they cornered him his wife got on the phone. Help showed up. The robbers fled. One of the trucks broke down, and the whole caper unraveled. The sentences handed down were stiff, especially for the ringleader, Bruce F. McLaughlin, a Pennsylvania man who'd been displaying a good deal of industriousness toward criminality in Baltimore for the past several months. McLaughlin had been a key figure in the Harvest Moon Shore case. The stash from that case had been linked to the robbery of the booze warehouse at Camp Holabird. McLaughlin was already in hot water for the Harvest Moon Shore deal as well as the Camp Holabird heist as he faced the jury in U.S. court for the Carozza job. While on liberty for a few days during the Camp Holabird–Harvest Moon Shore trial, McLaughlin had led the gang out to Carozza's. He was fined five thousand dollars and sentenced to two years in the federal penitentiary at Atlanta, Georgia. The Fort McHenry soldiers all showed up for trial in their uniforms. They all went to jail, their sentences ranging from five days to six months. The soldier who got five days lucked out because the court felt lenient toward him: he was eighteen years old.

"Don't think I'm foolish enough to believe that there are no violations of the Prohibition law," U.S. Prohibition Commissioner John F. Kramer said to an April gathering of the Federation of Men's Bible Classes in East Baltimore. "We can't change the moral map of the nation in a few weeks or months. But, if the liquor traffic can be ironed out in a generation, it will be the greatest work any generation ever did."

Internal revenue inspectors Edward Z. Parker and William L. Hawkins had quit the service and had been floating back and forth between Washington and Baltimore, with trips to other cities, for six weeks. Veteran Department of Justice secret agents had been quietly flocking to Baltimore for two weeks. It was late February 1920. The secret agents were tracking leads that led from Baltimore to the west and from Baltimore to tropical islands. It was an ever-widening case involving millions of dollars' worth of illegal booze deals, and at the heart of it were the two recently resigned revenue men. Parker and Hawkins tried to hop a train to Florida on February 19, 1920. Agents swooped in and arrested them. Said one agent after the arrest of Hawkins and Parker, "Both men have been spending money for several weeks like drunken sailors." Also arrested was G. Rudolph Vincenti, a top executive of the Triaca Company, the large wholesale-liquor outfit. The ex-revenue men and the distributor were at the heart of a conspiracy that was immensely profitable yet essentially simple. Since 1919, huge shipments of alcohol earmarked for export had been diverted into clandestine U.S. storage for subsequent black-market distribution. Whiskey consigned by its owners for export was diverted at Camden Yards by Triaca Company agents, who shipped the stuff to New York and Washington instead for astronomical profits. It was a gold-mine scam, thanks to the collusion of the false-report-filing revenue men. It was the biggest case of its kind that federal investigators had seen—so far.

"Farewell, you good-for-nothing, God-forsaken, iniquitous, blear-eyed, bloated-faced old imp of perdition," said Billy Sunday. "Farewell. Boys, let's all sing 'Praise God From Whom All Blessings Flow.'"

The preacher grabbed the American flag and climbed on top of his pulpit. While the great audience struck up the strain of the hymn, Sunday waved the flag in rhythm with the music, and his voice could be heard, loudest of all, above the crowd.

Liquor had been shipped out from Baltimore, and a backwash of it was returning with the tide: Canadian whiskey on the steamer *Firmore;* gin on the steamer *Mangore;* cognac on the steamer *Lake Gilta;* cognac on the steamer *Lake St. Claire.* Most of the smuggled liquor, it was reported, had been part of the recent huge export cargoes.

It was shipped out, and it was being shipped right back in, illegal now, but no less in demand. Chesapeake Bay—heavily trafficked, teeming with maritime commerce, centrally located in the populous East—quickly was proving to be a natural hot spot for illegal liquid imports. An epitaph was prophetic: in a mock funeral ceremony that predated Billy Sunday's Norfolk ritual (and had as its intent a sentiment opposite to Sunday's), a funeral for John Barleycorn had been held at John T. Roddy's Greenmount Avenue saloon in Baltimore in 1919. After the service, the alcohol-god's corpse was buried in a vacant lot on East Twenty-third Street. In the week before the funeral, the corpse had been on display in the window of Roddy's saloon. Hundreds had paused to pay their respects, and to read the inscription on the coffin:

"Good-bye, old John Barleycorn, good-bye. You've been a mighty good old pal and they've knocked you out. We'll bury you, but you'll come back. . ."

CHAPTER TWO

"ONE HUNDRED ILLEGAL STILLS WHERE THERE WAS ONLY ONE"

Booze bandits weren't the only ones hurting liquor-warehouse inventories. To Richard S. Dodson's profound chagrin, there suddenly was a superabundance of medical prescriptions as dubious as a football bat.

Dodson was a rich retired Eastern Shore banker fated to be first in a succession of men with a headache job: Prohibition Commissioner for Maryland, a state politically rebellious toward and socially resistant to Volsteadism. Internal Revenue Commissioner Daniel C. Roper appointed Dodson in February 1920 after a considerable delay caused partially, according to the *Baltimore Sun,* by the fact that "the political leaders in the State failed to give the Commissioner any assistance in naming the new official." Or, as the *Easton Star-Democrat* explained, "The position has been hard to fill because of the disinclination of any of the Democratic members of Congress to recommend a man for the job. They were, it seems, afraid to do it, believing that the wrath of the voters would descend on any man who showed any activity in putting into operation the restrictive provisions of the Volstead Enforcement Act." Someone finally put Roper on to Dodson, and Dodson made sense: former state senator from Talbot County, former member of the House of

Delegates, a well-liked pillar of Eastern Shore society who, despite his solidly antisaloon voting record, was "not a crank on the subject," as he himself put it. Dodson made sense; he wouldn't draw down intense opposition.

He dutifully accepted, left his comfortable home overlooking St. Michaels Harbor, and relocated to Baltimore, where stacks of backed-up mail greeted his arrival. From his cramped temporary headquarters at Room 202, Customs House, he told the press on his first day on the job, "I expect to enforce the law to the letter." By mid-March, still hampered by tiny office space and an equally tiny staff, Maryland's "dry chief" was bringing into focus the landscape of still-legal liquor trafficking. In Maryland and the District of Columbia (also Dodson's bailiwick) 629 physicians were licensed to dole out prescriptions for liquor, and 1,000 pharmacies had liquor-dispensing permits. Business naturally boomed for said doctors and druggists, and the rush was on among their colleagues to join the list of the lucky and the licensed. "That sort of thing will be my work," Dodson said. "It is my duty to see to the licensing of doctors, druggists, manufacturers for medicinal, sacramental and culinary purposes, and all others coming under special provisions of the law." But it soon would become blatantly apparent that the little "medicinal purposes" loophole in the law was really a gaping cavernous maw through which rivers of whiskey were flowing.

Reports were coming from Washington that March of a profiteering doctor who had "pint patients" lined up outside his door. In Baltimore, there were grumblings about pharmacists gouging customers to the tune of $5.00 or $6.00 a pint. The black-market mentality had taken over; the necessity of having a fair price commissioner quickly became evident. In March, the honest rate for medicinal whiskey was set at $2.00 to $2.50 a pint. "We made a thorough investigation," said Walter J. Bienemann, executive secretary of the Fair Price Commission. "... While it may seem strange to be fixing a fair price for whisky, it, nevertheless, is regarded as a medical necessity, and we have decided to tolerate no profiteering because of prohibition. The man who has to pay more than $2.50 for a pint of medicinal whisky should report it to our office at once."

By the end of March, the entire Maryland–D.C. supply of seventy thousand whiskey prescription blanks had been exhausted. Prohibition Commissioner Dodson was getting suspicious of the physicians doing the exhausting. "I don't want to see anyone get in trouble, and I will try to do all I can to save them, but if the stories told me are true, I want to say that those at fault had better go a little slow," the dry chief admonished. "I have had complaints reach me about the flagrant abuse of the law by doctors and druggists, as well as by persons obtaining prescriptions. A man told me the other day that one of his friends had shown him half a dozen prescriptions that he was carrying in his pocket. I have been told also that people are giving false names and addresses.

"I would advise those who think that they can make a joke of this law to watch their step."

The liquor prescription form was quite lovely to look upon: pink, grandiosely ornamented with an excess of fancy whirls and scrolls. A $2.00 office visit and a convincing gripe scored the necessary doctor's signature, with some random dosage instructions, "one ounce three times daily," or some such regimen. The prescription had to be filled within three days, so a hasty jaunt to the pharmacist's was in order. He would duly file the duplicate forms, log the transaction, take the "patient's" $2.50, go open the cast-iron safe, and get out a pint of 100-proof whiskey, bottled in bond. Paul Jones, Four Roses, and O.S.C. were prominent Bay brands. The pint labels were rather aesthetically rendered for something ostensibly marketed solely for medicinal purposes.

From January 17 to March 17, 1920, a total of 7,191 gallons of whiskey were evacuated from federal bonded warehouses in Maryland for the medicinal trade. "If there are abuses," Dodson warned, "somebody may get hurt." In April 1920 the warehouse-withdrawal figure jumped exponentially to a staggering 110,201 gallons for that one month alone. Most of it wasn't for Maryland consumption; truckloads of the stuff went to New York and Pennsylvania. But the local portion of 21,888 gallons still showed about a threefold increase in one month over the previous three months. "At this rate," the *Baltimore Sun* reported, "all the whisky in the bonded warehouses in this district—which represents a liberal portion of the whole of the supply in the country—will be gone in about 55 months, or less than five years." At the end of April Dodson issued a notice to the physicians and pharmacists of his district: No druggist would be allowed to purchase more than a hundred gallons of medicinal booze per three months; if his business was legitimate, that amount should be ample. "Druggists are cautioned to scan very closely all prescriptions for spiritous liquor," decreed Dodson. "It is my belief that most druggists are not only willing but anxious to comply with the law in dispensing liquors, but, unfortunately, some are lax in their methods, and do not scrutinize all prescriptions as carefully as they are required to do. Any omissions in such respect make the druggist equally culpable with the offending physician who stoops to commercialize his profession by prescribing spiritous liquor practically for the fee he collects.

"Whenever cases are brought to my attention involving dereliction of druggists and physicians in pandering to the mere appetites of liquor addicts I shall recommend revocation of their permits and also prosecution where the evidence justifies such action."

Within days the dry chief made good on his threat. Three physicians accused of nakedly commercializing their signatory powers had their liquor-prescribing permits revoked, and a druggist accused of drinking sixteen quarts of his own whiskey was also called to the woodshed. Dodson's inspectors soon turned up other abuses: counterfeit prescription blanks, bogus warehouse-removal orders (some from other states), and, audacity of audacities, liquor prescriptions filled for a pet dog.

In his zeal, Dodson incurred the wrath of the Washington Medical Society, which protested his characterization of D.C. doctors as caring "more for the dollar than their profession." Dodson took criticism in stride as he pursued his futile effort to keep the dry lid tightened. Whiskey removal from bonded warehouses in Maryland had reached a rate of three thousand gallons a day, calculated Deputy Collector of Internal Revenue Lewis M. Milbourne in that first springtime of the new dry age. Bereft of the saloon, the people were turning to the drug store as one of numerous new alternatives.

What medical excuses garnered a patient his whiskey allotment? Samuel Jeppi, who owned and ran a drugstore on Bloomingdale Road in the Walbrook section of Baltimore, reminisced decades later. "A man went to his physician, and if he were sick enough or a good enough actor, he might convince the physician he was debilitated and needed a tonic, was dyspeptic enough to require a stomachic, or depressed enough to require something for elevating the spirit.

"The desired prescription for any of these, and for many more real and imaginary ills, was a bottle of whiskey."

The pharmacist added, "Needless to say, these ills seemed to manifest themselves almost exclusively on weekends and holidays."

"The Volstead law can never be enforced; the people believe it is unjust," wrote Charles F. Davidson, M.D., of Easton, Maryland, in a 1922 letter to the editor of the *Baltimore Sun.* The Eastern Shore doctor had become an outspoken foe of Prohibition as he watched the Noble Experiment, and the concomitant underworld it spawned, redefining tidewater life in nasty and unintended ways. "A person who commits robbery believes he does wrong; the normal person that drinks a glass of beer believes that he does right. He has been taught so by his fathers, and the American people are not going to stand for a law that takes away their birthright."

For all the facile corruption inherent in the medicinal-alcohol loophole, all the pink prescription slips the Treasury Department cared to print couldn't begin to fill the widespread demand for spirits. There was profit begging to be plucked now, by anyone who could rig the copper contraption and keep the fire stoked properly beneath; mash meant money, and illegal distilling operations, both slipshod and slick, cropped up everywhere, from city walk-up to farm-country outbuilding, along winding, wooded waterways and hidden in the mosquito-thick remoteness of the marshy boondocks. Throughout the Chesapeake, stills abounded. It was almost as if because one wasn't allowed to buy alcohol now, more and more people, young and old, *were* buying alcohol now, keeping the stills solvent.

"I am in a position to know that we not only have the same old drunks, but, I am sorry to say, many more of them," Dr. Davidson wrote to his hometown newspaper, the *Star-Democrat*, in 1922. "Men used to get drunk and get sober; now they get drunk and get crazy. The person that thinks drunkenness is not on the increase is trifling with the truth. It has been estimated by responsible men that there are now one hundred illegal stills where there was only one illegal still before the Volstead law; and they seem to be like flies—a dozen appear for every one that is destroyed."

The Chesapeake Bay country was ideal for the creation and dissemination of illegal booze. Here was a land of farmers and watermen, of manufacturers and distributors. It was a tidewater maze of clannish, close-mouthed communities where entrepreneurship coexisted with a bemused sense of defiance, a spirit ingrained to the point of being unspoken tradition. Crop country plus water access plus independent-minded locals with boats spelled moonshiner's paradise and rumrunner's Riviera. Add some nearby urban Sodoms and Gomorrahs clamoring for hooch, and the Chesapeake's criminal subculture of the Roaring Twenties was bound to be born. It was born fat, and it grew fast.

It was there from the start. On Prohibition Eve, January 16, 1920, as Billy Sunday stood before thousands in his Norfolk tabernacle and shouted joyful pronouncements about the great awakening of an alcohol-free America, federal agents not far away were busy breaking up stills in the Great Dismal Swamp. The moonshiners of that area would continue to supply Norfolk and the lower Chesapeake despite efforts to stomp them out. It was too good a setup: hidden deep in a thick tangle of swampland, but just a boat ride away from the money. On January 16, as Billy Sunday celebrated the end of alcohol, the feds saw smoke and smashed two stills in an old swamp shack. Two men vanished in the trees as the officers found another still in the process of being built, the half-completed rig surrounded by barrels of ingredients and a pile of unassembled components.

The basic still setup is simple; it is small wonder the distiller's art is an ancient one. There's the main boiler kettle, called the "cooker," or "can." In here is the grain—cornmeal, rye, barley, whatever—mixed with distilled water, sugar, and, though purists would argue but expediency would dictate, yeast to cause alcoholic fermentation. This slurry mixture, which has been allowed to sit and ferment for several days, is called mash. It cooks at a low, steady boil, with the ideal temperature somewhere between 173 degrees Fahrenheit (the boiling point for alcohol) and 212 degrees (the boiling point for water). What's desired is alcohol steam, not water steam. Atop the cooker is the nozzled still head, which feeds into a midpoint receptacle, either a "slobber box" on a smaller apparatus, or a "thump keg" (named for the pleasant rumbling sound it makes when the rig's going full blast) on a larger operation. Next, the hot mix travels through a copper coil encased in a vat of cold water. This is the all-important condenser phase. The coil ends in a tap protruding from the lower part of the cold-water vat; from here, the spirits flow.

Distilling is an art infinite in its capacity for variation, experimentation, and fine-tuning. This malleability applies to recipes, methods, and the contraption itself, for a still can be fashioned from many things. College students could make them from laboratory glassware. The ideal moonshiner's still is made entirely of copper parts and is thoroughly leak-proof all down the line, though such perfection is rarely realized; a lot of makeshift patching-up takes place as the still churns along. At any rate, the parts of a still can be improvised, and as Prohibition settled in over the land, a whole lot of improvisation was going on as people learned to make do with the materials at hand. In Powhatan, a tidewater "negro settlement" near Petersburg, Virginia, authorities confiscated a 50-gallon still and arrested sixty-year-old Andrew Brown and his son Angus when Prohibition was but five days young. For the cooker, the Browns were using a big copper milk container that had every appearance of having been nicked from the Norfolk and Western Railroad. A moonshiner near Suffolk, Virginia, used gun barrels in his bizarre still construction. The double-barreled invention was nabbed by the law in

September 1920. Reported the *Norfolk Virginian-Pilot,* "The still was unique, the first of its kind the federal officers have seen, and they have looked on many." There were two cookers instead of one; both fed into the same slobber box, in this case a coffeepot. The gun barrels connected the cookers to the coffeepot. "The distilled stuff, according to the federal officer, by this doubling up, was twice as strong and had 'a kick like a mule.' The manufacturer was there, and the stuff was on the fire boiling merrily, but he was a long rangy man, and ran like a scared rabbit."

Spiritous liquid emerges from the coil as clear as water. It can be sold this way—the infamous "white lightning"—as cheap but effective stuff for the low-end market. More expensive, and better to the palate, is moonshine that has been aged in charred wooden barrels until it achieves that beautiful amber hue that most civilized people associate with drinkable whiskey. In an illicit-trafficking environment, anything that sped up the aging process was a boon. Arrayed on sawhorses in a hot attic for about nine days, the charred kegs' contents would have acquired enough quick coloration and flavor improvement to sell as "aged." A popular aging method in southern Maryland and on the Eastern Shore was to store the barrels aboard oyster boats, otherwise unemployed through the hot summer. The gentle rocking of the waves helped the maturation along in fine fashion. "Best way to age it," said Geneva Hall, former wife of a top Eastern Shore moonshiner, "leave it on a boat for that constant slosh, slosh, slosh."

The initial batch of still runoff is called "singlings." If from a good, airtight still, this first-run stuff is marketable, but not as palatable as it could be, even for moonshine. A good moonshiner gathers enough singlings to charge the cooker and runs it all through again, producing "doublings," or "double-run whiskey." It looks the same—clear before it's been aged—but it tastes better. Cornmeal or whole-kernel corn, toasted cornmeal or raw, molasses or granulated sugar, rye or corn, corn or barley—there are as many recipes for moonshine as there are recipes for crab cakes. In Prohibition, with more and more citizens dabbling in distilling, a superlative whiskey formula was information of widespread interest. In November 1921, during the trial of a black Eastern Shore moonshiner, a black woman familiar with the man's methods was called to the witness stand of the Talbot County Court House. She not only snitched out a roll call of the moonshiner's clientele—a healthily diverse biracial consumer base—but revealed his distilling secrets. She gave forth the precious secret details of his recipe and his process, and a court reporter chronicled that "there were numerous notes made on cuffs and backs of letters during this part of the recital."

While moonshining proliferated throughout the Bay country, certain sections especially were hotbeds. The Norfolk–Hampton Roads environs constituted major still country. Miscreants ranged from small-time back-water do-it-yourselfers to landed, prosperous gents such as C. H. Powell, arrested with his son C. D. Powell, when federal officials found two working stills—and evidence of several others used previously—on the Powells' 1,000-acre farm estate in Norfolk County, near Butts Crossing, in January 1920. Some twelve hundred gallons of mash were ready for the runoff. The stills were stoked by a 5-horsepower steam boiler.

Country boys didn't have all the fun. One of the biggest and best-rigged moonshine outfits the feds ever confiscated in the area was in the basement of a house at 4200 Granby Street off Ocean View Boulevard in Norfolk. It was the home of William L. Reteneller, owner of the Cut Price Tire Company. It was known that Reteneller ran the moonshine plant with two black assistants; he refused to divulge their names when he was arrested in December 1922. It was a large-scale operation for a city cellar: a 100-gallon still, a U-cut pipe linked to the chimney to suck off the stinking fumes, and a drain through the cellar floor to carry telltale refuse to a little swamp patch about 50 yards past the back door. In twenty-nine barrels and six vats, there were twenty-three hundred gallons of mash. Neatly aligned bins held the necessary ingredients: a hundred pounds of sugar and ample stashes of meal and yeast. There was enough stuff to pull off a hundred-gallon run a day for a good long time. And there were twenty-five gallons of freshly made corn whiskey ready to peddle.

The stench was Reteneller's downfall. Cooking mash reeks like stale beer, only worse. And though Reteneller had arranged for the rank steam to be chimneyed off into the acrid skies above Norfolk, the elements conspired against him one damp December day. The heavy weather held the escaping fumes groundward, and federal agents heading along Ocean View Boulevard caught the incriminating whiff.

That one fell into their lap; lawmen usually had to work harder to score a bust. When they nailed the biggest still ever taken in the vicinity, federal agents had to crawl through 100 yards of thick, dank swamp to get to the 300-gallon monstrosity near Butts Station in January 1923. It was a behemoth rig; the coil was 20 feet long and 3 inches in diameter. As they approached, the agents eyed the two men, one black and one white, who operated the swamp giant. The moonshiners hightailed it. They didn't get far. The Butts Station raid was part of a busy month for federal dry agents operating in the lower Chesapeake. In four weeks they captured and demolished more than twenty stills in Virginia's Bayfront counties. It was not a staggering number, actually, for a region so rife with moonshiners.

Farther up the Bay there was a territory where moonshining was even more widespread. The Northern Neck of Virginia and the Potomac shoreline of southern Maryland comprised a great nerve center of regional moonshining activity. Statistics suggest that a full 55 percent of those living along this river stretch were involved in moonshining during the Prohibition years. "If you didn't have a still, you weren't anybody," recalled St. Mary's County resident Bruce Scheible. "Everybody had a still. That was automatic, like planting a garden."

Southern Maryland product was considered high-quality, and the place was well situated for marketing in every direction. Southward, by boat and by car, the Potomac counties' moonshine traveled to beckoning Richmond. Eastward, the highly respected hooch traveled via rumrunning watermen to the Eastern Shore and from there, by road and rail to all points north. Westward, transported likewise by industrious watermen, the product went to the docks of Washington and Alexandria, where oysters were off-loaded only to get to the booze-filled Mason jars hidden underneath. Northward, up the Chesapeake by sailboat, speedboat, barge, and steamer, the stuff made it to Baltimore. And while rumrunners carried it along the water highway, their cousins in crime, the new breed of "automobile rumrunners," were loading their flivvers and zooming up the state's new blacktop. Its real name was Crain Highway, but it was known as Bootleggers' Boulevard.

Meanwhile, Baltimore's own distilling underground was growing apace with the rest of the region's. Like elsewhere, it started humbly—the first still raid, in February 1920, was on a dinky peach-brandy operation on Lexington Street—and grew like Jack's beanstalk. By January 1924 federal agents were raiding elaborate factories like the one at 825 Greenmount Avenue, where a pair of 200-gallon stills and a full-flown bottling plant took up the second floor, and eighty-one barrels of mash and two hundred gallons of product were stored on the third floor. If Baltimore had its share of stills, it had more than its share of beer-brewing initiatives. Baltimore was traditionally a big beer town, robustly so, with its strong German and Irish influences and a renowned zest for steamed-crab consumption. Once Prohibition kicked in, a whole lot of Baltimoreans were making a stab at brewing beer—potent suds, not the all-but-fake "near beer" the Volstead Act allowed. Many a Baltimore basement was converted into a home-brewing operation in rebuttal to Prohibition. H. L. Mencken, the resident genius-journalist and all-around witty bon vivant, claimed he was "the first man south of the Mason and Dixon line to brew a drinkable home brew." The Sage of Baltimore was magnanimous in sharing the secrets of his beer-making skill. "My native Baltimore smelled powerfully of malt and hops during the whole horror, for I did not keep my art to myself, but imparted it to anyone who could be trusted—which meant anyone save a few abandoned Methodists, Baptists and Presbyterians. . . . My seminary was run on a sort of chain-letter plan. That is to say, I took ten pupils, and then each of the ten took ten, and so on *ad infinitum.*" And so the streets of the city were occupied increasingly by citizen-brewers, adding their product's bouquet to the growing stench-aura created by the citizen-distillers.

A significant advantage that country moonshiners had over their city confreres involved the disposal problem. It is a principal difficulty in running an illegal still: how to get rid of all that used mash, a big, smelly, incriminating mess, without giving oneself away. One solution in a watery labyrinth such as the Chesapeake country was to pipe the slop out to the nearest stream, creek, bog, or river branch. Another, more universal, solution in rural areas always has been to feed the mash slop to the hogs, or chickens, or other barnyard denizens. As strong as the mash smells, when dumped into a pig pen it just becomes part of a greater funk. The hogs chow down on it, and it's bye-bye evidence, hello drunken porkers. Thus, a hog farm is an advantageous site for running a still. The W. L. Vellines farm in Norfolk County, raided by federal agents in June 1923, is an example. The farm was home to a sizable distilling outfit: two 120-gallon stills, a 6-horsepower steam boiler, a freshwater supply pipelined from a conveniently situated brook, the whole shebang going full blast when the federal men showed up. The farm, in addition to being home to the big still, was home to three hundred head of well-fed hogs. Along the Potomac, folklore suggests that a goodly number of the famed southern Maryland hams had a distinct and not at all unpleasant corn-whiskey flavoring during the Prohibition years.

Law enforcement agents in the Chesapeake region learned that when it came to running after moonshiners, there was no finish line. Racing with the moonshiners was as will-o'-the-wispy as racing with the moon. Stills proliferated faster than they could be destroyed, and the quarry was slippery. In a typical Eastern Shore dragnet in June 1922, Queen Anne's County officers and federal agents swooped down on several known offenders, but as the magistrate averred, "evidently they were innocent or else slick enough to hide their wares." Farther down the Shore, federally directed raids in December 1922 actually yielded a slew of arrests, fines, and jail sentences, but it was, as succinctly noted in the press, a Pyrrhic victory: "Immediately after this the stills began again."

The hunters had to aspire to the same levels of craftiness and deception as the hunted. For a couple of police officers in Cape Charles, Virginia, the hunt motif itself became the deception, and the chase acquired a definitively regional flair. It was December 1922. A pair of stills were churning out the 'shine in Hollywood, a forested patch outside Cape Charles at the entrance to Chesapeake Bay. It was winter on the Chesapeake, so what better cover for a pair of stalking lawmen than to pose as waterfowlers? It was intended to throw off any sympathetic locals who might tip the moonshiners as well as to fool the moonshiners themselves. The officers disguised themselves as Shore sportsmen, complete with gunning attire, shotguns, and hunting dogs. They bagged no birds, but they did bag three moonshiners, two 50-gallon stills, 104 gallons of corn whiskey, 2,000 gallons of mash, and 700 pounds of sugar.

Stills peppered the countryside to the extent that it wasn't unheard of for the law to stumble upon one serendipitously. An Eastern Shore manhunt led to a moonshine pinch in February 1923. John Raisin was on the lam after a Saturday-night brawl in Chestertown. Raisin had shot and nearly killed his brother-in-law. Raisin already had a long rap sheet, so he made himself scarce. With a posse of Chestertown and Centreville police officers after him, he holed up in an old shack on the fringe of the woods near Ewington. The posse tracked him down. Raisin considered fighting, weighed the odds, and surrendered. The Centreville constable searched the hideout. It was home to a stash of mash and a pair of stills that appeared to have been in operation for a long time. Inadvertently, the shooter had led them to a moonshine shack. There were more unexpected places than that to come across an apparatus. William T. Earle of Seaford, Delaware, took a short cut and discovered a slick-looking still in the abandoned cemetery of the Macedonia A.M.E. Church in July 1923. By the time the authorities got there, the graveyard still was gone.

In a steep southern Maryland ravine, hidden by thick woods more than a mile off the main road from La Plata to Bryantown, Prohibition agents in May 1923 nailed the biggest still found in Maryland up to that time. The agents described the 2,000-gallon Charles County rig as "unique, ingenious and stupendous." The still was so massive that they couldn't find a truck big enough to transport it in one piece to Baltimore, so they broke the thing down to haul it out. The moonshiners, absent and uncaught, had dammed a small stream, creating a pond that fed the condensing phase courtesy of 40 feet of 2-inch copper piping. A 40-horsepower boiler stoked the mash. Two large tents stood nearby, one for living quarters, the other for storage. It was the seventh moonshine raid in Charles County within one month. Agents suspected the ravine still was being run by a gang of southern Maryland bootleggers in the business of keeping Washington, D.C., slaked.

Good moonshiners were proud of their product and prospered because of satisfied customers and repeat business. Southern Marylanders and Virginia Northern Neckers thrived on the good word-of-mouth their moonshine inspired. The "St. Mary's Sampler," exclusive to the swamp stills of that Maryland county, was the secret rage at Washington's famed Willard Hotel. At fine Richmond lodgings, the preferred outlaw brand was the "Nomini Mix," named after the creek that fed into the Chesapeake. Potomac men, it has been said, made more money during Prohibition than at any other time, by making high-grade hooch, making boat delivery runs, or both.

A perilous phenomenon of Prohibition, though, was that skillful distillers were far outnumbered by ignorant amateurs and amoral profiteers who didn't think twice about polluting product to milk more mileage out of it or make it look like something it wasn't. These two groups, the stupid and the sleazy, turned the distilling art lethal, for it is an art infinite in its capacity for miscalculation, dishonest manipulation, and fatal poisoning. This fallability applies to recipes, methods, and the contraption itself, for a bad still can be a deadly thing. Rotgut alcohol cut death trails; it came in a number of corrosive varieties: moonshine corrupted by metal in dangerously ill-constructed stills; wood alcohol, pure poison that reprehensible dealers nonetheless doctored up and sold; and liquor containing noxious additives, bumped into the juice either by the lower class of moonshiner or a bootlegging middleman.

U.S. Surgeon General Rupert Blue was already voicing a frightening caution in January 1920:

There is such an alarming increase in the number of victims of wood-alcohol poisoning, caused by unscrupulous persons using it in the manufacture of "bootleg whisky," that it is wise to issue a word of warning. There is only one safe course, and that is to leave it alone, for even the smallest quantity, such as a teaspoonful, taken internally, is enough to cause blindness, and a larger quantity, such as a good swallow, is sufficient to cause death. After it is taken it is too late, usually, for the physician to save the eyesight.

The effect of wood-alcohol poisoning is quick. Within a few hours after drinking there is an acute headache and attacks of vomiting, pains in the body, particularly about the kidneys, with accompanying dizziness. The symptoms are certain and unmistakable.

Wood alcohol is made from the distillation of wood. Until recent years it could be very easily distinguished from grain alcohol, but refinements in its manufacture have made it look and smell much more like grain alcohol. It is intended for a commercial use only, and under no circumstances can it be taken internally without grave consequences. In fact, its external use is attended with grave danger.

. . . Don't take any chances. Better to be safe than sorry, blind or worse.

Wood alcohol: aka methyl alcohol or methanol. Main uses: an antifreeze, a denaturing agent for ethyl alcohol, or a raw material in the production of formaldehyde. Made by heating hardwood sawdust in a process called "destructive distillation." Can dissolve varnish, fats, and oils. Colorless. Used by laboratories to preserve anatomical specimens. If ingested, can definitely turn a live human being into a dead anatomical specimen. If it doesn't kill, it at least attacks the optic nerve. And as the surgeon general indicated, it can even be poisonous through skin contact.

It was used in bad liquor by those who were out for a fast buck and who didn't care so much, obviously, about repeat business.

Within days of Blue's warning, an eighteen-year-old Baltimore housemaid was rushed from the Park Heights Avenue home she served to Franklin Square Hospital. She was a victim of wood-alcohol poisoning, and other cases soon followed. It was bad enough that poison peddlers were about. Matters were worsened by hapless experimenters who, in their desperation for mind-altering drink, concocted nightmarish potions out of badly chosen ingredients. A Delmarva man brought up on drunken-and-disorderly charges in September 1920 had gone wild on his own homemade blend of various fruits, fruit skins, brown sugar—and gasoline. Even when ingredients were fine, an error in the science of still construction could render a death-dealing runoff. A barnyard turkey ended up like the proverbial coal-mine canary that croaked when it ate mash from an Eastern Shore still raided by local and federal officers at Starr, in Queen Anne's County, in 1923. The gobbler dipped its beak in the mash and keeled over dead. The still was made of sheet iron, a big no-no; only copper was surefire safe. There had been successive waves of poisonings caused by metal-still moonshine, or "monkey rum," in various part of the Chesapeake since 1920.

Its change to illegal status didn't end the liquor industry; it merely deregulated it. There was so much that could go wrong, so many things that could queer a batch and turn it foul. A wave of poison corn liquor hit the Eastern Shore in July 1922. The offending compound was zinc acetate. It didn't come from a bad still, and it wasn't added by a runner. It came from the screw tops for the Mason jars that carried the hooch. The liquor worked itself under the jar's porcelain cap and corroded its zinc lining. This created high levels of the acetate in the beverage, producing severe nausea and violent vomiting. By the beginning of 1923 the Talbot County Health Department was issuing statistics and declaring that bad moonshine was increasing the death rate, through damage to vital organs such as the kidneys. The Health Department especially warned citizens to avoid the "green whiskey" currently making the rounds.

It was enough to make a law-ignoring imbiber think, "Thank God for offshore rumrunners." Mysterious vessels—larger cousins to, and partners in crime with, indigenous Bay craft engaged in the lucrative trade—were making the Chesapeake part of their territory now. The large-scale runners were becoming the pipeline for the real thing—bonded, well-made, safer, and tastier, brought over the waves from the rest of a world that hadn't descended into dryness. Unfortunately, there was no such thing as a sure thing; just because it was smuggled in from abroad didn't ensure quality. Early on, the *Hwah Jah* incident had shown the certainty of that uncertainty. *Hwah Jah* was a Chinese steamship that arrived in Norfolk from Saigon, French Indo-China, by way of Havana in August 1920. She was in the Chesapeake to take on a cargo of cigarettes for shipment to Shanghai. Her manifest quite legally listed several sealed cases of liquor. But she carried more, smuggled aboard somewhere by Chinese crewmen and now being smuggled ashore at Norfolk. Customs got wise, pulled a search, seized thirty-six cases, and ran a sample analysis: wood alcohol. Thus, "from offshore" was no guarantee in and of itself. But as they became more available, offshore goods would become the buyer's best bet. And in the dry spells between shipments, the second best bet was to know an alky-cooker whose stuff was reliable, stick with him, and hope the law didn't shut him down.

The Virginia House of Delegates responded to the monkey-rum menace with an amendment written into the Layman Senate Prohibition Bill in March 1924. The manufacture or sale of lethally poisonous liquor was now considered first-degree murder in the Old Dominion. If the customer-victim was poisoned but not killed, the maker or seller could be charged with attempted murder.

It was a timely law. "The entire Atlantic seaboard is being deluged with a vast tidal wave of booze bearing death and destruction," it had been reported in December 1923. From Baltimore to the Eastern Shore, on up to Philadelphia and beyond, poison whiskey sliced a swath of dead and blind victims that winter. Not all came from a single source, but rather from a growing trend: the use of concentrated lye in the mash. Lye triggered quick fermentation, but lye also made moonshine lethal. Several deaths were reported in Baltimore, Salisbury, Philadelphia, and other eastern cities. Philadelphia seemed hardest hit: seven deaths in one day, one hundred critically ill, more than five hundred arrests. A typical victim was Eastern Shoreman Adam Meekins, forty-seven, a farmer living near Worton in Kent County. He went on a Yuletide bender that left him loaded with lye. "Meekins had been under the influence of the liquor for about a week," reported the *Centreville Record,* "and on Christmas day he celebrated with an overdose."

"The Internal Revenue chemist reports that less than 1 percent of the products of these stills is honest liquor, and that the other 99 percent is poison," wrote Dr. Charles F. Davidson, the outspoken Eastern Shore Prohibition foe. "The Volstead law is directly responsible, for before it there was no market for this stuff; now the owners of these stills are making hundreds of thousands of dollars."

Rotgut fostered madness. The *Easton Star-Democrat* cited authorities who believed the preponderance of bad hooch was "responsible for much of the increase in insanity." Talbot County was spending about nine thousand dollars a year for the maintenance of a growing roster of booze-spawned mental patients, some kept in adjacent Dorchester County at the Cambridge Hospital, the rest scattered across the state at the Crownsville and Springfield facilities.

Dr. Davidson inveighed against "poisonous stuff that is being poured down the throats of our people, wrecking their bodies and weakening their minds. What sort of a race will we be in twenty-five years if this evil increases. . . ? It is our duty to let our Congressmen and Senators know that they must eliminate the bootlegger and the moonshiner by passing sane laws governing our liquor traffic in place of laws made by political cowards who were afraid they would not be sent back to Washington if they disobeyed the orders of an organization composed of fanatics."

When the Woman's Christian Temperance Union held an all-day institute at the Ebenezer Methodist Episcopal Church in Easton on May 2, 1922, delegates from all nine Eastern Shore counties as well as Harford County were in attendance, and the topic was meaty: how to enforce the Eighteenth Amendment. The delegates formed a "law enforcement league," in which fifty women enlisted, and it was hoped the seed had been planted for a movement that would spread statewide. Particularly invigorating was the address delivered by Mrs. Ab Bibbins of Baltimore, who pointed out that, alarmingly, there were thirty organizations in Maryland enjoined in the battle to have the Volstead Law either repealed or rendered toothless. The time was now, Mrs. Bibbins said, for women to unite to fight those who would smite progress. The press came under fire for its unfair distortions about Prohibition. Mrs. Milton Stewart of Baltimore gave a talk on Christian citizenship. The afternoon session featured a lecture by Mrs. J. S. Taylor, who said there were other causes for the united women to take on, other victories to be won, other goals to get to, including the next great crusade: the outlawing of tobacco.

The evening session featured the awarding of cash prizes for the best essays written on "The First Two Years of Prohibition and What It Means to This Country."

Dry crusaders were right to be worried over Maryland, where their hold was tenuous. The voting clout that rural areas had over Baltimore and environs had pushed the state in a dry direction, but wets of both political parties were prominent and outspoken in Maryland politics, and the opposition to Prohibition was nowhere more exemplified than in the governor himself.

Albert C. Ritchie—patrician, aristocratically handsome, a Democrat—achieved national prominence for eloquently espousing anti-Prohibition views long before it became the politically popular thing to do. Nominated for governor in 1919 and winning by the merest margin, Ritchie would become the great Maryland statesman of his generation. He would become revered by the wets and despised by the drys. President Warren G. Harding, pro-dry Republican, invited Ritchie to a governors' luncheon in May 1922. Harding orated about the need for states to get behind Volstead enforcement. After the president sat down, there was a silence that seemed to suggest tacit agreement. Then Ritchie rose. When he spoke, it was the articulation of defiance, and a political star was born:

"The Eighteenth Amendment is an unnecessary invasion of states' rights. The people of Maryland inherit a tradition of temperance, and we were effectively solving the liquor problem by local option. When a community wanted prohibition, it got it. Now, however, that the federal government has usurped the power and functions of the state, we hold that enforcement is the business of federal officials." Lecture invitations flowed in from across the country now for the Maryland governor who refused to sign into state law any sort of "baby Volstead Act."

Through Ritchie's attorney general, Maryland police were told they needn't bend over backwards to help enforce the federal liquor-restriction statutes. A federal law? "Let the feds deal with it" remained the Ritchie administration's states-rights stance. National dry leaders bemoaned Maryland's refusal to board the Prohibition-enforcement bandwagon. But Hamilton Owens, editor of the pro-wet *Baltimore Evening Sun,* was inspired to dub Maryland "the Free State," a nickname that stuck. Maryland Anti-Saloon League President George W. Crabbe may have damned Albert C. Ritchie as "a menace to the good morals of the state of Maryland," but the majority populace of said state evidently disagreed. In 1923 Ritchie was reelected governor in a state that rarely did so; he was the first Maryland governor to be voted into a second term since 1838. Ritchie would go on to serve an unprecedented four consecutive terms.

Ritchie had taken center stage in a national debate that continued with the same hotheadedness and divisive absolutism that had defined it before national Prohibition became a reality. The law was here, but the fight wasn't over. Both sides deftly played the statistics game, spouting facts and figures to support either view. Prohibition is working: see these statistics. Prohibition is not working: see these statistics. But one would have to have been blinder than a wood-alcohol drinker to miss seeing the rise in crime. In Baltimore, for example, more arrests were made in 1923 than in any year in the history of the Baltimore Police Department up to that time. And the figure had been climbing steadily since the onset of Prohibition: 41,988 arrests in 1920; 54,602 arrests in 1921; 60,947 in 1922; and the record-breaking 74,285 in 1923. Police Commissioner Charles D. Gaither directly attributed the increase to "bootleg liquor and the general disregard of law" and noted that liquor trafficking "is now worse than it ever has been."

"Crime is increasing," stated Dr. Charles Davidson from his Eastern Shore vantage. "Unless something is done to modify the tyrannical provisions of the Volstead law there is going to be a revolution more bloody than the one that is going on."

The revolution in criminality was partner to a revolution in style, manners, and morals. Illegal liquor fueled both revolutionary fronts. Bootleggers were making a killing thanks to the law that had created their career and to a hedonistic postwar *zeitgeist*, an attitude epitomized by a younger generation that was fast, loose, out for kicks, and immoral as hell. The World War had gutted the old order; the jaded young laughed drunkenly at their parents' strictures of decorum. Young ladies cut their hair in short, flirtatious bobs; they went wild with the mascara, lipstick, and rouge; their shocking, slinky dresses showed lots of leg. They were the flappers, vampish and ultramodern, and their young men had fast cars, cigarettes to share, and a penchant for taboo music. The Jazz Age was a youth revolution, and the hip flask was standard equipment.

It was a frightening period for those who remained true to the moral codes of yore. It was enough to make a Virginia college president rail about the army of "hard-drinking, cigarette-puffing, licentious Amazons" who had taken over the American campus. As he delivered the opening address of the National Lutheran Educational Conference held in New York in January 1924, Roanoke College's Dr. Charles J. Smith attacked the zealous boozing, risqué dancing, and widespread lack of carnal restraint that were destroying college life. "What can we do," asked the Virginia educator, "when daughters of the so-called best people come out attired scantily in clothing, but abundantly in paint, carry a bottle of liquor, dance as voluptuously as possible, quench their thirst, and engage in violent petting parties?"

The young, of course, don't invent sin; they only think they do. And the wild youth of the Roaring Twenties weren't the only drinkers, of course. The older generation, too, was doing its part to keep the bootleggers solvent. And if they were shocked at the younger generation's excesses, they doubtless were a little titillated, a little inspired, as well. In Norfolk, the mainstream audience turned out in droves to peek at sexy

Colleen Moore starring in *Flaming Youth,* the scandalous movie based on Warren Fabian's scandalous novel about rambunctious Jazz Age thrill-seekers. The Norfolk crowds filled the Norva Theatre to capacity night after night, and it's doubtful that they were there for the *Our Gang* short that preceded the sizzling melodrama. In Baltimore, the everyday readers who thrilled voyeuristically to the serial-fiction exploits of "The Flapper Bride" in the *Baltimore Daily Post* weren't all flappers themselves, but they sure enjoyed reading about one.

Symbols of the rebellion—the flapper's hairstyle, for one, and women smoking, for another—soon worked their way into the mainstream. It may have been upsetting for the more Puritanically minded of the age to witness the mainstream veering toward such scandalous motifs, to detect the tantalizing whiff of sinfulness creeping into the center of everyday life like that. But it was an ironic by-product of the Puritans' political success. For via Volstead, lawbreaking itself had entered the mainstream. The once-simple act of acquiring a bottle had been embossed with a patina of daring, of naughtiness, of adventure. It was a little thrill that many in the mainstream were learning to experience, a little jolt of badness that in their minds linked them, however fleetingly, to the wild young element setting the era's tone. And, most perversely, there was something in all the lurid booze-trafficking news for even a Puritan to surreptitiously savor. However indignant the whole sordid scene made him, a Puritan, noted H. L. Mencken, nonetheless "reads with prurient glee every account of a federal agent being murdered, police searching a woman's underwear for liquor, or officials raiding a yacht."

Baltimore customs officials, ardent in their efforts to curb the influx of liquor on ships, extended their net of suspicion to include a dead sailor among all the live ones engaged in smuggling. Seaman H. G. Wriglands died of peritonitis at Bermuda in April 1920. The U.S. consul asked the master of the steamer *Lake Flushing,* coaling up for the Baltimore run, to take the American's corpse stateside. The seaman's remains were encased in an airtight coffin that was boxed up for shipment. At Baltimore, an undertaker was supposed to take charge of the dead cargo and ready it for westward transport to the waiting family. But the sailor's final return home had to be delayed. Customs wouldn't let the coffin go until after it had been pried open and searched for liquid contraband. The dead man, it turned out, was clean.

The absolute thoroughness that poking about in coffins implies would suggest that not much got past the men charged with halting the booze flow in the Chesapeake, but such was not the case. The volume of illicit trafficking rose in concert with the rising volume of illicit manufacturing and with the rising volume of offshore importation. Oystering season emerged as a particularly good time for rum-running on the Chesapeake Bay. Bushels full of oysters made a first-class booze cover. On a cold, nasty day, what inspector wanted to root through boat after boat of oyster mess hoping to nail the one skipjack in the fleet that was hauling the hooch?

Vessel types native to Chesapeake waters were well suited for rum-running, especially when customized for the purpose. At boatyards from Coan River to Colonial Beach, from Smith Creek to Combs Creek, and elsewhere throughout tidewater, Bay boats were being built with extra cargo space, artfully hidden, for the burgeoning cottage industry of maritime liquor traffic. The Prohibition-era vessels had false bottoms built to fit cases of Mason jars, a dozen jars to the case.

Motorcraft naturally became the workboats of the emerging Chesapeake rum-running fleet. Fast, able to run in and out virtually anywhere along the water's jagged rim, a motorized vessel manned by a waterman was a formidable foe for the feds. The Hooper Island draketail—narrow, shallow-draft, with plenty of cargo space but built for speed—was a graceful design relatively new at the time and a fine craft for outrunning a patrol boat. The draketail *Dixie*—32 feet long, 6 feet wide, built in 1915 by Elijah Wallace of Fishing Creek, Hooper Island—was a recurring winner at the Choptank River workboat races. She was light and lean enough that a single-cylinder Palmer engine was all she needed to earn her reputation for good speed. For a certain type of nightwork, therefore, she was a natural. Sleek, swift *Dixie* was owned by Dorchester

County waterman Alonza Elliott. "He had that boat built for a crab boat, and he was crabbin' all his life. . . ." recalled Alonza's son Milford Elliott. "Prohibition went into effect, so he had a chance to run some whiskey—it was quick money and plenty of whiskey to drink."

With Milford's brother Rufus, Alonza Elliott made nocturnal sorties across the Bay to southern Maryland. The Elliotts ran white lightning and got paid by the trip: twenty-five dollars (and moonshine, all they could drink, gratis) to haul a four-barrel load, fifty-five gallons a barrel. The southern Maryland pickup spot was on the Bay shore below Solomons Island—"back in the woods," said Milford Elliott, "no revenue man dared to go back there"—at Cedar Point, future site of the Patuxent Naval Air Station. The Eastern Shore drop-off spots were at Church Creek and Shoal Creek. Somewhere around the midnight hour, the watermen would hook up with bootleggers who would load the contraband onto a waiting truck. Elliott's main buyer was a four-man Dorchester County syndicate. The syndicate divvied up the product into bottle apportionments and made sure lightning always struck in Cambridge. "Them fellas sold it out of their own homes," said Milford Elliott. ". . . You'd go there and buy your pint or half-pint and put it in your pocket and go off with it."

The southern Maryland–to–Eastern Shore run was one of many trade routes developing on the Chesapeake. They ran every which way. An import region was also an export region. An area receiving certain goods would manufacture and ship out other goods. It was all quite scattershot and informal at first. As the Prohibition years went on, order would emerge from the chaos. Crime would become organized. But be it anarchy or criminal hierarchy, the bottom line was that sailboats and speedboats, workboats and yachts all had a whole new avenue of income in Chesapeake waters.

Their cousins in crime were the rumrunners of the road. The land traffic in liquor flourished as part of the amphibious journey—once the boats off-loaded, the highway brigade took over—as well as along its own strictly terra firma trading paths. More than before the great war, the automobile was becoming a fixture in American life, and even in horse-and-carriage backwaters such as the Delmarva Peninsula, the motorcar was a more common sight. Add the explosion in bootlegging activity to the growing presence of the automobile, and it comes clear that the machine and the moment were met.

The newish profession of chauffer, its ranks filled with ex-doughboys and various other desperate, rowdy young men, was an advantageous cover job for a runner. Sometimes they got caught, like the Baltimore chauffeur nailed by motorcycle cops while en route to the Bowie racetrack with a carload of whiskey. Other times they slipped away, like the enigmatic black chauffeur cruising around the Eastern Shore in a large car and calling out to passersby that he had whiskey for sale, bottled in bond, ten dollars a quart. He was openly dealing right on the state road, doing a brisk business, making his rounds with impunity until the law got wind of him in Royal Oak. The officers gave chase, but the bootlegger's wheels were too fast for them, and after miles of eating his dust, they gave up.

In Maryland and Virginia, on both sides of the Bay, there proliferated a dusty, noisy new phenomenon: the car chase. Norfolk motorcycle officers bagged a pair of automobile rumrunners in one afternoon. The first car, a Studebaker, was loaded down with forty-five gallons of corn liquor; the second, a Ford, was hauling twenty gallons. They caught the Studebaker near the railroad tracks on the waterworks road. The runners—the owner and an auto mechanic—were arrested on charges of "transporting ardent spirits." The cycle cops caught up to the Ford in Campostella. Two men jumped out, ditched the car, and took off through the woods, leaving the police with the goods. The Ford was sporting a stolen license plate from Cleveland.

Prohibition agents tracked a bootlegging ring and got after three of its members in a high-speed chase on a Delaware causeway. The agents fired their revolvers at the fleeing, whiskey-laden vehicle. The runners shot back. Up ahead, a Pennsylvania freight train was moving on the railroad track. With bullets flying and a wall of train up ahead, the runners bailed. They jumped and the whiskey car smashed into the train. The runners threw themselves down the embankment and disappeared in the Christiana Creek marshes.

Bootleggers led police on a high-speed twenty-five-mile chase through Washington, D.C., Ellicott City, and beyond, running red lights, ignoring one-way signs, bombarding the squad car with flying whiskey bottles, and further confusing the situation with a smoke-screen device. A half-gallon whiskey jar smashed through the windshield of the pursuit vehicle, which was forced to hurl its way down crowded D.C. streets at fifty miles an hour not to lose its crazy quarry. The judge called the bootleggers "a distinct menace to society" and sentenced them to five years at Atlanta.

After staging a raid in Wicomico County on the lower Eastern Shore, Prohibition agents stopped in Easton to grab some eats at the Puritan Restaurant. It was getting dark. While the agents ate, someone broke into their car and liberated seventeen bottles of whiskey, just confiscated in Wicomico. People wondered, "How did the thief know?" A reporter mused, "Someone in Easton certainly has a keen sense of discernment."

Audacity was the way to play it, to an extent. In Baltimore, a limousine pulled up for a booze score. But it was a setup, and it led to the arrest of Jacob Cohen, with twelve hundred dollars cash in his pocket and a brazen racket going. Cohen was selling medicinal whiskey allotted for use by Dr. Morris Schlaen, pharmacist. The kicker was this: Cohen was selling the whiskey right out the back door of Schlaen's house, while the doctor was out and Mrs. Schlaen was snoozing upstairs.

The traffic thrived on such inventiveness and individual creativity. When revenue men busted James Wray, alias John Miller, in his digs at 1504 West Fayette Street in Baltimore, they found a crafty setup. The dapper Wray, ostensibly a salesman, had a traveling case and a trunk. In the case, the agents found a 3-gallon copper tank full of whiskey. In the trunk, they found layers of padded sheaths stuffed with bottles of whiskey. They found a leather belt with sneak-pockets for half a dozen flasks. And they found a roll of greenbacks, twenties, fifties, and hundreds so fat it wouldn't fit in a pocket.

Runners didn't come more ingenious than Burwell L. Jones, finally nailed by the Norfolk police behind his residence at 915 Boissevain Avenue with a siphon full of moonshine in his hand. Jones had come up with the most devilish way to stash and transport liquor the law had yet seen. One end of his car's gasoline tank contained gas. The other end contained whiskey. To access the camouflaged whiskey tank, a small opening capped by a screw bolt was hidden behind a steel strip. A rubber tube served to transfer the cargo to jugs for sale. The space-efficiency didn't end there. Jones also had another hidden tank full of whiskey nestled behind the backseat cushion.

Captain J. L. Doxey was officer of the Norfolk police boat, which was kept quite busy in these times. He happened on another artfully conceived scam at the Ghent Bridge. Howard F. Crosby was fishing late one Sunday night. He hooked a big one and struggled. Doxey was watching it all, making ready to help the citizen haul in his catch. Then Crosby brought it up, a monstrous thing. A row of garages sat by the bridge. Crosby made for a garage with his weird catch. Doxey caught up to him and caught him red-handed with ten gallons of whiskey that had been hooked up to his line by someone on the water. In the garage, Doxey found more of the stuff. It was an elaborate setup, and it was the second time in a fortnight that Crosby had been nailed for bootlegging. In the previous run-in, he led detectives on an insane chase down city streets, the cops firing at Crosby's auto and Crosby trying to trash the whiskey cargo while flying through Norfolk thoroughfares.

A group of Norfolk police officers, including Captain Doxey and the legendary Detective Leon "No Whiskers" Nowitzky, closed in on 1620 Castner Street in December 1922. They were here to bust a moonshine plant. They went in. A seventy-year-old woman hobbled off. It was sad, really, watching the old lady shouting feeble warnings that the police were there. She was the wife of Fred Bruckner, who at seventy years of age was about to become the oldest moonshiner ever arrested in the area. Upstairs, the police found two young black men and a 30-gallon copper still. One of the black men, Leroy Campbell, offered himself up in sacrifice, trying to insist that the still was his and his alone. But the cops weren't buying it. Old Bruckner was hauled in. The house where the Brucknerslived and ran their still was at Lamberts Point, near the

Norfolk and Western Railroad. It was a small house, and the railroad owned it. Bruckner was a retired railroad employee. Of his twenty-five-dollar-a-month pension from the railroad company, five dollars a month went back to the railroad company for rent. The house had no electricity or running water. To operate the still, they hauled water in from the nearby Railroad YMCA. The court approved of Detective Nowitzky's action involving the old lady; the lawman admitted that he "didn't have the heart to arrest Bruckner's wife."

On the other end of the demographic spectrum was Preston Posey. He sold some corn liquor in January 1924, and the police got wise. He barricaded himself in a boat on the Potomac River as the officers closed in. They caught him, and he was arraigned and turned over to his mother pending further investigation. He was the youngest bootlegger ever captured in the region. He was thirteen years old.

"Not long since I learned of a boy 17 and another 15 who were drunk," said Dr. Charles Davidson in Easton. "I have found a boy 11 years old with a pint bottle of whisky on his hip. Every drunkard is still drinking; the difference is that now he seldom gets sober. I was called by a woman to treat her husband; he had been drunk for two months with Jamaica ginger. I attended another man whose stomach had been so ruined by dangerous whisky that it would not retain water and that he was regurgitating blood.

"You can imagine how bad the thing is when you learn that automobiles of bootleggers back up in front of the doors at our public dances. People are coming to realize these things and sentiment is surely turning against the Volstead Act."

Confusion was inherent in any attempt to enforce the sweeping law. A bottle of whiskey was brought in as evidence against a Baltimore saloonkeeper. The United States commissioner ended up dismissing the case. The bottle of evidence technically was the legal property of the exonerated man, but he refused to take it. As he explained to the court, by carrying it on his person on the street, he would be transporting it and thus would be liable for arrest. The Baltimore police wanted nothing to do with it, nor did the internal revenue agents. Finally, the revenue agents agreed to take the bottle and destroy it before it ever had a chance to get onto the streets. "How it was destroyed," mused the *Sun,* "is not known."

Among law enforcers the tangle of legalistic confusion led to disillusionment, and frustration led to temptation. The traffic meant easy money, and police payoffs were part of the natural rhythm of things. There were bootleg-related police-department shake-ups on the Eastern Shore and in Baltimore, Newport News, and Norfolk. J. A. Davenport was booted off the Norfolk Police Department and brought before Corporation Court after it was ascertained that for more than half a year he had been engaged in the business of transporting liquor while wearing his police uniform. The assistant commonwealth attorney condemned Davenport's actions as "comparable to treason in the army." Davenport explained that his "salary as a policeman was insufficient" to support his big family.

Cash under the table, untaxed and in obscene quantities, was proving a greater tempter, a viler corrupter, than John Barleycorn himself.

She was hailed as one of the best women orators ever to address an Eastern Shore audience when she spoke at Easton's New Theatre in October 1922. She was Miss Roena E. Shaner, national vice president of the Woman's Christian Temperance Union, and she thrilled the audience packed into the movie house at the corner of Dover and Harrison streets. She urged "every law-abiding citizen to report every violation of the law . . . and be ready to appear in court if need be." Miss Shaner declared that "law enforcement officers have a far more dangerous position than the boys who went across the sea." For it was evident, as the WCTU vice president pointed out, that those "who are doing their best to enforce the law" were up against a foe who "will not hesitate at even murder."

The Reverend J. Richard Bicking, pastor of the Salem Methodist Episcopal Church in Pocomoke City, Maryland, delivered a sermon condemning the "bootleggers and lawbreakers of Pocomoke" in July 1923. Here, amid the proliferation of stills and backwater speakeasies, and the increasingly active rum-running junctions of the lower Eastern Shore, the Reverend Bicking became a temperance warrior. His crusade arose with a concomitant change in the nature of the criminality around him. The lower Shore's horizons were being broadened. "At first when bootlegging was conducted by town characters who had their own little stills to make 'corn' everyone more or less winked at their activities as the natural result of Prohibition," said the *Crisfield Times*. "But during the past few months a decided change has come over the profession of bootlegging. A regular deluge of illicit whiskey flooded the surrounding country, with Pocomoke as its distributing point."

The rural underworld was showing off new muscle and exercising its power to make its adversaries shut up or suffer. Noted the *Times*, "Men who attempted to check or protest against the state of affairs received threatening letters warning them to desist." Yet here was the Reverend Bicking—undaunted, outspoken, bold, foolish. Bad moonshine killed a youngster, and the pastor went on the warpath. He led raids on stills, he preached with noisy anger, he pointed the damning finger. And his enemies fought back.

They drilled four holes in the hull of the Reverend Bicking's cabin motorboat *Elsie B.*, scuttling her. She was found, fixable, along the shore on the edge of town. Friends helped the preacher raise her. He got her back home and patched her up. One night, about a week later, noises came from the wharf. The preacher grabbed his shotgun and went to take a look. Men were in his boat. The preacher aimed and fired. Bullets whipped past his face in response. The boat thieves headed downriver in *Elsie B.* They torched her, and there was nothing left but smoke and cinders when she was found. The theft and arson were no deterrents. The Reverend Bicking informed the public he was "in the fight to the end."

A few weeks later, the preacher's wife, Mrs. Elsie Bicking, an invalid due to withering illness, woke her husband around four in the morning. She smelled smoke. The Bickings' house was on fire. The fire siren and the night officer's gun roused the town. A bucket brigade was formed.

The Reverend Bicking dashed from the blazing parsonage with his wife in his arms. Already deathly ill, she was now in shock. The Bickings' two sons caught fire as they fled. Paul suffered severe burns on his arms, back, and legs when his nightshirt flamed. Willard, the older son, was burned on the face, then lacerated by glass as he threw himself through a closed window. The bucket brigade was futile. The house was destroyed. Mrs. Bicking died.

The Board of Trustees of the Salem Methodist Episcopal Church offered a thousand-dollar reward for information leading to the arrest of the arsonist or arsonists. The Town Council offered up another thousand. Despite his loss, the Reverend Bicking stood tough. His "activities against the lawless of the community will never cease," he declared. "Threats against my life, the death of my wife and even perils to my boys will not deter me from continuing my war against the Pocomoke vice ring."

The preacher was on the verge of a breakdown, but he declared that he would deliver his Sunday sermon as usual. The church's board of trustees wouldn't allow him to do so; he was in no condition, it was clear. The Wilmington Methodist Episcopal Preachers' Association issued a support statement for the Reverend Bicking: "He has the spirit of the old reformers and martyrs. He has nobly maintained the best traditions of Methodism in his fight against all evil practice, individual or organized. . . . We are proud of him and his brave family, who have carried a load sufficient to break any man's courage."

The state's attorney's office worked with local lawmen and arrested three boys. Two of the boys were Pocomoke natives; the third boy was from Baltimore. They confessed that Elwood Bevans of Pocomoke had paid them to torch the preacher's boat and house. The boys were thrown in the Snow Hill jail and more arrests were made, including not only Elwood but a couple of other Bevanses as well, in addition to another half dozen or so members of the local bootlegging subculture. The state's attorney developed a witness list, and as people prepared to testify before the Worcester County Grand Jury in session at Snow Hill, the intimidation campaign began.

Colmore E. Byrd, cashier of the Citizens' National Bank of Pocomoke City, was called to testify, and someone stole his boat. Someone damaged the motorcar of Adolph Bye, another threat target. Sylvester W. Messick, a policeman assigned to breaking up the bootlegging cabal, was set to testify, and he was the next victim. At two in the morning, as Messick, his wife, and daughter lay sleeping, someone blew up Messick's newly built stable. The explosion rocked Messick's house, shook nearby buildings, shattered several windowpanes in the area, and filled the sky with demolished lumber shrapnel. The saboteur knew what he was doing. Had the dynamite charge been placed on the ground in the stable, the concussion would have merely spat dirt and made a hole. But the explosive had been expertly hung from a second-floor joist, bursting the stable skyward and blanketing the surrounding land with a rainstorm of timber and splinters.

Sentences eventually handed down in the case ranged from fines to jail time. Elwood Bevans, the alleged instigator, was released due to lack of evidence. The war was frustratingly inconclusive. The press had paraphrased the Reverend Bicking stating that "affairs in Pocomoke had reached such a state that all who stood idly and did not take part in the battle against the bootleggers were equally culpable with them."

Those who had tried to do their part had found their mettle tested by death threats, larceny, arson, and terrorism. As the situation neared anarchy, the Ku Klux Klan, its roster swelling to record numbers in those days, volunteered to help restore order.

"Where do they get the whiskey?" asked the *Easton Star-Democrat* as the ranks of the inebriated grew. "This is the question that many . . . would like to have answered. It seems to come in large lots, for there are a number of persons arrested at the same time for being drunk, and it appears that after that there is no more evidence of liquor until another crowd is under its influence a week or so later."

It came from the neighborhood druggist and the neighborhood moonshiner. It came from Baltimore and New Jersey, courtesy of the automobile-propelled hawkers. And, increasingly, as the Easton paper noted, there were signs that "a new epoch" was dawning in the traffic, as, with increasing regularity, "whiskey was being brought in motor boats and sold."

The earliest rumrunners of the Chesapeake waterways, locals moving local product, were becoming part of a larger world, a world in which fast, indigenous boats were the all-important consorts to large, ocean-going deliverers from far-flung ports. As 1923 heated up, the *Norfolk Virginian-Pilot* reported: "Federal agents have begun to unfold a story of organized outlawry which puts to shame, for sheer technique and audacity, the grimmest tales of buccaneering on the high seas in the days of Captain Kidd."

No liquid lunch allowed: Prohibition officers raid Hammel's Lunchroom in Washington in 1923. Courtesy Library of Congress (LC-USZ62-95478).

Revelers on a joyride enjoy a jug at Bay Ridge, Annapolis, in 1925. Courtesy Maryland State Archives (MSA SC 2140-181).

Backwoods stills such as this rig proliferated in the Bay country during Prohibition. Courtesy Doug Bast, Boonsborough Museum of History, and Maryland State Archives (MSA SC 4073-44).

Dry agents in 1922 pose after shutting down the largest still raided up to that time in Washington. Courtesy Library of Congress (LC-USZ62-95475).

A moonshine-sniffing "hooch hound" patrols the Potomac in 1923. Courtesy Library of Congress (LC-USZ62-96300).

A flapper of the region shows off a fashionable, functional accessory—her garter flask. Courtesy Library of Congress (LC-USZ62-99952).

A bootlegger's smoke screen clouds the view of D.C. motorcycle police during a high-speed chase in 1923. Courtesy Library of Congress (LC-F801-26020).

A "rumrunner of the road" is wrecked after a chase through Washington in 1922. Courtesy Library of Congress (LC-USZ62-96758).

Norfolk dry agents dump out the liquid contraband of the captured rumrunner *Silver Spray.* Courtesy The Mariners' Museum, Newport News, Virginia.

Pocomoke City temperance gathering, 1908. Courtesy Maryland State Archives (MSA SC 1477-4960).

As Chesapeake rumrunners grew more brazen, U.S. Coast Guard Commandant F.C. Billard advocated "the liberal use of gunfire."

Pleading for more vessels, Commander Lucien J. Ker of Section Base Eight, Norfolk, avowed that the number of boats he had were "barely sufficient to maintain a Chesapeake Bay patrol."

Speaking of the Chesapeake rumrunners, Sixth District Commander Irwin B. Steele said, "It is our duty to catch them, and *catch them we must.*"

The Coast Guard cutter *Winnisimet* was a Chesapeake sentinel. Courtesy National Archives.

The Baltimore-based Coast Guard cutter *Apache* roamed the Bay as a rum-chaser. She was built in Baltimore in the early 1890s. Courtesy National Archives.

The Coast Guard cutter *Yamacraw* saw service in the Chesapeake and was involved in the *Glen Beulah* incident. *Top:* Courtesy National Archives.

The Coast Guard cutter *Manning* patrolled along the Chesapeake Capes. Built in 1897, she was a veteran of the Spanish-American War and World War I. Courtesy National Archives.

The patrol boat *CG-182* was constructed at Newport News during the great federal rum-war force buildup of 1924. Courtesy The Mariners' Museum, Newport News, Virginia.

The 38-foot *CG-2385* exemplified the rum-chasing picket boat.

In a typical 1927 mid-Atlantic scene, a Coast Guard picket boat chases and fires upon a rumrunner. Courtesy National Archives.

This page and top photo on facing page: Some didn't make it through the gauntlet: officials off-load rum boats captured in the lower Bay. Courtesy The Mariners' Museum, Newport News, Virginia.

A Coast Guard vessel and smuggling schooner take part in a classic 1920s sea chase.

CHAPTER THREE

SCOTCH AND WATER

Rum ships hovered at the mouth of Chesapeake Bay. There were four of them, British, hanging back beyond the 3-mile limit with combined booze cargoes worth an estimated $1 million. It was May 1923, and the quartet of rummies anchored off the Virginia Capes had, according to the Norfolk press, a clear-cut aim: "flooding Washington with whisky." The biggest and most infamous of the four was the steam yacht *Istar*, aka "queen of the rum-runners" and "flagship of the rum fleet." *Istar* had arrived at the Chesapeake with thirty-three thousand cases of the quality stuff from Glasgow; speedboats had already managed to run about five or six thousand cases to Washington by Friday, May 25, when federal Prohibition agents brandishing warrants swooped down on the Atlantic Hotel in Norfolk and arrested a woman and two men. One of the men declared himself to be "second in command of the Atlantic Coast rum fleet." As he spilled his story to the feds, Coast Guard vessels swarmed the Chesapeake entrance in hopes of stemming the incoming alcohol tide.

The rum war was on.

In the Atlantic Ocean, from New England to the Virginia Capes and on southward, an ad hoc international fleet congregated. The vessels came from Canada, England, France, Bermuda, the Bahamas, Cuba, and, of course, the United States. The vessel types and ports of origin varied, but they had key things in common: speed and illegal cargo. They stayed far enough out to dodge authority, but came close enough in for small, quick craft to race out, load up on liquor, and run for shore. In the Atlantic Ocean, a long line had been drawn by outlaw crews, and they called it Rum Row.

Throughout the Roaring Twenties, the United States Coast Guard would fight the so-called rum war; it was the Coast Guard versus a motley shadow society of foes who were highly organized, rich, and getting richer all the time. From its roiling epicenter off New York, Rum Row stretched north to Maine, south past the Delaware breakwater, and beyond the Chesapeake Bay to the Carolina coast. Along the Chesapeake region's Atlantic spine, the rum war would be fought by the men of the U.S. Coast Guard Sixth District, with stations aligned down the shore from Lewes, Delaware, to Chincoteague and the Virginia Eastern Shore. At the entrance to Chesapeake Bay, which was emerging as a popular point of entry for Rum Row vessels by 1923, the patrolling duties would fall to U.S. Coast Guard crews stationed at Norfolk and Hampton Roads, buttressed in times of emergency by Baltimore-based vessels that were rushed down the Bay, particularly that durable Coast Guard warhorse *Apache*. A special headquarters—Section Base Eight, Norfolk Division—would be created as the rum war heated up.

It was heating up fast in the spring of 1923. Rum-running activity had been heavy off New Jersey; the law was cracking down. Whiskey-laden vessels shimmied down the coast and did their imitation of John Smith: they discovered Chesapeake Bay. Others had come before. The foursome converging off the Bay that May learned what other rum-runners already knew: the inland sea offered optimum smuggling opportunities. The lucrative Washington and Baltimore markets beckoned, and there were loads of locals with fast boats and a fluency in the art of outsmarting the powers that be. The British rumrunners anchored offshore as their land agents cut deals in Norfolk. The million-dollar cargo was perfect for Washington; the national Shriners Convention was coming to town, and D.C. booze-suppliers were clamoring for a big score. While *Istar* off-loaded, federal agents zeroed in. The Coast Guard and the Norfolk district attorney's office pitched in on the investigation, culminating in the three-way sting at the Atlantic Hotel on May 25.

The Norfolk arrests yielded alarming information. The rumrunners at the Chesapeake entrance were part of a fleet that, according to the *Norfolk Virginian-Pilot*, "constitutes one of the most powerful and most completely financed enterprises of its kind in the history of outlawry. So huge is the enterprise, in fact, that it takes on a semblance of the old privateer days, when rich and smug citizens financed pirate ships which plied their nefarious trade on all the seas." The rum fleet was "managed and financed by men of means who held high positions and who take little, if any, of the risk involved in conducting their business in direct defiance of the American laws." It was "a gigantic smuggling syndicate with important branches in New York, Canada, London, Scotland and the Bermudas . . . The syndicate . . . is comprised of prominent men in New York City and abroad. The membership is said to include fifty-four men, the majority of whom represent large financial interests." The rum ships anchored off the Chesapeake were "members of a powerfully organized combine, with unlimited financial backing and with a definite, well defined program in view." The Norfolk arrests were the first step in "an effort to grasp the leaders in what is termed the most powerful ring of rum-smugglers in the world."

The arrestees, charged with "unlawfully conspiring to smuggle and transfer intoxicating liquors into the United States," were New Yorkers William E. Baker, alias William L. Burwell; his wife, Elizabeth Baker; and Rex D. Sheldon. The lawmen had Baker pegged as "One Eye Burwell," a figure in the high-profile Becker-Rosenthal New York murder case. Police Lieutenant Charles Becker had ordered a hit on gambler Herman Rosenthal. Rosenthal was snuffed, Becker was executed, and One Eye Burwell, who walked free after being hit with nothing worse than a false-affidavit beef, was suspected of being one of Becker's hired guns.

Rex Sheldon, a former member of the infamous Montague Gang (New York "society bootleggers"), was still a wanted man along the Hudson. He and two other rum smugglers had been indicted; trial was held, Sheldon pulled a failure-to-appear fast one, and his cronies took the fall.

The Norfolk feds found William Baker talkative. He detailed the Chesapeake setup. For two weeks, he and other top "agents of the liquor fleet" had been in Norfolk negotiating transactions and arranging for the transport of goods from ship to shore and on to the nation's capital. Among other things, Baker was responsible for rounding up local talent for speedboat delivery duty. Sheldon, the supply purchasing agent, was also known as "the fixer." It was his job to hobnob with officialdom and grease the right palms "to make it possible to smuggle liquor without fear of arrest."

Elizabeth Baker, a mother of three when not fulfilling the role of rumrunner's moll, claimed to be ignorant of the details of her husband's business, and she was suspected of being, at most, a go-between, a messenger. "She is quiet in demeanor," reported the *Virginian-Pilot*, "and somewhat reserved in contrast to the male prisoners, whose fondness for talking was said by the Federal authorities to have aided in their own undoing."

Baker and Sheldon explained standard procedures. The main bootleggers in a given city would pool cash and hammer out a deal with a rum ship's business agent for the whole cargo. Meanwhile, the business agents would use a secret code to communicate via wireless to the ship captains, "informing them when to expect visits and the character of the visits."

Istar and the other rum ships—the steam yachts *Cartona* and *Strand Hill* and the schooner *Mary Beatrice*—were under close scrutiny now; by all reports, only *Istar* had managed to disgorge cargo before the Coast Guard clampdown. And as they hovered off the Chesapeake, there was the impending threat of "international complications" in the form of a gun—not a harmless, acceptable, yachtsman's one-pounder mounted forward for common saluting purposes, but rather a serious-business six-pounder, or three-inch rifle, perhaps—mounted on *Istar*'s aft deck, sighted by the Coast Guard vessel *Mascoutin*. The State Department had concerns. Here, lying just outside U.S. territorial waters, was a ship flying the British flag and sporting a nasty piece of aft-mounted artillery. The issue turned moot. The rumrunners disappeared.

Federal agents had intercepted ship-to-shore messages. They grilled the Norfolk three and cajoled Baker into kicking forth with the key to the code. *Istar* was bound for Bermuda, the deciphered missives indicated. Later, the feds would figure out that the coded messages were just a dodge, a crafty feint; *Istar* had moved up the coast, after having unloaded onto *Strand Hill* and *Mary Beatrice* the remainder of the booze she hadn't already shipped landward. They were still out there, somewhere.

"The story of the first effective raid on the Atlantic coast rum smugglers is but the opening chapter of a history which may be written of the rum trade that has been lifted from the plane of the bootlegger and converted into high finance," said the *Virginian-Pilot.* "It is a history that bids fair to take place alongside those vivid chronicles of the slave trade of the old days, or the ravage of that coterie of romantic scoundrels and privateers headed by Stede Bonnet, Captain Teach and the renowned Captain Kidd. . . . the steam yacht *Istar* and her following of lesser craft are nothing more nor less than the privateers of other days, modernized for the sake of expediency. . . . these ships are ships of prey no less than was the memorable *Revenge* of Captain Bonnet."

Rum Row's archetypal hero also happened to be its reputed founder: Big Bill McCoy, a strapping American who loved the adventure of it all and lost interest as mercenary fat cats inevitably came to dominate the smuggling scene. Tough, smart, a bit of a romantic, McCoy was top dog among the brethren of the coast during Rum Row's formative period. In the crime-spawning hothouse environment of Prohibition, some sort of Rum Row was destined to be born. It happened to be Big Bill McCoy who would deliver the first profitable offshore booze shipment that inspired the rapid growth of rum-running. As McCoy recounted it, the birth of Rum Row was on the New York coast, which, of course, would later become the heart of it. But it was almost initiated at the Chesapeake Bay.

McCoy's first load was fifteen hundred cases of Old Granddad rye, property of the Vance brothers, who had got it out of the States aboard the steamer *Baltimore* and had it stashed in a Bahamian bonded warehouse. McCoy's original intention was to run the cargo in at the Virginia Capes: "We battened down the hatch, put the rags on her, and went breezing up the warm blue road of the Gulf Stream, Norfolk bound." While McCoy's yacht *Henry L. Marshall* waited off Cape Charles, McCoy hitched a ride landward on a fishing schooner; the fare was a case of whiskey for the schooner captain. McCoy's connection was waiting for him in Norfolk with a pair of Italian gentlemen "who were to become leaders in the distributing end of the bootlegging industry." The bottom line, though, was that Norfolk interests didn't want to cough up the cash this go-round. So it was on to New York, and "thus *Marshall* founded Rum Row," said McCoy. If that seminal shipment had offloaded as originally planned, the Chesapeake, from the very beginning, would have been more at the center of Rum Row than along its southern edge. But Chesapeake Bay's emergence as Rum Row's back-door entrance was star status enough; by 1923 it was so inundated with smuggling action anyway that patrol boats couldn't keep up. It was a wide-open back door.

"The *Apache*, with a machine gun on her forward deck and with her six-pounders uncovered, tonight patrols the mouth of the Chesapeake Bay hunting an expected rendezvous between rum ships and supply boats," said *Baltimore Sun* correspondent Raymond S. Tompkins, filing his on-deck report by wireless to Hampton Roads. It was May 25, 1923, and *Apache* had come down the Bay to help hunt *Istar* and her consorts. "The Baltimore ship on this five-day vigil rolls heavily in the high seas at the Capes and everything is lashed down. Officers and crew, most of them Baltimoreans, are cruising under wartime sea rules. No smoking is allowed on deck and port hole lights are out as the *Apache* sneaks at seven knots across the 10-mile sea gate. . . . The *Istar*, flagship of the rum fleet, is said to have a big gun on the aft deck. If she fires a shot, however, . . . the Baltimore gunners will sink her. Among the crew of the *Apache* are veterans who took part in many submarine hunts during the World War and are eager for a scrap."

A great deal of alcohol had made it ashore. Some of *Istar*'s cargo was seized in Baltimore. And some of it, reported the *Virginian-Pilot*, had "seeped into Norfolk from the quiet-looking little ships that played hide and seek with the revenue cutters out there beyond the 'dead line.'" As for the main destination, Washington, the Bay's speedboat smugglers ultimately succeeded in running an estimated eight thousand cases up the Potomac. The *Washington Post* reported that D.C. bootleggers were getting $85 to $120 a case for *Istar*'s whiskey, and that the town seemed amply stocked for the upcoming Shriners Convention. Even though she and her consorts had been driven off before completely unloading, *Istar* had succeeded, said the *Virginian-Pilot*, in "flooding Washington with the biggest liquor supply it has had since the country went dry."

The feds suspected that even more cargo had been discharged somewhere in the lower Chesapeake, and that it was stashed and awaiting shipment to Washington, Baltimore, New York, and other profitably thirsty towns. And it came to light that even before *Istar*'s arrival, other rumrunners had made recent huge deliveries to Baltimore and Washington, and that liquor had been moving through Hampton Roads night after night.

Prohibition officials conceded that trying to staunch the flow of whiskey from ship to shore was growing ever more daunting. Coast Guard officers estimated that some twenty patrol vessels would be needed to thwart the small-craft rumrunners darting in and out of the Chesapeake Bay entrance with ever-greater frequency. Significant amounts of liquor were making it into the Bay; this much the Coast Guardsmen knew. They also knew they just couldn't seem to stop it.

Apache's back-and-forth Bay-entrance sentinel duty had yielded zero. Raymond Tompkins reported over the wireless: "To date since this handsome white ship dashed away from Baltimore to chase rum pirates out to sea, we have caught four fish. We have not caught any pirates, nor found any rum.

"... A brave sortie out upon the waters, with a commission pennon flying from the peak and men polishing long slim guns on the decks, and the promise of swift brushes with the long, low rakish craft of the Johnnie Walker Navy, has become a fishing party off Cobb's Island."

The Baltimore crew had started out with gusto and itchy trigger fingers. "The ship cruised back and forth, back and forth, between Cape Charles and Cape Henry. There were rumors, 'They are going to try it tonight!' Ship's lights were low and hope of a scrap ran high." But days of ennui had eroded their objectives. "Today we will punch any rum-runner in the jaw, not for carrying liquor, but for scaring the fish."

Tedious vessel searches had defined the *Apache*'s Virginia Capes assignment, not the thrilling rum-pirate shoot-outs that were expected. The Baltimore correspondent griped, "Compared to fighting off the U-boat hornets on a wild night off Portugal, this business of trying to keep out of the Chesapeake a few thousand bottles of diluted whisky carried by a fleet of sneaking mongrels of the sea is, well, Sherlock Holmes walking a beat in the Northern district." The constant reports of liquor cargoes arriving in the Chesapeake exasperated the crew. Their logical reaction was disbelief. They were stopping and searching every boat they saw, and swifter Coast Guard craft were on the prowl farther out. They couldn't believe the liquor was getting past them. It was. While the men patrolling the Chesapeake entrance cast fishing lines and griped of boredom, the rum fleet outflanked them, finding, as it were, the back door to the back door.

Residents along the Chesapeake and Albemarle Canal had been reporting an unusually high volume of water traffic, and federal officials gradually got wise. The rum ships had dropped down the coast and hooked up with North Carolina motorboaters. Fast boats took on liquor loads, threaded through Currituck Sound, dashed up the Chesapeake and Albemarle Canal to the Elizabeth River and on into Chesapeake Bay. There they either made shoreline drop-offs or went ahead to Washington and the cash-waving bootleggers still stockpiling potables for Shriners Convention mania.

Meanwhile, at the mouth of the Chesapeake, a thick fog settled in. On *Apache*, Ray Tompkins remarked that the fog rendered any rum fleet that might be out there "as invisible as a flapper's natural complexion."

The fog was a moot point, or a metaphor, or both, for as Tompkins pointed out, "So far as the *Apache* was concerned the rum navy had been invisible from the start."

Investigators became convinced that the headquarters of the rum-running outfit was in London. It was known that the top man in the *Istar* operation had made $250,000 off the Chesapeake run. Baker admitted that the top man had been in Norfolk, also. The feds knew it all too well. They had tried to nab the elusive top man, but he got past them both in Norfolk and in Washington, to which he traveled by boat at one point during the deal-making. The authorities knew he was going there and still failed to nail him. Baker tried to convince his interrogators that this enigmatic "man higher up" had ordered Sheldon to "bump Baker off."

Even on a run largely aborted by Coast Guard vigilance, some rum-syndicate big shot had managed to sail away from the Chesapeake Bay with a cool quarter-million. Who was this mysterious mastermind? During *Istar*'s Virginia Capes sojourn, a lot of Norfolk people had boated out to visit, set up deals, buy product, arrange to deliver product, and such. A Norfolk citizen who visited *Istar* came back and told the press that "at least one man aboard the ship had held a seat in the British Parliament, and that all with whom he came in contact bore evidence of excellent breeding and wealth."

U.S. Coast Guard instructions eventually were issued to crews patrolling the entrance to the Chesapeake Bay:

> You will be particularly vigilant in the boarding and examination of vessels, especially motor-boats, tug boats, sailing vessels and barges. Such vessels should be boarded frequently and every effort made to see that they are observing the law in every respect.

Chesapeake patrol-boat crewmen bunked on board, ready to fuel up at Hampton Roads Naval Supply Station and race to sea on short notice. "You will be required to keep your boat in readiness for immediate service at all times." Enlisted men got a subsistence allowance of a dollar a day. The officer in charge pooled money and bought all the food. As for drink options, "The use of intoxicating liquors will not be tolerated," the orders admonished, lest anyone forget that contraband was contraband, and not booty to be savored. ". . . Each person shall so conduct himself as not to bring discredit or adverse comment . . . upon the Coast Guard."

Beyond honor, the reasons for sober deportment were pragmatic from a publicity standpoint:

The personnel of section bases and of boats attached thereto will be constantly under observation by the public. Their conduct and appearance will be noted by everybody in the community in which the base is located, including many persons unfriendly to the mission and who will be only too pleased to "get something" on the men. Absolute integrity, exemplary conduct, scrupulous neatness, and care and discretion in picking associates are matters of vital importance.

The chase, of course, was the main thing:

You should be able to remain at sea for several days at a time, under reasonable weather conditions, and you shall keep on board at all times sufficient fresh and dry stores to enable you to do so.

When assigned to watch a rum ship you should remain at your post under all weather conditions under which rum running launches can operate. When the weather is so bad that it is evident that small vessels cannot take a cargo from a rum ship, you should seek shelter.

. . . When on patrol you should endeavor:

a) To quickly discover newly arrived rum ships.

b) To watch all rum ships and prevent any intercourse with them by craft from shore.

c) To keep them from disposing of their cargoes.

d) To "hang on" the rum ship unceasingly, day and night, following her up when she changes position, and to wear the rum ship out.

e) To stop, board and seize (if circumstances warrant) all craft suspected of rum running.

f) To prevent entrance into inlets, rivers, or bays, or landing of liquor on the beach, by rum running craft that have eluded or escaped from our forces offshore.

g) To harass the enemy.

The 50-ton sloop *Glen Beulah* was looming with eighteen hundred cases of Lewis Hunter rye whiskey in the haze-thick darkness off the Virginia Capes when an unidentified "mystery ship" rammed her and sank her on Saturday night, June 2, 1923. *Glen Beulah* went down in less than fifteen minutes. Her nine crewmen were in their pajamas in a rowboat with one oar when rescued by the Coast Guard cutter *Yamacraw*. The predominantly American crew of the British vessel with papers out of the Bahamas spent Sunday in the Norfolk city jail.

Protestations were loud and profanity-laced in the jail: *Glen Beulah* was not engaged in illicit rum-trafficking, but had merely stopped for engine repairs at the entrance to the Chesapeake while en route from Nassau to Canada, asserted her captain. He also asserted, with damning invective, that it was the Coast Guard vessel *Mascoutin* that had sent *Glen Beulah* and her cargo beneath the waves.

"Ridiculous," countered Lieutenant Commander C. S. Root, acting head of Coast Guard operations in the vicinity. "We have reason to know that the *Mascoutin* was well within the Capes when the collision occurred. The *Glen Beulah* was anchored ten miles southeast of the Cape Charles Lightship when she was sunk." Furthermore, Lieutenant Commander W. P. Wishaar, skipper of the crew-rescuing *Yamacraw*, had caught a glimpse of the mystery ship speeding off after crashing *Glen Beulah*. It was a two-masted yacht, stated Wishaar; the Coast Guard's *Mascoutin* was a one-masted tug.

Not so, countered Captain George Kelly, the master of *Glen Beulah*. He was a big burly Floridian, a crusty sea veteran in his fifties with deep-tanned skin and a mop of black hair going gray. "The *Mascoutin* hit us and ran off like a dog to leave us to our fate," Captain Kelly said. ". . . I tell you, we were lucky we were not drowned. . . . I know it was the *Mascoutin*, because I had been watching that boat ever since we anchored. She was cruising around out there. She had a black hull and one mast and the boat that hit us was the same boat. I was close enough to see her as she pulled away."

When confronted with the information that *Mascoutin* had been sent into the Bay at six-thirty in the evening, hours before the collision, Captain Kelly replied, "She must be an airship."

While definite in his accusations, Captain Kelly was vague in many of his answers. He said he couldn't remember the name of *Glen Beulah*'s owner, the man who had hired him to haul the liquor. He said he didn't know how much the cargo was worth, only that he was being paid $250 to transport it and would get "other considerations" on completion of delivery. He was somewhat cavalier about the fact that his name was on the government's list of suspected rumrunners. "Going to sea is my business. If a man hires me to run his boat I am likely to take the job." Formerly, he had operated out of Pamlico Sound in his own boat, *The Buccaneer*. "In appearance, the grizzled master of the wrecked sloop suggests the characters that have been made famous by authors of romantic tales of the sea," a Norfolk reporter wrote. "He is equipped with a seagoing vocabulary, which he drew upon unreservedly and unblushingly."

Prohibition agents were authorized to detain suspects for twenty-four hours. Captain Kelly and his crew were released after twenty-three hours and thirty minutes. Still dressed in the ill-fitting, random duds they had been given to wear when picked up by *Yamacraw*, they went straight to the British Consulate and stuck to their version of the events. As a matter of routine, British Consul Barton Myers forwarded their story of the shipwreck to the British Embassy. But he also forwarded the official report of Lieutenant Commander Wishaar of *Yamacraw*.

The rum-chaser had first sighted *Glen Beulah* on May 29, Wishaar stated, and when asked what his cargo was, Captain Kelly had shouted back, "I'll give you one guess."

She was British and beyond the 3-mile limit, so she stayed unmolested, said Wishaar. But "the fact that she should remain at anchor so close to the United States, with a cargo which it was quite safe to assume was liquor, led to the belief that she was waiting for an opportunity to land liquor in the United States illegally by means of either transferring it to other craft, by buoying for other craft to pick up, or by running into some convenient harbor with the liquor itself to unload it.

"Because of this belief, the Coast Guard units operating in that vicinity decided to keep an exceptionally close watch on her. This watch was maintained for several days, and during this time several suspicious incidents were observed. . . One night the *Glen Beulah* was seen to signal with a closed-in light to somebody at sea, sending a succession of four flashes at intervals. On another night a vessel . . . with no lights showing, was seen in the vicinity, but because of the Coast Guard unit's presence did not approach the *Glen Beulah*."

On June 2 the mystery ship struck *Glen Beulah* portside aft of amidships, reported Wishaar. "Evidently fearing detention and arrest by the Coast Guard cutter, the unknown vessel did not stop, but immediately proceeded in a northerly direction and was lost to view." By the time *Glen Beulah*'s crew had been rescued, pursuit of the mystery ship was pointless.

"The early suspicions concerning the mission of the *Glen Beulah* were further increased by actual contact with her crew," said Wishaar. "It seems quite evident now that this aggregation was gotten together for the explicit purpose of endeavoring to evade the United States Prohibition Act, the Volstead law, and any other state or federal act which has to do with prohibiting the bringing-in of liquor to the country. It is hard to understand how an American crew can be permitted to completely man a British vessel and how they can obtain honest clearance."

Silhouetted in *Yamacraw*'s powerful searchlight, the fleeing mystery ship had strongly resembled *Istar*. The Coast Guard's theory was that *Istar* or some other similar rum ship was pulling up alongside *Glen Beulah* for a cargo transfer. The Coast Guard vessel's approach put the kibosh to the proceedings, and in a panic to get lost, one rumrunner rammed the other.

The Coast Guard ordered Chesapeake Bay patrol-boat officers and crew to be on constant lookout for vessels in suspicious rendezvous:

> The general plan is to watch rum ships so closely and so continually that no boat from shore can go alongside them, so that there shall be no more cases before the courts of vessels, or boats, seized for rum running. Pending the consummation of this plan, if any boat from the shore does receive liquor from a rum ship, see that the boat does not get to the shore with that liquor in her. If the fleeing rum runner throws her cargo overboard, pick up only enough for evidence if required, and sink the rest. Your mission is to prevent a drop of liquor from getting ashore from the rum ships.

The British steamship *Rowan Park* was in the Atlantic Ocean off Diamond Shoals, near the entrance to the Chesapeake Bay, when she spied a schooner showing a distress signal. *Rowan Park* came alongside the schooner. The schooner's skipper identified his craft as *Leader;* she'd lost her rudder, he said. They were trying to maneuver her by sails alone, he said. The officers of *Rowan Park* invited the rudderless sailors aboard. They said they didn't want to abandon their vessel. But could *Rowan Park* radio the Coast Guard for help?

Rowan Park made the radio call and went on her way. Responding to the call, the Coast Guard cutter *Manning,* on patrol nearby, headed out to the struggling schooner's aid. But as the Coast Guard cutter headed out, the schooner headed in. The schooner wasn't damaged. The schooner wasn't called *Leader,* either. She was *Julito,* Honduran registry, a rumrunner with a perfectly healthy rudder and a cargo consisting of two thousand cases of champagne, gin, and raw alcohol. She scooted through the Virginia Capes and headed up the Chesapeake Bay. By the time she got to the Poquoson River she had two Coast Guard patrol boats on her tail. The patrol boats gave chase, overtook the rumrunner, and boarded her. A dog barked and scampered. Bacon and eggs crackled in a frying pan on the galley stove. The crew had disappeared.

Standard procedure in chasing a suspected smuggler: fire a warning shot; if it does no good, then give forth with live shot. It was all spelled out in Section 2765 of the Revised Statutes:

> Whenever any vessel liable to seizure or examination does not bring-to, on being required to do so, or on being chased by a cutter or boat . . . of the Coast Guard, the master of such cutter or boat may fire at or into such vessel which does not bring-to, after . . . pendant and ensign has been hoisted and a gun has been fired . . . as a signal; . . . If any person is killed or wounded by such firing, and the master is prosecuted or arrested therefor, he shall be forthwith admitted to bail.

Chesapeake crews were given instructions stressing that guardsmen's intentions must be clear:

> The Coast Guard intends to stop rum running at sea, and it intends to make any vessel bring-to that is liable to seizure or examination. Be sure that the vessel pursued knows that you are calling upon her to stop. Blow the whistle and fire a number of shots across her bow. When this has been done and you are entirely satisfied that the vessel pursued knows that you mean for her to stop, if she continues to flee you are fully authorized under the law, in the opinion of Headquarters, to "fire at or into such vessel."
> . . . If it becomes necessary to fire at or into a vessel to bring her to or to prevent her escape, be sure to fire several warning shots across her bow to attract her attention before firing into her. If you have to fire into her, try to disable her steering gear, rudder, etc., and not fire into a group of men unnecessarily.

When the British two-masted rum schooner *Mary Beatrice* was anchored at the mouth of the Chesapeake in late May 1923, no one who came in contact with her noticed a gang of illegal aliens on board. The vessel vanished with *Istar* and the other rum ships, and when she showed up in New York two weeks later, she had no cargo, no papers, no captain, no crew, and no compass. But she did have fifteen confused

Chinese passengers on board. Asked about the missing crew, one of the men answered by pointing over the side.

Mary Beatrice had become, as the New York press dubbed her, "a strange ship with a weird tale of the sea." Immigration inspectors brought in an interpreter and the Chinese gave their bloody account. Other rumrunners had reported no trace of the illegal aliens on board *Mary Beatrice* while she was anchored off the Virginia Capes. If so, then it had to have been some other vessel the Chinese boarded in Havana, twenty of them paying the unidentified man $250 apiece to smuggle them into the United States. At some point after disappearing from the Virginia Capes, *Mary Beatrice* took on the illegal aliens. And somewhere off the New Jersey coast, an unidentified woman and an unnamed "stool pigeon" boated out to *Mary Beatrice*. They got back off as the situation grew nasty. The "tall sailorman" absconded with the passage money, abandoning the ship and its human cargo to their fate. Food and water were running low. The mate now demanded an additional $250 apiece from the increasingly desperate immigrants. A bloody hand-to-hand battle broke out between the Chinese passengers and the four-man crew. The fighting raged with axes, razors, knives, marlinspikes. The crew was slaughtered; they took five Chinese with them. The Chinese survivors threw the corpses overboard and drifted.

Reports were coming in from Rum Row that other smuggling vessels were likewise diversifying. According to the U.S. attorney's office, *Strand Hill*, which had lain at anchor off the Chesapeake with *Istar* and *Mary Beatrice*, was among the craft that had illegal immigrants aboard waiting to be smuggled ashore. Narcotics also were creeping into the repertoire, federal officials noted warily.

Coast Guard orders gave a clear mandate—cast a net of suspicion widely:

It is of the utmost importance that single barges in tow of tug boats bound into Chesapeake Bay be stopped, boarded and examined. This is especially necessary when such barge appears to be light or only lightly laden.

While on patrol all motor boats, fishing vessels, small sail vessels and single barges in tow of tugs shall be stopped, boarded and thoroughly examined to see that they have the necessary marine documents, have no contraband liquor or drugs on board, and are complying with the laws in all respects.

Thanks to Rum Row, Nassau, Bahamas, became a boom town, a rumrunners' haven crowded with British distillery agents and American profiteer-adventurers. During the "first wave of the boom," recalled McCoy, "Bay Street, usually somnolent, grew active. Liquor dealers enlarged their quarters. Murphy, an American and later my main source of supply, bought a quantity of rye in Baltimore. A United States Shipping Board vessel brought the cargo over and landed it in Nassau. Every case of it thereafter went back to the United States via Rum Row."

Another speck on the map that flourished was a bleak granite island in the cold north: St. Pierre, largest chunk of rock in a cluster of French islands off Newfoundland. St. Pierre was a remote outpost of impoverished codfishermen; it became a multimillion dollar liquor-traffic junction, "Nassau's chief rival for the rum trade," said McCoy. Crates of booze proudly bearing St. Pierre's name regularly turned up as far south on Rum Row as the Chesapeake.

A pioneer of Chesapeake booze smuggling may have been a Scotsman named Alastair Moray who, according to local accounts, came across the Atlantic in the four-masted schooner *Cask* with twenty thousand cases of whiskey from Glasgow, entered the Virginia Capes, and anchored off Point Lookout, Maryland, in December 1922. Speedboats, drafted into service out of Baltimore and Washington, were ready and waiting to greet the Scottish four-master. They ran the whiskey in at Smith Creek. Trucks loaded up and hauled the Scotch to Washington.

As Moray recounted it, he had been minding his business, walking along a Glasgow street one day when a friend approached him with a job offer. The friend hooked Moray up with a rum-ship owner seeking an officer to handle the cargo. Moray signed on as such; the vessel was the aptly

christened *Cask*. Moray immediately got to work stocking up on supplies: "I purchased six .450 Webley revolvers, one Colt .450, an automatic .38, and plenty of ammunition." As *Cask* departed Glasgow, drifting down the Clyde, off to America, "Our progress down the river was nothing if not pleasant and successful, after the pilot had told the skipper that he wouldn't go any further unless a sober man was at the wheel. After some search, a gentleman answering to that description was found."

To stave off ocean-voyage monotony, Moray brought along his bagpipes. While at sea, he composed a pipe tune he called "Bootleggers' March," or "March to Rum Row." "With a few alterations, it will not be bad—at least, that is the composer's opinion," he told his journal. In addition to bagpiping, there was another Caledonian antidote for high-seas boredom. "We have mapped out a golf course on the poop. We play with a rope ring and a T-shaped bit of stick, with circles marked on the deck with chalk for holes. At present I hold the championship with a score of twenty-five for nine holes."

There were, of course, more disruptive means of fun-seeking on a vessel that happened to be hauling twenty thousand cases of the amber. "Someone with malice aforethought managed to get a couple of bottles into the fo'c'sle this afternoon; result, a certain amount of rowdiness," Moray chronicled. "Second mate was nearly mad—in fact, for a bit he was mad—throwing knives at the mess-boy . . . until he was forcibly restrained . . . The mess-boy's face is considerably scarred owing to this afternoon's amusement."

Moray, according to Chesapeake accounts, made his money and got out. He went on to augment his prosperity on the Bermuda–to–New York run.

"It is necessary to exercise the utmost vigil," Coast Guard orders stressed,

> to see that no vessel with prohibited cargo on board enter or pass up Chesapeake Bay. To this end your attention is again called to your authority to use force to stop and board vessels under the United States flag wherever

found, and to board and examine foreign vessels whenever found within three nautical miles of the coast of the United States. At the entrance of Chesapeake Bay a foreign vessel found within three nautical miles of a straight line drawn from the Easterly edge of Cape Henry to the Easterly Edge of Smith's Island shall be boarded and examined, and if found to have intoxicating liquor on board, she shall be seized and brought into port.

The Norfolk city police gunboat was doing its part, giving chase to the small, creek-and-cove rumrunners serving as the distribution pipeline for the large, offshore rumrunners. And as always, in addition to the bonded booze from abroad, there was, in the Chesapeake, much liquor "of the unimported variety" being boated about as well. When the officers of the police boat spied *Alma Lee,* a 35-foot motor launch, anchored in Tanner's Creek on May 28, 1923, they got suspicious. The launch's crew departed in a rowboat. Officers boarded *Alma Lee* and found eighty-five gallons of corn whiskey in 5-gallon cans. Two patrolmen hid in the launch's cabin. The police boat pulled off. That night, a man rowed back out to the launch. He boarded. The police nabbed him. There was whiskey in the rowboat, too. Elmer Wallace, thirty-one, of Norfolk was charged with trafficking and possession. Such was the nature of rumrunning on the Chesapeake: it existed in layers. From the sleek oceangoing corsairs of Rum Row to the indigenous Bay craft that plied the brackish backwaters, they were rumrunners all, part of the same Darwinian food chain of supply, demand, and black-market protocols. And whether the smuggled product was Highland malt or swamp white lightning, the risk and the profit potential defined the life.

"The successful accomplishment of the mission calls for complete loyalty on the part of all," read Coast Guard orders,

and requires the closest cooperation between all shore units and floating unit commanders. . . .

It is expected that the Officer in Charge of each unit shall throw himself, heart and soul, into the successful accomplishment of the mission; that he shall display energy, initiative, and resourcefulness; that he shall not be afraid of responsibility; and that he shall thoroughly indoctrinate the men under his command.

These orders must be held strictly confidential, and no information concerning them shall be permitted to get into the hands of persons outside the Coast Guard.

Coast Guard officials were getting reports that fully laden rum ships from Nassau and Bermuda were approaching the Virginia Capes in June 1923. Instructions were to seize the British auxiliary schooner *Monarch* if she crossed the 3-mile limit for any reason, and to keep a lookout for the steamship *Mauhav,* thought to be heading for the Virginia Capes. All cutters were put on full alert. They cruised a 50-mile radius off Cape Henry by day, huddled in tightly to stop small craft from running between the Virginia Capes by night. Meanwhile, *Istar* and others were said to be out there still. Masters of passing vessels had sighted the queen of the rum fleet and said she was starting to look ragged, with great, gashing scars in the paint on her hull, and her decks a mess from the sliding and crashing about of thousands of liquor cases. Said one report, "she resembles nothing so much as a rum warehouse in distress."

Bracing for the next wave of rumrunners, and still anticipating the unfinished business of *Istar,* the Coast Guard established special land patrols from Cape Hatteras to Delaware. It was reported that a major off-loading would be attempted somewhere along the Delaware coast.

The idea made sense from a smuggler's standpoint. From the mouth of the Chesapeake on up the Atlantic beaches to Delaware Bay, the land was perfect for sneaking contraband into the United States. The ingredients were there: miles and miles of desolate shoreline, and a native populace well versed in the intricacies of coastal travel and not averse to seeking extra income.

In April 1923, at the Coast Guard's Sixth District headquarters in Lewes, Delaware, acting commandant Captain A. J. Henderson issued orders to those Coast Guardsmen charged with policing the long sandy smugglers' paradise stretching from below the New Jersey coast down to the Virginia Capes:

> Headquarters desires to impress upon you the necessity of the crews of stations in your district exercising extraordinary vigilance in the enforcement of the customs and prohibition laws, to the end that violators of those laws may be apprehended. . . . When a motorboat or other vessel is rendered assistance of any kind opportunity should be taken to board and examine the vessel, and, if the weather and other circumstances permit, to search her thoroughly for prohibited liquors.
>
> Each officer in charge should be instructed to carefully board and examine each motor boat or other craft found in any of the inlets in the vicinity of this station and to be particularly vigilant in observing and reporting any rockets, flares, or other signals made by vessels off the coast.

The rum fleet was growing; it had become obvious by 1924 that the rum-chaser fleet had to grow, too. At Milford, Delaware, at Annapolis, Maryland, at the Colonna Marine Railway Company in Norfolk, and at other yards around the country, 75-foot patrol boats were being built for use by the Coast Guard in chasing the rumrunners. President Calvin Coolidge had sent Congress an appropriation proposal of $13,853,989 in February 1924. Part of the sum was to finance the building and outfitting of 223 cabin cruisers at a cost of $37,500 each, and 100 smaller Seabright dory-type motorcraft costing $8,000 each, all to be added to an ever-growing rum-chasing armada. The one positive side effect of rampant maritime criminality was the lucrative increase in business for area boatyards, such as the Vineyard Shipbuilding Company in Milford, which realized government contracts worth a quarter of a million dollars in June 1924. Remarked a Delmarva reporter, "This will mean plenty of work for Milford ship carpenters for many months."

Another part of Coolidge's rum-war appropriation was the creation of twenty-four new section bases; the rum chasers being built at Annapolis in 1924 were earmarked for the new Norfolk Section Base Eight, born to battle the increasing rum-running villainy in the lower

Chesapeake. The Annapolis-constructed vessels, *CG-193* to *CG-196* inclusive, would form the nucleus of a Bay fleet that would be kept busy in the gin-soaked years ahead.

Command of Section Base Eight was assigned to Captain A. J. Henderson, the aforementioned acting commandant of USCG Sixth District. Henderson was a forty-year veteran of the service and one of its most highly respected senior men. "Captain Henderson is an officer in whom I have the fullest confidence," declared U.S. Coast Guard Commandant F. C. Billard in an internal communiqué. "He is able, conscientious and devoted to duty, and is scrupulously particular in carrying out to the letter all orders emanating from this office and all instructions contained in the Regulations. As a matter of fact, Captain Henderson, while on duty in Washington, practically wrote the Regulations in their present form."

The place and the moment called for a tough chief. "Captain Henderson is one of the very best officers in the Coast Guard," said Billard, "and one who maintains proper discipline and requires efficient performance of duty by the men under him."

The new leader spelled things out for his officers. A patrol boat assigned to Base Eight was ordered to "cruise in the waters adjacent to the entrance of Chesapeake Bay, and the waters of Hampton Roads and the Harbors of Norfolk and Newport News, Va., as may be directed. Her duties will consist of . . . the enforcement of the Customs Laws, especially the laws relating to the illegal importation of intoxicating liquors and other merchandise."

The rum war escalated. The Coast Guard reported in 1924 that the rum fleet had grown to include some 158 vessels, and their success at importation was on the increase. In the last three months of 1923, imports from Scotland alone had amounted to 415,703 gallons in bulk and 26,755 cases. In late 1924 the Treasury Department issued a statement: "The administration is determined to make every effort with the material it has to combat, and, if possible, to break up the rum fleets which have become a national disgrace." One of the foremost "troublesome locations" cited in a concomitant Coast Guard report was the smugglers' coast that stretched from the Delaware shore to the Chesapeake Bay.

"Just because you happen to know a boat, or the crew of a boat that is plying in and out your inlet, is not sufficient excuse for not boarding and searching . . . day or night," stressed acting Sixth District Superintendent Irwin B. Steele in October 1924 orders to Assateague Beach Station. To emphasize his point, the superintendent cited a recent Sixth District sting:

> Had the officer in charge taken it for granted, that because he knew and had known the crew of a certain boat all his life, that it was useless to board and search or to exercise a strict watch over her, he would have missed the opportunity of seizing six hundred gallons of alcohol, and at the same time let go unmolested persons connected with some of the best families of his state, who were flagrantly violating the laws. So you see the necessity of observing the strictest watch possible on all classes of boats.

Steele was talking about the capture of the 8-horsepower motorboat *X 10 US*—39 feet long, sloop-rigged, like so many rumrunners, "painted a lead color"—chased down by members of the Lewes Station crew on October 17, 1924. They caught her, hauling twelve quarts of dry gin in addition to the six hundred gallons of raw alcohol, near the entrance to Lewes Canal; they arrested her captain/owner, E. G. Edgens, and mate Daniel Schmierer. The men said they had bought the load off the British schooner *Tessie Aubrey,* anchored out about 14 miles east by south. They were supposed to make the drop-off "somewhere on Milton Creek," and from there the firewater would travel by truck to Philadelphia. The authorities knew *Tessie Aubrey:* a two-master, 94½ feet long, Nova Scotian registry. A confidential Coast Guard missive tagged her "a very suspicious craft." In this she was not alone.

"This office has received information . . . that vessels were lying off the Virginia Capes and disposing of their cargoes of spiritous liquors which were brought into the Chespeak [sic] Bay by motor boats," warned Assistant Collector W. W. Vipond of the U.S. Customs Service at Norfolk, writing to Captain Henderson in 1924. "The place most often mentioned in connection with these rumors is Chincoteague Island. In addition to this we have received information that schooners laden with spiritous liquors come into the Chespeak [sic] Bay and bring their cargoes up to points within a radius of twenty-five miles of Baltimore where they are unladen."

Some rumrunners, of course, didn't stop short. They headed right for Baltimore Harbor, especially if they were of Baltimore registry. Officers of the Baltimore police boat *Lannan* seized a launch laden with six thousand dollars worth of Black and White Scotch docked at the end of Chester Street on June 15, 1925. The launch was deserted. Her crew reportedly had been tipped off that the sting was imminent. The hunt had been on since three o'clock that morning, when *Lannan*'s officers got reports of a vessel without lights sneaking into the harbor. The craft was registered to Baltimorean Frank Machs of the 1800 block of Aliceanna Street in Fells Point. The sting was bad timing: Machs was due to appear in federal court that day on charges of smuggling some months earlier, using the same vessel. The current load, it was suspected, had come off a Baltimore freighter in the Jamaica trade, which had lain offshore while boats such as Machs's had run in the whiskey cargo.

Baltimore was being supplied from all directions. It came by land, from farmland Pennsylvania and the mountains of Virginia, West Virginia, and western Maryland. High-grade 'shine pushed the 200-proof mark (strong enough for the middleman to water it down by half and still have something that would curl consumers' toes). Shipped in square 5-gallon tins, it rolled into town in Cadillac touring cars, phony hearses, bogus milk trucks, fake bread trucks with fictitious bakery names painted on the sides, and flatbeds hauling more than the legitimate lumber and hay loads that showed on top. It came by sea, through the Chesapeake and Delaware Canal and up the Chesapeake Bay in sailboats, motorboats, passenger steamers, barges, tugboats, and any other floating conveyance imaginable. There was an eclectic, unceasing supply of potables, good offshore bonded stuff and high-powered homemade product from the moonshine meccas of southern Maryland and the Eastern Shore. Not least of all, Baltimore was being supplied by Baltimoreans.

A dubious pharmacy prescription was no longer required to get drunk in Baltimore. If a man deserved a drink, he could get one here, the saying went. With a governor standing in open defiance to federal Prohibition, with an acid-penned, beer-loving wit named Mencken as its leading resident man of letters, Baltimore was a town rebellious, recalcitrant, and well-lubricated throughout the Noble Experiment. It was a personality befitting its role as the principal import-export center of what was called the wettest state in the Union during those ostensibly dry years.

Federal Prohibition agents working the city found themselves akin to an occupation force in hostile territory. A routine raid could lead to street violence in a hurry, as angry mobs gathered to disrupt attempts to enforce the law. The level of public disapproval ranged from the merely disrespectful to the truly life-threatening. Sometimes it was just vocal, as when hundreds of onlookers gathered in West Pratt Street on June 2, 1922, to jeer at the agents demolishing Jacob Miller's whiskey-making operation. They found and destroyed one hundred gallons of rye whiskey, fifteen gallon jugs of corn liquor, five hundred gallons of mash, and a substantial distillery setup in the allegedly vacant house in the 1000 block of West Pratt, and they arrested Miller as he tried to hightail it over the back fence. The night air was filled with the sound of copper stills being smashed and glass bottles being shattered, and as a counterpoint, the hateful shouts of the hostile crowd amassing in the street.

Sometimes the mobs were bigger, rowdier, scarier. Some five thousand raucous Baltimoreans laid siege to Henry Shalitsky's saloon at St. Peter and Barre streets on the night of October 7, 1922, hurling bricks and brandishing clubs for more than two hours. Inside Shalitsky's, eight Prohibition agents crouched in mortal fear, begging to be rescued by the Baltimore cops and the troops at Fort Holabird. G. E. Ensor, the head dry agent trapped in Shalitsky's, later said, "If the man we were raiding had not protected us we never could have got out alive."

They didn't always emerge unscathed. A dry agent was driving down North Pearl Street on May 29, 1925, when he saw a man toting what looked like an alcohol stash. The agent parked, got out, and followed the suspect. The agent hadn't gone a block when he was surrounded by a crowd of about two hundred. He drew his gun. He backed up against a wall. The mob rushed him. They shoved him down and trampled him. They threw rocks on him and kicked his teeth loose. He lay there, severely injured, till a Baltimore police sergeant and three patrolmen stormed forth, swinging billy clubs and hacking a path through the crowd. They got the dry agent to the station house. When time came to move him, a police escort unit still had to fend off the waiting horde. Meanwhile, back in the dry agent's car, there had been twenty gallons of seized booze. The mob made off with all of it.

For the thirsty, the city's night life thrived. Anybody who was somebody imbibed at the Fiorella Club, Johnny Butta's swank speakeasy on Albemarle Street in Little Italy. Or there was Braumeister's beer saloon on Gay Street, catering to discriminating palates with the finest Bohemian hops. Or the legendary "beautiful blonde bootlegger's" joint on Cathedral. Or the bookshop on North Charles with a bar in back, one of many sort-of-secret watering holes where Mencken and his merry band congregated for conviviality. There was even a floating establishment, a "chain saloon" that changed locations as survival demanded. Dry agents caught on when they shut down the same proprietor, first on Oak Street, then on Falls Road shortly thereafter. Carl Burger was released each time, but his bail jumped from one thousand to four thousand dollars. Even the penny-ante saloonkeepers in Baltimore were raking in a thousand dollars a night, but the overhead was high; landlords knew the score, and gouged. And there were lawmen and fire inspectors to pay off, of course. A lot of cash was moving around.

Bootleggers and dry agents were part of the same surreal universe where adversaries often knew one another and engaged in cat-and-mouse contests. When the feds raided Rudolph Ruhling and Frederick McGinn's joint on Dolphin Street in May 1925, the sting, as re-created later in court, unfolded thusly:

Two dry agents entered: "Coupla shots."

Ruhling poured the drinks, set them on the bar, and said, "Well, your faces are familiar . . ."

Cash register: "Bing!"

Ruhling: "I remember! You're dry agents. Gimme those shots!"

He grabbed. The agents set down the empty glasses and said, "Too late."

They left. Then came the raid.

Within a four-week period, federal agents busted fifty Baltimore saloons. But the saloon-shutdown injunction proceedings crowding the federal court docket in January 1924 were leading to a rise in the private-club style of speakeasy in Baltimore homes. The *Baltimore Sun* reported a federal agent's claim that "for every saloon closed . . . two speakeasies open." Speakeasies were harder to raid because you had to be known or know someone reliable to get in. Said the agent, "Saloon men who switch from a public to a private base for their illicit operations do not do as much business as formerly, but profits are so large they do not seem to mind this." The federals' widespread saloon crackdown was not eliminating booze joints in Baltimore; it was merely moving them into harder-to-monitor corners. "The danger lies . . . in scattering the evil of the low groggery into residential sections. . . . for the present I am somewhat afraid the cure will be worse than the disease."

Crackdowns aside, drinking joints abounded in Baltimore: John C. Munder's saloon at 4536 Harford Road, Jerry Bee's saloon at 2000 West Lanvale Street, the Iola Athletic and Pleasure Club at 109 Parkin Street, the Hotel Leland bar at 1610 Pennsylvania Avenue, the Biddle Street Saloon, the Laurens Street Saloon, Seymour's Mulberry Street watering hole, Nixon's Café, the black saloon on the corner of Gough and Dallas streets, the Diamond Café at 311 West Franklin, Ivory Booker's beer hall at 15 North Frederick, Maurice Finn and Charlie Mitchel's place at 3 North Frederick, Eddie Vaeth's saloon at 300 Light Street, and the Lithuanian Hall barroom at Hollins and Parkins, where men congregated to play cards and knock back beer and mash.

In Baltimore, a red crab in the window meant "saloon in the back room." A sign advertising "seafood" meant likewise. Speakeasies and beer halls proliferated in a city that, in terms of both geography and temperament, was well situated to remain well supplied. Pennsylvania home brew and mountain corn liquor kept pouring in from the overland routes. Rum from the Caribbean, whiskey from Scotland and Canada, champagne from France, and beer from Germany kept sailing in courtesy of the rogue ships at sea.

But Baltimore was a great producer as well as consumer. It had abundant stills, naturally, and above all, it had the mighty United States Industrial Alcohol Corporation (USIA), a government-sanctioned operation headquartered at Curtis Bay that yearly churned out millions of gallons of 185-proof grain alcohol for the legal medicinal trade. Entrepreneurs of the amoral persuasion couldn't pass up such a mother lode ripe for the skimming. Massive amounts of USIA product got diverted into the black market. A gallon of USIA grain spirits had a street value of about three dollars in Baltimore. The customer would cut it with water, add glycerine drops (available at the friendly neighborhood pharmacist's), cork the mixture in a bottle, roll the bottle on the floor for that ideal blending effect, let it age for, say, half an hour, and, voila—gin—or some gut-sloughing facsimile thereof.

Serious money was being made by those engaged in the illicit trafficking of USIA spirits. When federal agents discovered a whole train-carload—8,000 gallons—of USIA alcohol labeled "olive oil" in the President Street Station, it led to the arrest and conviction of a six-man ring on charges of having diverted 110,000 gallons of the Curtis Bay grain with an estimated value of $2.5 million.

Baltimore's status as exporter was nowhere more evident than in its relationship with Norfolk. The Norfolk vice squad seized 40 gallons of Baltimore liquor at the Old Bay Line steamboat wharf in February 1924; Norfolk police seized 250 gallons of alcohol shipped from Baltimore in paint cans in February 1925. Such dockside raids had been going on for years. Baltimore was one of the main suppliers Norfolk bootleggers could always count on. Anticipating the arrival of a beverage consignment from

Baltimore, a Norfolk bootlegger would hand the claim check to a drayman and send him to the waterfront. The drayman would take the cargo to a preordained spot and unload it, and the bootlegger would emerge only after assuring himself the coast was clear. "We couldn't stop it if we had a policeman on every corner of this city," a Norfolk inspector said. "I doubt if we could stop it if we put a policeman in front of every house in Norfolk."

Norfolk after hours hopped with opportunities for the parched and the randy. Bellhops and cabbies led salesmen, sailors, and slumming society kids to outlying roadhouses where drinks and doxies beckoned. There was Charlie Zadzook's "house of ill fame" at Ocean View, or John Trimble's "disorderly house" at Chesapeake Beach, or Mrs. Bristol's Norfolk County brothel, or diverse other wayside vice dens where epic drunken brawls capped off many a rowdy night. But the heart of the Norfolk *demimonde* was downtown in the so-called "Black Belt," where booze flowed like rivers and the music was dangerously hot. Things got really wild after midnight. "RACES AND SEXES MIX AMID LIQUOR AND JAZZ," screamed the headline of a Norfolk exposé. "Old Tenderloin Resort Now Negro Cabaret Where White Men and Women Watch Jungle Dances and Get Drinks That Cheer."

Within a flagrantly close radius of the second precinct police headquarters on Queen Street, the speakeasies flourished; one of the busiest, Gus Perry's, was packing them in right across the street from the police station. "Babylon had her wild orgies and Rome her bacchanalian revels, but neither of them probably had anything on the frenzied spectacles that are to be witnessed nightly in the triumvirate temples of Venus, Bacchus, and the great god Jazz right here in the heart of Norfolk," declared the *Virginian-Pilot.* "A bubbling spring of liquor and licentiousness in the midst of a land seeped dry. . . , Norfolk's underworld is now the Mecca toward which lines of closed automobiles speed under the cover of darkness . . . while the rest of the city is sleeping—dreaming mayhap of the lasting good wrought by the Eighteenth Amendment."

Here in the Black Belt, as newspaper staffers learned through participatory journalism, "blood is flushed to fever heat by beverages that have been banned by law and by dances that have all the sensuous vulgarity of the jungle."

On Lincoln Street, two blocks from the cops, John Pope's Cabaret in its own outlaw way was helping to erode the race restrictions that ruled the world. Pope, who claimed to be one of the most money-making blacks around, ran a nightclub where his white friends could cut loose side by side with the black clientele. This was the old red-light district; Pope's was located in what used to be Jennie Williams's posh whorehouse. The name "J. Williams" lived on in the tiled flooring of the vestibule. From out in the street, you could hear a chanteuse moaning the blues. At the thick front door, a sliding peephole greeted the would-be joy boy.

To get the true lowdown on Norfolk's illicit night life, a *Virginian-Pilot* reporter and three of his willing and able colleagues infiltrated Pope's. It was all drunkenness and nasty movement and loud crazy music, and whites and blacks mingling, reveling at adjacent tables, no less. "A 'jazz' band bangs and rattles 'jazz' music, and negro men and negro women, the latter with their skirts held up around their waists, dance 'jazz' dances. And then the white couples take the floor and, if the word may be used, dance.

"Between times, everybody drinks."

There were potted palms everywhere; colored paper dangled from the ceiling; surrounding the dance floor, tables were filled with chorus girls, seamen, and sundry flappers and gadabouts. Three vice-squad detectives were hanging out, so booze purchases were a little more surreptitious than usual: down the hall, second door on the left, seven dollars a pint, poured into ginger ale bottles for the sake of appearance. People were smashed and were loving life, "watching with languid eyes the muscle-quivering antics of a colored girl in the middle of the floor, who appeared in imminent peril of wriggling out of her clothes." The floor-show goddess was a revelation. "As the dancer succumbed more and more to the spell of the sensuous jazz, dancing with an abandon never surpassed by the wildest bacchante of ancient Rome, men—white and black—about the tables flung coins at her feet."

She gathered up her money and finished with a flurry of high kicks. The crowd went wild. A drunken white lad got up and tried to do justice to the shimmy dance. The crowd whooped. The music changed. "The pianist struck up a melody with all the haunting, mystical appeal of the Orient in its sensuous rhythm; the drummer got a fresh hold on his sticks, and the spectators fell under the spell of the music."

As the syncopated song percolated, "a young negro strutted into the room, and the ensuing exhibition of shivering has never been surpassed, even by St. Vitus himself. That young fellow wriggled every muscle in his body, and finally in an apparent delirium of ecstasy, stood perfectly still and 'shimmied' with his ears. Such muscular control as he demonstrated was marvelous. His shoulders, breast and lower portions of his body going through the undulations of the sea in a storm, the young negro leaned over toward one of the tables occupied by a group of young white men and girls. He wriggled suggestively, and an answering contortion was performed by a girl with the face of a saint."

The four reporters scored a bottle; now they were popular. "A fascinating blonde at the table in the rear of the room who had been dividing her attention between a sailor and a civilian, looked over and smiled invitingly. And after she had witnessed the seeming satisfaction with which the highballs were sampled, she left her companions and sauntered over to the table of the newspapermen." She singled one out, draped her arms around him, and started planting kisses. "Oh, I just adore children," she breathed. The lucky one's comrades watched, rapt.

The master of ceremonies gestured; the jazz band kicked in with "Swanee." Couples rushed the dance floor. Someone grabbed the blonde, and "she hoisted her skirts up to her knees, revealing a fetching view of socks and a generous glimpse of what they partially enclosed."

As the debauch escalated, a police sergeant and two patrolmen came in and watched, and did nothing.

For publicity purposes, the law would stage a raid, one calculated to find no evidence of sin. A widely announced shakedown to take place at 10:30 P.M. was disingenuous when everyone knew the real party started after 12. But the crusade was becoming more genuine by

early 1924, as a freshly formed Norfolk vice squad began cracking down on booze joints with the aid of the U.S. Navy. Police gave sailors marked money and sent them to suspected dives. The mission: to spend liberally on libations and disseminate the incriminating currency. The effort netted several arrests from the get-go. The police praised the enthusiastic cooperation of Fifth Naval District Commandant Rear Admiral Roger Welles, who was "anxious that vice conditions be cleaned up for the good of the men of the service who make Norfolk their mecca when on liberty."

While Norfolk, Baltimore, and points in between continued to be awash in the liquid that cheers, Coast Guardsmen continued to maintain strict vigilance from the Virginia Capes to Chincoteague Inlet to Assateague Harbor to the Delaware beaches. The highly publicized rum war continued through peaks and valleys of heightened activity and lulling interludes.

On March 5, 1924, it heated up again with a vengeance. Shrouded by dense fog, twenty-one vessels materialized off the New Jersey coast, dropped anchor, and made ready to flood the mid-Atlantic region with 160,000 cases—$8 million worth—of liquor. By the next day, seven more foreign ships had arrived, and the totals jumped to 224,000 cases with an estimated potential value of $11 million. Who better to head up the looming rum fleet than the queen herself? *Istar* had returned.

What had become of her master, the mysterious top man who had sidestepped the Norfolk sting that took down his second-in-command in May 1923? Who was the top man?

In May 1923 the mystery man had headed in from *Istar* on a surf boat that capsized. He got ashore at Cape Henry, and by midnight, a man in wet clothes was checking into a Norfolk hotel. The next day he walked into a Norfolk bank and plunked down $250,000 cash. As the bank converted the money to English currency for him, the man boasted of his plan to make one more run before retiring a millionaire. A ship's chandler supplied the launch that transported the man, English pounds sterling and draft notes in tow, back to sea.

Sir Broderick Cecil Denham Arkwright Hartwell, Fourth Baronet—late a captain in the Leicestershire Regiment, a decorated veteran of the Boer War and the World War—was back on Rum Row in March 1924, back at the helm of *Istar,* his syndicate's flagship.

Sir Broderick was a mystery man no more; he was taking his Scotch-export enterprise public. In February 1924, prior to making his latest transatlantic run, he even issued an investors' prospectus, assuring "a certain 20 percent profit on capital every 60 days" to those British who cared to buy into the venture. "I have arranged with an American syndicate to take from me at least 10,000 cases of high-class Scotch whisky a month," read the prospectus. ". . . I sell this syndicate at an agreed price—my sale is guaranteed and certain, and my profit is equally sure. The cargo will be fully insured against all marine risks."

Each shipment, said the rum-running baronet, would tie up an investor's capital for approximately ninety days. "This allows a month for bottling, labeling and packing, a month for transport and a month lying off the coast for unloading."

As they prepared to dispense the $11 million cargo from the fleet anchored off New Jersey, the rum crews were jovial. They opened hatches with a "yo heave-ho!" and stacked booze on deck. A new treaty had extended the U.S. 3-mile limit to 12 miles, but no one seemed hampered. The feds intercepted radio messages inviting lady friends to come out to the rum fleet that night for dinner and dancing.

"She is a wicked old sinner. Coast Guard get after her," said a message from the Department of Justice, targeting *Istar.* Sir Broderick was sighted on her deck, supervising transactions. He liked to stress that out there past the U.S. boundary, he was breaking no law. Yet, as he had shown in Norfolk, Sir Broderick had a smooth talent for being scarce when necessary. *Istar,* minus Sir Broderick, was nabbed by Canadian customs men at St. John, New Brunswick, on April 26, 1924.

The Coast Guard compiled telling figures that spring: it was evident that the number of rum-running ships nearly equaled the number of active ships in the U.S. Navy. Officials announced they had certain knowl-

edge of 270 ships engaged in the illegal liquor trade, and figured there
had to be hundreds more they didn't know about. "Almost every nation
in the world is said to be represented in the huge fleet," the *Virginian-
Pilot* reported, "with vessels flying the British flag predominating."

Eric Sherbrooke Walker was representative of the English rum-
running roguery. He entered into his first venture following a gathering
of like-minded profiteers at a posh London gentlemen's club. He said
that he was often asked questions like, "How could you bring yourself to
hinder the Americans in their plucky efforts to cope with one of the
greatest of present-day evils?"

"My reply," said Walker, "is that if they were making a genuine effort, nothing would have induced me to go into the business. But Prohibition is a gigantic farce which is being used by hundreds of thousands of
Americans for enriching themselves. Go to the houses of any prominent
politicians or senators in Washington . . . and in eight out of ten of them
you will be pressed to drink whiskey, gin, or champagne with an insis-
tence to be found in no European country. . . .

"So who can blame an Englishman for joining in a game which pro-
vides the American nation with good liquor instead of bad, and himself
with adventure and profit?"

For all the Coast Guard's vigilance, for all the extra federal dollars
appropriated for the war on rum, was the rum war being won? Perhaps it
was the elusive, amorphous sort of war that couldn't be won at all. If victory were to be measured by completely stopping the rumrunners from
punching through their deliveries, then it most certainly was the sort of
war that couldn't be won. If victory were to be measured by at least making procedure more difficult for the rum ships and their speedboat consorts, then maybe it was a war worth fighting.

A flotilla of rum smugglers had gathered in Assateague Harbor,
reported the new USCG Sixth District Superintendent, James F.
Phillips, in January 1925. "A liquor-laden vessel" recently had been
spotted offshore, and now, the former World War I subchaser *Hiwal,*
the schooner *Katie C.,* and the motorboats *Higherhopes* and *Bie &*

Schott, "all notorious and practically admitted rum-runners," were at Assateague. Naturally, the crews submitted to boarding and examination, and naturally, they were, at present, clean. And because they were momentarily between cargoes they could afford to be brazen. "The crews admitted that they were in the rum-running business and were carrying their cargoes up the Delaware River and Chesapeake Bay," said Phillips.

It was not a question of winning a war, but of at least minimizing the scale of the inevitable. The words of Phillips's predecessor, acting Sixth District Superintendent Irwin Steele, echoed along the coast:

"These boats may be coming in through any of the inlets from Chincoteague to Smith Island, and it's a sure thing that they are coming in through some of them. It is our duty to catch them, and *catch them we must.*"

CHAPTER FOUR

WADING IN WHISKEY

"National prohibition is based upon a false philosophy of human conduct, has proved an utter failure as an ally of human morality, and has
had no practical effect except that of adding many new forms of lawlessness, social scandal and official corruption."

The Honorable William Cabell Bruce, United States senator from
Maryland, addressed the delegates of the Home Rule Convention of the
Eastern Shore at the Atlantic Hotel in Ocean City on August 29, 1925.
The Coast Guard's "heightened blockade" initiative of the past year had
garnered plenty of positive press for the war on alcohol. Now, a similar
beefing-up on the land front was being launched by the federal government. And here, standing at a podium in the heart of the smugglers'
coast, Senator Bruce threw a wet blanket on the rum-war publicity
hoopla and delivered his eloquent diatribe, titled with Ritchie-era
Maryland frankness, "Federal Invasions of State Rights."

"I imagine that very few persons, who have not had some special reason for making a study of the subject, have formed any proper concep-
tion of the extent to which the Federal authority has expanded since the
beginning of the Civil War," the senator remarked. "Of all federal intru-
sions into the field of state jurisdiction, the Eighteenth Amendment, of
course, is the most arrogant. It wholly ignores the dissimilar manners
and social usages, which distinguish not only the different states, but

even urban and rural communities in the same state, from each other. It penetrates to the very core of state autonomy; it violates every elementary principle of personal liberty. The time will come when the disaster that it has brought to the human character and human laws in the United States will be the study not so much of the political historian as of the political pathologist. It may be aptly termed in the words of Milton: 'That fatal, that perfidious bark, Built in the eclipse, and rigged with curses dark.'"

The Prohibition enforcement entities were being overhauled that summer. Enlistment was expiring for some four thousand extra crewmen recruited to jack up the Coast Guard's rum-chasing efforts; the official word was, "Job well done," but no one seemed to be going thirsty. "The progress of enforcement throughout the country has been immeasurably helped by the Coast Guard blockade," Prohibition Commissioner Roy A. Haynes had declared that spring. Haynes, due to be stripped of his powers on September 1 when Prohibition policing duties would go to regional departments, felt confident that, thanks to the Coast Guard, it was now "possible for the land forces to concentrate on inland problems." A lot of Volstead champions disagreed, though; Washington officials were paraphrased as saying the coastal campaign had been "more spectacular than important." It was a dim view shared by Wayne B. Wheeler of the Anti-Saloon League. Wheeler's philosophical opposites, men such as the esteemed senator from Maryland, likewise sensed futility in the policing efforts thus far, but beyond the futility, perceived fundamental injustice as well. And now, as Assistant Treasury Secretary General Lincoln C. Andrews, the brains behind the maritime rum war, set his sights landward, Senator Bruce used statistics to buttress cynicism:

"The Department of Justice has recently reported that, since the enactment of the Volstead Act, liquor violators have been prosecuted in such increasing numbers that now their cases make up 50 per cent, or more than half of all the cases presented to the Federal Courts in 71 out of 81 districts in the United States proper. . . . In Maryland, our Federal District Court, too, is calling lustily for the appointment of at least one additional Judge. It is justly entitled to him; for, while only 409 persons were convicted of violations of the Volstead Act, in Maryland, in 1922, in the year ending June 30, 1925, this number increased to 1,065. Under these conditions, the Federal penitentiaries are naturally enough so full of inmates that their wardens are perplexed to know how they are to meet the still greater strain upon their cubic space that is expected to result from the vigorous administration of the Volstead Act by General Andrews."

A bead was being drawn on targets large and small. There was the industrial-alcohol skim racket, such as Curtis Bay's bootlegger-coveted USIA grain alcohol output—according to some estimates, about six million gallons of industrial alcohol had been detoured by bootleggers in 1924. And in cities, towns, and countryside, the outlaw distilleries continued in abundance, their once-disparate efforts becoming increasingly more coordinated. Lincoln Andrews was gearing up to make a wholesale sweep of a criminal class that since 1920 had ballooned to include farmers, storekeepers, watermen, business tycoons, and everyday citizens of every stripe.

"In the heart of every human society there is a body of men who, to use the vivid language of Shakespeare, are no friends of the world or the world's law," said Senator Bruce. "That such a body of social mutineers and outlaws exists in the United States no one can deny. Indeed, it is now but a trite thing to say that in no civilized country of the world is crime of the deepest dye so rife as in ours, or so often unpunished. . . . it may be truly affirmed that, at the present time, a criminal spirit, wholly abnormal is abroad . . . in the United States. Are the Eighteenth Amendment and the Volstead Act to continue to make a vast addition each year to this element of our population which is no friend of the world or the world's law? Are the thousands of young men, who are often impelled to violate such an impossible measure as the Volstead Act by love of excitement and adventure as much as by desire of pecuniary gain, and who might have been respectable and useful citizens but for the depraving solicitations of this Act, to continue to be converted by fine and imprisonment into hardened criminals; from bootleggers into robbers and murderers?"

Protestations aside, "the land offensive against bootleggers" was on, decreed Prohibition Commissioner Haynes. The great federal maritime effort would be matched onshore. The timing was based on the illusion that the offshore rum fleet had been shattered and scattered for good. "With the cutting off of the foreign supply," proclaimed Haynes, "local operations will be increasingly difficult for bootleggers." The Coast Guard crackdown had indeed changed the nature of the maritime liquor commerce; gone were the flagrant, nose-thumbing days of Rum Row in its openly defiant early incarnation. "With the weight of the whole American government behind them, the cutters literally starved out the old-time Row, broke it up, and chased it away," said Big Bill McCoy. All the Coast Guard had succeeded in doing, really, was to break up a raucous floating party that stretched down the coast, a party that had grown so flashy that it had its own caterers and prostitutes. The Coast Guard war did little more than teach the rumrunners to be more secretive, more elusive than ever before. It had dispersed them, but it hadn't put them out of business.

And with or without the Coast Guard's interference, Rum Row was evolving along its own natural course, growing more streamlined, more consolidated, more rigidly organized. The changes drove out Big Bill McCoy. The New Jersey syndicate tried to bring him into the fold, but he turned them down, preferring his independence. He would always remain convinced that his refusal to join led to his downfall, that the Jersey mob flexed monetary muscle, bought law enforcement cooperation, and set McCoy up. He did jail time, got out, and stayed out of the business he had helped define.

As the offshore liquor trade became more aggressively corporate, the quality of the product dipped. Untrampled good stuff became an ever rarer commodity, and the term "off the boat" became a hollow one. A newspaper correspondent came ashore from a Rum Row sojourn with a story shocking to those who had put their faith and funds in imported goods. It was reported in Baltimore that rumrunners off Jersey had become "maritime moonshiners," replete with elaborate shipboard stills and fake-label operations. "The real McCoy"—a term said to have orig-

inated in reference to Big Bill, who had always stood behind the quality
of his imports—was getting harder to find by 1924. The syndicates taking over Rum Row were putting the lie to the newly minted slang. "They
exist right off the Jersey coast," said the reporter on returning from his
revelatory excursion. "I know, because I have seen their stills in operation, have watched the manufacture of 'white mule' and the printing of
labels and tinfoil caps to which even wary drinkers would point with
pride, remarking: 'Have another drink. Safe? Sure! This stuff is imported.'"

The reporter visited two rumrunners and uncovered two swindles:
(1) altering genuine product to milk more mileage out of it, and (2)
cranking out complete counterfeits. On the first vessel, they were
dumping bottles of the good stuff into a big tub, adding equal parts water and pure alcohol, then rebottling the dilution. On the second vessel,
a schooner, the aft hold housed a half-dozen stills, while in the forward
hold, a hand press printed out phony labels. Counterfeiting bona fide
brand-name labels was a snap, according to the captain, and "anyhow,
people don't care what the label says; they want the kick." Also in bogus
manufacture were the foil seals that, atop the bottle cap, connoted new-
ness. The skipper indicated that the schooner did quite a side business,
selling fake labels and foil seals to the other ships of the rum fleet.

The reporter asked one of the captains how much genuine liquor actually was making it to shore. "Any good liquor? Son, I will stake my
ship and all that goes with it that there is not a pint of 'uncut' whisky in
the country outside of what people had before Prohibition," the captain
answered. "And gin? No real gin at all. Everybody can make it too
cheap."

There were some exceptions, though, asserted Scottish rumrunner
Alastair Moray. "A great deal of the whisky sold out here reaches the
consumer as it leaves us, that is, if it is going to one of the good clubs,
first-class hotels or any of the wealthier homes or good restaurants; all of
them have their own private bootlegger or firm of bootleggers, who deliver the proper goods. But, on the other hand, a great quantity . . . is
blended with crude alcohol and heaven knows what else—one bottle of,

say, Old Smuggler making four bottles of what the consumer thinks is Old Smuggler."

Diluted or not, illegal imports constituted a $40 million business in 1924. Another way that legitimate bottled product entered the States was aboard legitimate ships unknowingly engaged in smuggling. Tramp steamers, ocean liners, even naval vessels continued to be a means of transport for booze coming into U.S. ports. It had been going on since Prohibition's outset, and it was a significant enough problem to warrant the launching of a major drive in 1925 to stop the flow. With this beefed-up federal dry enforcement program, arrests ranged from nabbing a sailor in Norfolk for dispensing Johnnie Walker Red Label Scotch, to busting a sailor in Baltimore for smuggling whiskey to shore in bread cans. A more dynamic controversy involved the case of the U.S. Naval Transport *Beaufort,* stung for smuggling fifty cases of whiskey into the Chesapeake Bay from the West Indies in February 1925. Naval courts-martial held in Norfolk that May yielded several guilty convictions; those caught in the sweep included a lieutenant and the ship's medical officer.

Such was the scene in that midpoint year of the Roaring Twenties, as U.S. officials proclaimed victory in the maritime rum war and turned their sights landward. "As I speak, the government is mobilizing its Prohibition force of some 10,000 men for another concentrated attack upon the bootleg industry," said Senator Bruce from his Ocean City podium. "Like the naval demonstration against rum-running which recently took place along our North Atlantic seaboard, this movement is to be led not by a Prohibition evangelist, but by an able and experienced soldier [Lincoln C. Andrews], with the aid of 24 district administrators, of whom not less than five are former army officers. This last fact, of course, supplies but another proof that the assaults of the government upon the bootleg industry are more and more assuming the character of military dragonades.

"Far be it from me to speak disrespectfully of General Andrews; everything that I have ever heard of him tends to inspire me with a marked respect for him. I think that it was a generous thing of him to notify the bootleggers that he intended to move against them in full battle array on next Tuesday. By doing so he gave them full time to make their wills.

"This act reminds me of those chivalrous aborigines of New Zealand, the Maoris, who were so considerate, until experience made them wiser, as to make a practice of letting the British enemy know in advance just when they would descend upon him from the mountains.

"I also think that it is highly creditable to the candor of General Andrews that he should have frankly stated, as he has, that he does not know whether the late naval demonstration off our North Atlantic seacoast had any practical effect or not.

"When thrust out the front door, the Rum-Devil has an irritating way of creeping around to the back door."

Like its nautical equivalent, the land campaign of the war on alcohol was fought by the expected cross section: the zealous, the corruptible, the inept, the ingenious. Some of the front-line lawmen were so crafty and creative as to become national celebrities. Izzy Einstein and Moe Smith, a pair of rotund New York cutups who proved to be masters of disguise, achieved fame for their comical bootlegger-nabbing escapades based on often outrageous masquerades. The Chesapeake region had its own such hero-trickster in the person of Lone Wolf Asher.

Virginia-born Asher was the consummate "liquor sleuth," racking up a string of successes in several major cities. He was heavyset, medium height, and friendly-faced, with a frank, open disposition that enabled him to gain the trust of strangers and an acumen for deception that enabled him to dupe even longtime acquaintances. In undercover efforts in his native Richmond, efforts that led to widespread arrests, Asher was able to convince people he had known for twenty years that he was not Asher, but "Brown," a steelworker. Whatever city he tackled, Asher had a flair for insinuating himself into the underworld. "I use old ruses that have worked as long as detecting has been a business, but usually they work just the same," he said. "For instance, I go into a town unannounced and most of the time totally unknown. Under various disguises I mix and mingle with sources of information. Dressed as a laborer or common bum, I often hang around street corners and other places where the riffraff of men and women gather. When I see a likely informant I go up to him."

Once he'd scoped his mark, Asher would lay it on thick with the dry-throated routine. "Say, buddy, wonder what's the chances for a thirsty man to get a drink?" he would say. "Know of any right handy place? If you do, come on, let's go get a shot or two. Been traveling a long way, don't know anybody here and need a drink powerful." It was the simplest of deceptions, and it worked consistently. "In nearly every case where the man addressed does not know of a place to get drinks," said Asher, "he will direct me where someone does know."

Infiltrating the speakeasy, Asher had to belly up to the bar to keep the illusion alive. Though his work involved frequenting many a booze den and ordering many a round, the detective was able to state, "I never drink the poison." During the 1925 trial of saloonkeeper John Sullivan, Asher demonstrated for the Baltimore jury just how it was that he managed to stay dry. He poured a glass of water and raised it to his mouth. With a quick flip of the wrist, the liquid was gone—not down Asher's throat, but into a custom-made secret pouch in his coat pocket. It was fast enough legerdemain, he told the courtroom, to fool any bartender.

They called him the Lone Wolf, but he generally operated with a confederate. "Most of the time, I have a partner working with me. Between us we usually have the situation well in hand if any trouble should happen. Of course, we are often facing peculiar situations. In one city we were both arrested by a policeman who insisted that we were highwaymen, wanted for some big job that had been pulled off in that locality the night before. We were carried to jail and thrown into a cell. When the mayor heard of it (he and the chief of police were the only persons who knew who we were and what we were doing) he ordered us brought immediately to his office, where we were freed without the police knowing anything of it."

He lived in that shadowland between law enforcement and law-breaking for law enforcement's sake; his work by its nature involved walking the ethical edge. In a 1925 case in which Asher's undercover work led to the arrest of a Havre de Grace bootlegger, the federal court in Baltimore echoed with attacks on Asher's character. Damning testimony tied him to a roadhouse, and accused him of perjury and financial wrongdoing. But the jury disregarded the accusations against Asher and turned in a guilty verdict on Asher's quarry.

He was right for the life. Artful and quick-thinking, he could get out of a jam with admirable sangfroid. Working the Sullivan job in Baltimore, Asher almost got cornered like Daniel in the lion's den. He was gathering evidence in Sullivan's West Baltimore Street joint when a customer came in, saw him, and yelled out, "My God! You didn't sell him a drink? That's *Asher!*"

Lone Wolf stayed loose and said, "Who's Asher? I'm Connelly, from Delaware. Tell me about this guy Asher."

The man who had recognized him ended up apologizing. He even bought Asher a drink.

"I suppose I can say that I have a sort of natural gift for detective work," Asher said. "I have seen a great deal of life and had many valuable experiences. It stands me in good when playing at this game, and in a way, it is play."

Dry agents knew temptation well. With greenbacks being waved in their faces, many succumbed. Roughly one in twelve had to be ousted for bribe-taking, conspiracy, and sundry related charges. Corruption existed with breezy nonchalance on the local, county, state, and federal levels. In a 1925 Annapolis "rum ring exposé," the seven line-crossers brought before the Anne Arundel County grand jury included a county constable, an Annapolis cop, and a lady dry agent, Virginia Wilson. She was one of a group of area women gaining nationwide fame for running entrapment scams on bootleggers. It came out that they had accepted protection money from an Annapolis confectioner to keep his bootlegger brother out of hot water. It also came out that Virginia Wilson had a bootlegger for a sweetheart, and she lied to keep him out of the dry agents' snare. She was suspended from the dry force and charged with conspiring to defeat justice.

Temptation ran in the opposite direction, too, toward an excessive lust for victory. Wading through the underworld, a morally driven law enforcement agent naturally could become fed up with such frustrating impediments as proper procedure. Entrapment and other dirty tricks were the oft-used bad means to a good end. Government agents set up a bogus speakeasy in Norfolk; wires led from lamp shades to a Dictograph in a back-room where stenographers waited to transcribe all the damning info that bootleggers were duped into unwittingly spilling. But the entrapment setup was too extreme: the agents put up the money to set up the stills to supply the fake speakeasy, then nabbed the runners and corrupt cops who got involved in the trafficking. The scheme went too far, and the Prohibition Bureau closed the phony watering hole in 1926.

The prevailing image of the dry enforcer was not a flattering one. Certainly, dry agents were not all a bunch of rude, intrusive, uncouth, power-abusing, bribe-sucking, privacy-invading bullies, but such were the unsympathetic strokes defining the cartoon portrait of the dry agent in the public imagination. The community-relations nightmare had become so horrid that the Prohibition commissioner created a "traveling school" of ethics and decorum in hopes of smoothing rough edges off the dry enforcement ranks. Professors Webster Spates and Harry M. Dengler bustled to and fro nationwide conducting workshops for Prohibition agents. Personal behavior, deportment, arrest tactics, courtroom psychology, basic law—the professors crammed as much as they could into the four-session course. In Baltimore, they set up school at Fort McHenry, and about two dozen agents came to class. "Those opposed to the work you are doing," lectured Spates, "are ever ready to capitalize any defects they may be able to discover in your personal conduct." Dengler delved into the intricacies of case preparation and courtroom presentation. He rattled off pearls of sage advice as concise and crystallized as Confucian aphorisms: "Be careful. The persons you are asked to identify may be switched." And, "Don't read newspapers in the courtroom." And, "Don't go in the courtroom wearing boots, nor with your pistol displayed at a threatening angle and bumping about on the chair you are occupying; wear clean collars and be cleanly shaved."

And above all, when the oath was being administered, "Put your arm all the way up—like you expected to tell the truth."

If there was an underlying ideal to the professors' lessons, it was that if the war was to be won, the agents must first win over the hearts and minds of the people. "The only way to secure proper enforcement is to change public opinion," said Dengler. "If you can't change their senti-ment, it is at least possible by correct conduct of your affairs to change their opinion about the methods of enforcement. Respect of the com-munity is what is needed. We can't get the respect of the public, though, if our agents are going speeding through towns and when stopped show their badge to the policeman and go scott free. . . . Nor can we expect it if the agents attempt to badge their way into baseball games and similar events."

"Just one principle I want you to take away from here tonight," said Spates. "If you remember it always when engaged in your duties as en-forcement officers and when before the public eye, I feel that our hours spent lecturing you will have been well spent.

"It is this: You can't tell the public to go to hell and get away with it."

Lone Wolf Asher and those less successfully involved in the war were arrayed against an adversary more organized, connected, and flush with money—and its resultant influence—than ever before. Networks, combines, and syndicates of varying complexity had evolved out of the more anarchic early days of Prohibition. The days of a high-profile raid on a 50-gallon still had metamorphosed into the days of a routine raid on a 500-gallon still. On land as on water, the distribution network had matured to a higher level of sophistication. The land trade increasingly belonged to the likes of "society bootlegger" Joseph Conley, who rum-ran with a false bottom in his auto and supplied the toniest clientele in Philadelphia, Baltimore, and Washington. When the Philadelphia Po-lice Department finally nabbed Conley and turned him over to the feds, they found him with eighty-five gallons of grain alcohol as well as some "real fine old whiskey" sloshing about in the hidden crannies of his car. They also found a list of high-hat names that the police noted "included many persons well known in official and social circles of the three cities." On the inland waterways, meanwhile, the main smuggling routes had been established, and the aquatic runners, ever gaining in the lore of trickery and evasion, were an increasingly relied-upon link between suppliers and buyers. A swamp-country powerboat route feeding the lower Bay became mythic. Stories were told of the "moonshine city" that had grown up deep in the heart of Alligator Swamp, North Carolina. The swamp city had electricity and running water. Twenty big stills cranked out corn whiskey that was barreled up and sent shooting along a 5-mile flume to the drop-off where speedboats loaded up for the 90-mile run to Norfolk. After off-loading the swamp 'shine, the motorboats took on cargoes of corn mash and sugar, and hastened back to Alligator Swamp.

Moonshiners in general were improving as a breed. The market dictated that devil-may-care cutthroat poisoners and idiots out of their element be eliminated. "Bootleggers and moonshiners, from the kind of information now available in the laboratory, are making better stuff," the *Norfolk Virginian-Pilot* reported on the cusp of 1924–1925. "They are becoming more expert in the art of distilling booze, and are inclined less frequently to embody in their liquor any of the deadly poisons of the group of which wood alcohol is the chief. Now and then the police capture a malefactor who has smashed the prohibition laws, and find on his person a certain liquid which shows in analysis the presence of mineral compounds extremely injurious to the inner man. But the tribe is becoming smaller every month."

In that far-off era of a few years earlier, the city bacteriologist routinely had been swamped by citizens seeking sample-testing of the illegal alcohol they were about to imbibe. But "folks are taking their whisky in Norfolk these days as they find it, and are asking no questions." The only test requests anymore seemed to come from cops or from some potentially fortunate consumer who, with ever greater infrequence, may have stumbled upon some genuine prewar liquor, that holiest of grails among the drinking set. "The so-called 'good whisky,' the pre-war stuff, is . . . becoming a rare commodity. Now and then the laboratory has a call from some individual who has a supply of whisky which he has bought for the genuine commodity, but the authenticity of which he has reason to doubt. . . . He doesn't trust his bootlegger in such things, and while the stuff may smell right and look right, he is rather inclined to have the chemist go a little deeper before he subjects the concoction to the final analysis, that performed in the stomach. So he sends a sample, and as a very rare thing, it turns out to be real whisky, the kind that the bibulous now mourn in memory."

With or without prewar beverages, drinking was becoming safer and more palatable, thanks to the refinement of the moonshine subculture. "From all indications . . . people who formerly were extremely careful over the stuff they drank, or often paid a severe penalty for lack of care, now are inclined to take chances in the belief that whisky nowadays, in more experienced and more expert hands, is being made with fewer of the disastrous ingredients. Wood alcohol poisoning nowadays is seldom heard of."

It was Thanksgiving season 1924, and residents of Larchmont, Virginia, near Norfolk, were complaining of unmistakable still-stink hanging thickly on the autumn wind. Vice-squad cops combed posh Buckingham Avenue and zeroed in on the source: 1206 Buckingham, the beautiful home of H. L. Page, real estate big shot. The Pages were currently wintering in St. Petersburg, Florida; they had rented the Larchmont house to a man named Brown. A judge was on the prowl with the cops. He signed the warrant on the spot, and in they went.

Lights were on inside. The law banged on the door. Lights went out. Silence. The mash-stink was redolent. The cops jimmied their way in through the back door. Their noses led them upstairs. The second floor *chez* Page had been converted into a state-of-the-art distilling operation. The furniture in the three bedrooms had been shoved aside to make room for moonshine. The back bedroom, the one adjoining the bathroom, now sported a mighty still, its hefty cooker perched atop gas burners on a brick foundation. Five giant barrels stood upon a platform, while a system of pipes linked the barrels to one another and ultimately to the big cooker. Holes had been drilled into the wall. Rubber hoses fed in gas and water from the bathroom. Barrels of mash were lined up against the walls. The walls and the floor were nasty with mash-splatter, and the dense, nauseating stench was enough to gag a goat.

The cooker was hot. A run had been done just before the law broke in. Downstairs, in the kitchen, they found a hot pot of coffee and an unfinished plate of sausage. They went down into the basement. There, hiding amid the cobwebs, they found David Frank Willis, twenty-six. His cohort, the elusive Mr. Brown, had driven off ten minutes before the vice squad showed, said neighbors. When he learned of the Larchmont raid, H. E. Page, a relative of the absent homeowner, commented that it had gotten to the point where the population was "divided into two classes—bootleggers and bootleggers' customers."

The inspector said the raid on the big still was more important than arresting twenty bootleggers "because a plant of this size could keep more than twenty bootleggers supplied with liquor for the retail trade. If the source of supply is cut off, the rest of the liquor problem will take care of itself."

Along with motorcars, radios, motion pictures, and public utilities, bootlegging was a growth industry, one of the many noteworthy success stories of a robustly capitalist decade. That this particular growth industry had the stigma of being illegal seemed to hamper its quick development little if at all. Those in the trade tasted success, reinvested, and got ever fancier in the way they conducted the business. Prohibition agents in 1925 raided a still in the swamp at Titsel Farm near Glen Burnie, between Baltimore and Annapolis. The still was a behemoth: 1,000-gallon capacity, standing alongside vat after vat of readying mash, eighteen thousand gallons in all. So productive was the operation that it was served by its own private railway.

Another significant mid-decade distillery bust transpired at the old abandoned Baltimore City municipal pig farm in Anne Arundel County. The big piggery along Bodkin Creek had been a fiscal flop, and the physical plant—wooden building, concrete floor and foundation—had lain fallow until some visionary had seen its outstanding potential as a water-front moonshine factory. In the old days, the pigs there had been fed on Baltimore City garbage shipped on scows. Tracks leading to the wharf indicated that the piggery moonshine likewise was being transported by water. The seventeen-year-old stepson of the current property owner was caught running the 500-gallon still and was arrested. The property owner avowed ignorance; he was renting the building to a Baltimorean, he said.

Whiskey-making talent was drawn to the Bay region. On Maryland's upper Eastern Shore, one of the top moonshiners was an expatriate North Carolinian. A group of North Carolina brothers were active distillers on the lower Eastern Shore as well. And George Williams, a first-class mountain moonshiner from Virginia, was recruited to run a sizable mid-Shore operation. Expert distilling was a Williams family tradition. George's father was an esteemed master of the art; people in the Blue Ridge Mountains would travel far for a snort of old John's liquor. Geneva Hall, former wife of George Williams, remembered her old father-in-law: "He could just shake a bottle and tell you what proof it was." The Williams clan was large; young George displayed the distilling talent that was his familial hallmark. A prosperous Eastern Shore farmer named Dorsey Webb, one of the first men in the region to own an airplane, flew to Virginia to scout liquor talent for his growing Talbot County moonshine sideline. "Dorsey had that plane," recalled Geneva. "He flew George up and hired him to make whiskey."

Life was good for the young couple after they relocated from the mountains of Virginia to the flatlands of Maryland. Geneva helped her husband's operation in many ways. She'd make the roundabout overland run to Baltimore to stock up on yeast, a big yeast purchase drawing down less suspicion in the city. She'd make whiskey deliveries all over the area, from the farm-country Caroline-Talbot border to the black speakeasies of Easton to the remote reaches of Tilghman Island. The customer base spanned all economic strata. The well-to-do in the community bought their whiskey good and aged; for most, though, white lightning was the affordable option. The white lightning went for eight dollars for a 5-gallon can; the aged stuff was considerably higher, about fifty dollars for a 10-gallon keg. In addition to making home-delivery runs, the Williamses enjoyed a brisk walk-in trade. Customers ranged from a young couple courting, seeking a little libation for a sitting-session beneath a tree, to the black workers from the Phillips Packing Company in Cambridge, who would pool their resources and score a can of lightning for subsequent pay-by-the-glass dispensation among their comrades. Frequent visits, Geneva soon learned, could be expected from the local constabulary, not to arrest, but to indulge. The first time a policeman rode up on horseback and asked for a drink, Geneva was taken aback. But she got used to it. It was routine. It kept the wheels of commerce oiled. George would always give a policeman a drink, Geneva said, "and give him more than one drink if he wanted!"

Geneva came to realize that she needn't worry about the police while she was making her delivery runs. "I wasn't afraid. If I saw police walking right down the street, I knew they wouldn't bother me."

Federal investigators—the revenue men—these were to be feared and avoided. And even on the local level, there would always be some devoted lawmen one had to watch out for. But in most cases, the blind eye was what the down-home Officer Friendly would be expected to turn.

Milford Elliott, the son of rum-running waterman Alonza Elliott, remembered how Saturday was the big go-to-town day in Cambridge. As farmers and watermen made the weekly pilgrimage, bootleggers regularly enjoyed a peak business day. "Yessir, them pint bottles were flowing around," Milford Elliott said. But the Cambridge cops, "they didn't pay any attention. We had a few police, you know, out patrollin' the streets, whackin' his stick. He didn't care, as long as you didn't walk on him."

"See, the police in that time, they didn't give a durn," said Geneva Hall. "You could have the police lookin' right at you and it didn't matter."

In such a climate, the underground industry flourished on the Delmarva Peninsula. In Cecil County, stills proliferated and a sizable chunk of the population made a living from liquor. In Caroline County, moonshining had become a predominant way of life, with Caroline distillers supplying a region far beyond county borders. One particular distillery-intensive Caroline section was known as "Mexico." Another, near the town of Harmony, was called "Hell's Half-Acre." Bethlehem had a moonshiner, and across the Choptank River in Talbot County, near George Williams's moonshining turf, stills were run by George Alfred "Shot" Smith and the black moonshiner Levi Slaughter, who marketed his product under the quasi-brand names of Meal Wine, Meal Buck, and Cornstalk Buck. Dorchester, Somerset, and Wicomico counties all had their representatives in the moonshining ranks, and the names of fondly remembered rascals live on in local lore.

The restructured Prohibition Enforcement Bureau of late 1925 carved the nation into two dozen districts, one of which was composed of Delaware, Maryland, and Washington, D.C. Edgar Budnitz was named district chief, headquartered at Baltimore. He quickly set his sights on the Eastern Shore, mobilizing an army of two hundred agents, at their vanguard a "flying squadron" of advance alky-snoopers, for a wholesale Shore sweep, described as "a general cleanup of the bootlegging fraternity." Budnitz intended to hit fast and hard at the rampant Shore distilling scene, his master plan a threefold one:

1. To wipe out the source of supply of thousands of gallons of illicit and poisonous liquor manufactured in crudely constructed stills throughout the rural section of the Shore.
2. To round up the great horde of moonshine vendors, who have been practically unmolested and permitted to flagrantly violate the law in disposing of their illegal concocted combinations.
3. To complete unmistakable evidence against both manufacturers and vendors by sending an advance guard of inspectors and investigators, quickly followed by officials who will apprehend those against whom complaints have been lodged.

It so happened that Eastern Shore watermen at this time were going through a rough time. They were coming off a couple of lean years of harvesting Bay seafood, and they were about to begin what would be one of the worst oyster seasons (1925–1926) in years. The hard times were felt all down the line, from watermen to shuckers to packers. Will Gotman was a black waterman who came to Talbot County from Crisfield. He wasn't making any money, so he started making booze. A brisk trade ensued. Gotman's core client base consisted of down-on-their-luck shuckers who could ill afford such luxuries, but who's to judge? Gotman, at any rate, had found a way to eke out a living, until his arrest in early 1926. He was dealt a twelve-month sentence, taken to Baltimore, and thrown in stir.

For watermen, the liquor trade provided another moonlighting option, another diversification for men whose livelihood was based on diversifying. It was a tempting fast-cash proposition when oyster yields were lean, and a lucrative adventure even in better years. The Chesapeake waters themselves kept offering up mystic suggestions. Seth Haddaway was oyster-tonging in the Tred Avon River when his tongs brought up, instead of muddy bivalves, a tightly corked bottle filled with dark liquid. Uncorking unleashed an aroma that was wonderfully, unquestionably pre-Prohibition. "Mr. Haddaway," it was reported, "suddenly became a very popular man." Oxford oyster packer Oliver Gallup enjoyed displaying an empty half-pint liquor bottle brought up from beneath the waves. Oysters clung steadfastly to the bottle; the one at the mouth was the fattest of all. It was a funny find. It looked like the big oyster had drained the bottle of its contents. A waterman brought a similar artifact to an Oxford oyster house. It was a broken old whiskey jug. Seven great oysters were stuck around the jug's mouth "as if they tried to get into the jug after getting a whiff of what was once inside." Other oysters were attached to the side of the jug "looking as if they were waiting their turn to get inside." The watermen hung the old jug on the wall of the oyster house, and underneath the oysters they painted the word "Memories."

Another aspect of society was being affected. The Prohibition-induced drinking pandemic was flaking off the veneer of small-town racial coexistence. The friction could be seen throughout the Eastern Shore, home to an archetypical black-white culture. Illegal thirsts knew no boundaries of class or skin, and the illicit booze trade was carried on enthusiastically between the races. Tribalism was less important than supply and demand. But some white people dreaded alcohol's ability to create what they perceived as an increased bravado among the black people along the thoroughfare. Many of the white populace thought heavy drinking made black people "uppity," and moonshine's proliferation aroused Caucasian fearfulness. In Easton, the phobia's flashpoint was the east-end stretch of sin and depravity known as Graham's Alley, made especially infamous when Graham's Alley boozers were linked to the shooting of prominent citizen Samuel Hambleton in 1926. "There has [*sic*] been many fights, gun toting, and bootlegging in that alley for years," reported the *Star-Democrat,* "and at times its reputation has been such that no white person would venture into it after dark." The town elders finally declared war on the danger zone. To mop up Graham's Alley, the police presence was beefed up and would be kept so, it was declared, "until this long obnoxious section is made what it should be." Three brawny officers ventured down the alley on a typically insane Saturday night. They did succeed in making a number of street arrests, mainly on concealed-weapons charges. But "as soon as their presence was known the bootlegging joints were sealed tight. Lights were put out and doors locked and in a short time the alley was quiet as a tomb."

In St. Michaels, the irascible strip was Skinner Street, likened by the press to "a boil on a healthy person. It is one of the sore spots of the community . . . according to the better class of people." Indignant St. Michaels residents urged the state's attorney to take action against the bawdy-house boulevard that Skinner Street had become. "This street is back of the theatre. Colored people live there, and it is said operate drinking places where beverages stronger than lemonade are served. . . . conditions are so bad that parents are refusing to let their daughters attend the movies." Saturday nights in Trappe, too, had become notoriously rowdy. On Saturdays after dark, the ostensibly peaceful village on the north-south road between Easton and the Choptank River developed a dangerous, wild-west atmosphere. The streets were filled with surly shouting, interracial brawling, mass inebriation, and a complete lack of secretiveness on the part of drunkards. "Most of these were colored people, cursing and swearing and fighting late at night to such an extent that the white people could not sleep."

A merchant, who closed his store early due to violence escalating out front, said, "I never saw so much drinking in Trappe as I witnessed on Saturday night . . . the cursing and swearing and fighting going on just outside my door. I went outside and persuaded two colored men to go home before they got in trouble, and just about this time another man came along and we two managed to stop them fighting and sent them to their homes." A woman, frightened and stirred from her bed, went to the window and looked out: "There were both white and colored people in the crowd, but I could not make out any of them. They were fighting and swearing so that I could not sleep. It is time the authorities put a stop to this kind of business."

"The colored people seem to ignore the law more than ever," a Shore reporter griped, "and boast that the men they work for will get them out of trouble if they are arrested. Farm hands are scarce and when the colored help gets into the trouble the farmers as a rule help them out." A Trappe citizen was quoted saying, "If the magistrates would be more severe the trouble would soon be broken up. . . . it is hoped that the authorities will try and put a stop to the drinking and fighting and swearing along the streets, especially after the white folks have retired."

"Between convictions under the Volstead Act, and arrests for drunkenness," said Senator Bruce in his Ocean City speech, "it looks to me as if the time might come when one-half of our people will be in jail and the other half will be drunk; and there will be no one at all to look after the Commonwealth."

Edmund Budnitz's major Maryland-Delaware land offensive in the war on alcohol fizzled by May 1926, less than a year after it was launched with brio and zeal, stalled out by mundane bureaucratic entanglements having to do with forbidding agents to hire automobiles for investigative purposes. It was budget-tightening, or nitpicking over the Volstead Law (there was no authority written into it for the hiring of vehicles for investigators), but the result was that dry agents ended up having to limit their areas of operation to town limits, for now they were suddenly foot-soldiers, and foot-soldiers only, in the war. If they used their own vehicles, they would have to do so at their own expense. It was like telling a policeman he can't have a police car and has to prowl the beat in his own private chariot. What about all those stills bubbling away out in the boondocks? An agent on the Shore conceded "they will be let alone for the present."

So the land war was stymied. It had been launched on the assumption that the nautical phase of the war already had been won. The water war had, in fact, only just begun. The cocky, blatant Rum Row of old had been scattered, but it hadn't been destroyed, merely reconfigured. And as the government had geared up for its land offensive in the summer of 1925, the *Baltimore Daily-Post* already was reporting, "a renewed attempt of the rum fleet to swamp the coast with booze is anticipated."

"It still goes on," said Big Bill McCoy of the offshore rum traffic. "Officials may say that their five-ply sea blockade has wiped out the trade, but I know they are wrong, and they must, too. Their cutters and speedboats, their agents and spies have not decreased sea-borne liquor traffic. In spite of them all, liquor continues to stream in, but it comes through safer, better concealed, more thoroughly charted channels than in the old days. It never has been stopped, despite the hundreds of millions the government is spending and for which taxpayers are paying. It never will be."

"Prohibition is here to stay; it will stay as long as the stars and stripes fly over this country and that, my friends, is for some time to come." Thus had spoken the legendary William E. "Pussyfoot" Johnson, first a leader of the Anti-Saloon League, then a leading light in the World League Against Alcoholism, traveling and speaking on both sides of the Bay after returning from a tour of Africa in 1924. He had made an exhaustive antialcohol tour that traversed the African continent from south to north, from Cape Town to Zanzibar. His Chesapeake dates were part of an East Coast lecture itinerary that marked his triumphant return stateside. Before a large Eastern Shore crowd, the famed crusader called alcohol "one of Satan's tools" and said, "Had you been told twenty-five years ago that this country would be dry . . . would you have believed it? You would have said that it was a dream. Still the fact is here; this country is dry. Critics may say that a flood of liquor is inundating the country; that the young are learning to drink even more youthfully than in olden times, but will they say that conditions are any worse than they were under the old license system?"

Pussyfoot Johnson acknowledged that the Volstead Law was being broken daily, probably even hourly. "But we should not be discouraged. There isn't a law on the statute books which is not continually being violated. You cannot legislate a thing out of existence. Public opinion must back it up. . . .

"The matter has already passed the stage of being for or against Prohibition. You are either for the enforcement of all laws or against the Constitution. The Eighteenth Amendment is part of our Constitution and it will either stand or fall by it. I know the American people, and I know that the Constitution is here to stay. Prohibition is here to stay."

Years earlier, Pussyfoot Johnson had gone to England. He tried to launch a dry crusade. Blue-collar workmen got hostile. In the ensuing mob assault, Pussyfoot Johnson had lost an eye.

A week after Pussyfoot Johnson's Shore speech, a judge stood over a sewer hole in a pen at Norfolk Police Court and joked, "I have often heard of people who took baths in champagne in the good old days, though I never got to that stage myself." The judge was overseeing the sewer-dumping of about six hundred gallons of corn whiskey, grain alcohol, and bottled imports culled by the cops in several recent raids. "Yes, sir," said the judge, hoisting a gallon can and pouring liquor into his hand. He tossed the can, deftly rubbed his hands together, and treated himself to a sniff. "As I say, I have heard of people bathing in champagne, though I never got that far myself, but this is the first time I have ever washed my hands in liquor."

Several officers and court staffers had gathered to watch the pouring-out ritual. The drain-destined haul included more than twenty bottles of Canadian Club whiskey, proclaimed by experts to be the genuine article. As they broke the bottles and dumped them out, onlookers said, "It's a shame." Some couldn't watch anymore, and they ambled off, reiterating, "It's a shame, all right."

"Look out there, Judge!" the court officer yelled as he bunged open a 56-gallon barrel of booze. A thick stream of premium corn liquor shot forth. It surged and swirled about the judge's feet until they were submerged. Unfazed, the judge calmly finished dumping out the contents of a 5-gallon tin before stepping back, smiling.

"Well, I washed my hands in liquor for the first time," the judge said, "and now I am wading in liquor for the first time in my life—and to think we are living in a Prohibition age!"

CHAPTER FIVE

"SUBJECT: INCREASED ACTIVITY, RUMRUNNERS"

It was 1926. The nation was shaking to the latest dance craze, the Charleston. The sleek, slinky Charleston flare dress was de rigueur flapper couture. Henry Ford quit making Model T's and started making Model A's. New York and London were linked by telephone for the first time. Movie siren Clara Bow was dubbed "the It Girl," and the nickname stuck. Movie seducer Rudolph Valentino, "the Great Lover," died, and thousands who never knew him grieved with bizarre intensity. Gene Tunney beat Jack Dempsey to win the world heavyweight boxing title. U.S. Marines landed in Nicaragua. The stock market dipped, but it rebounded fairly quickly, and there seemed to be nothing to worry about. It was 1926, almost a year into the land phase of the war on alcohol, and the war's leader, General Lincoln C. Andrews, assistant secretary of the treasury, went before the Senate Judiciary Committee and admitted that it was a war fraught with seemingly insurmountable obstacles. Andrews testified to the committee that just in the past year he had been compelled to boot out 875 of his Prohibition agents for various forms of booze-related corruption. Bootleggers, meanwhile, were raking in more than $3.5 billion a year. The beleaguered federal forces, conceded Andrews, were intercepting only about 5 percent of the hooch. Also, said Andrews, the 175,000 stills destroyed in the past year probably amounted to no more than 10 percent of the stills in operation. President Coolidge told Congress the obvious: that the Volstead Act needed more enforcement muscle behind it. The president budgeted $30 million to beef up Prohibition crackdown efforts. It was 1926, and temperance leaders argued that there was less crime now, thanks to Prohibition. The Anti-Saloon League's Wayne B. Wheeler, meanwhile, confessed that the Anti-Saloon League had paid off certain congressmen to spew eloquence on behalf of the dry cause.

It was a year since it had been declared that the rum war on the waves was won, and the rum ships, gleefully ignorant of their own reported defeat, continued to infiltrate the coast. On the Chesapeake in the summer of 1926, the Coast Guard had its eye on a number of miscreant craft, including the Baltimore steam yacht *Sabalo* and her partner in crime, the two-masted motor schooner *Eugie*. Both were taking liquor off of Baltimore-bound rumrunners and bringing the stuff to Annapolis. Orders went out to vessels of Section Base Eight: eyes out for *Sabalo* and company. On June 29, 1926, patrol boat *CG-185* found *Sabalo* at anchor off Goodwin Island, near the mouth of the York River. *CG-185*'s officer in charge boarded the smuggler. Upon his unexpected arrival, he found creme de menthe, French brandy, vermouth, and a wild party going full force. The onboard revelers were swacked. The yacht was hauled to Norfolk, where the district attorney kicked forth arrogant: he tried to assert that the Coast Guard needed a search warrant to board any vessel (one can imagine what such leashing of authority would do to patrolling efforts). In addition, the district attorney stared at the Coast Guardsman present and made a remark about his uniform, a snide comment to the effect that it was like a penny-ante imitation of a real U.S. Navy uniform. It was just such an atmosphere that made the Coast Guard cynical about the prosecutorial machine handling the cases the guardsmen brought to land.

Among the Coast Guard, rumrunner lore was well entrenched by now. They called the smuggling vessels "blacks," short for "black ships," because of the dark paint-jobs so many rumrunners sported for obvious reasons. The runners long since had come up with a practical packaging method, a method that Big Bill McCoy himself claimed to have invented: the "sack," a big burlap bundle in which several bottles of booze were snugly encased, able to float and protected from breakage.

The Chesapeake's illegal maritime traffic continued to thrive as a two-tiered construct: (1) oceangoing vessels brought the product and either ran the Virginia Capes gauntlet themselves or, more often, served as mother ships for smaller craft waiting and willing to make the end run; and (2) the smaller craft, many of them native Bay boats, served as consorts to the foreign rumrunners and also carried on a prosperous enterprise transporting regionally made firewater from one part of the Chesapeake to another. Both tiers served to lubricate not only the Bay country, but a far larger territory, for Chesapeake Bay more and more was being appreciated by traffickers as an advantageous entrance to many major markets. This interest in the Bay was a distinct and trackable side-effect of the Coast Guard's breakup of the old Rum Row. After Coast Guard pressure increased on the offshore ships arrayed along the New Jersey and New York coasts, the fringe regions of Rum Row, including the Chesapeake, saw a marked increase in rum-running activity. The Bay in the late 1920s was more thickly trafficked by rum craft than ever before.

In Chesapeake waters, the stuff was going every which way, but certain routes did stand out as major booze-paths. The time-tested southern Maryland–Eastern Shore run was one such artery. "From information obtained it appears that corn liquor is frequently transported from points in the vicinity of St. Mary's River, Maryland, to Crisfield, Maryland, and distributed from that place," reported USCG Norfolk Division Commander A. J. Henderson in June 1926. "This information has been received from the masters of several boats operating in the vicinity of Crisfield, Maryland, who allege that they are opposed to illegal traffic in intoxicating liquors." Crisfield, of course, was but one of several Eastern Shore drop-off points for the coveted southern Maryland "tiger spit."

While southern Maryland was exporting great amounts of its celebrated corn mixture, the region also remained active as a major import nexus for transoceanic contraband Washington-bound. Foremost among the Potomac rumrunners was the 80-foot *Wild Rose*. With three Packard engines, she routinely made the 75-mile run to the high seas and would "take a load of booze off a ship and be back home by daybreak," said Bruce Scheible, whose mother-in-law was a waitress at the southern Maryland dockside restaurant that served as home port for *Wild Rose*. The legendary vessel, recalled Scheible, was "the fastest thing on the water at the time."

After being shipped eastward across the Chesapeake, most of the southern Maryland product was trucked to the beckoning markets of the northeast, but some also was earmarked for local consumption, such as the stuff brought by Dorchester rumrunner Alonza Elliott for his local-distribution clients. The Eastern Shore was producing bounteous amounts of its own homemade distillate, but the southern Maryland moonshine nonetheless enjoyed a devoted Shore following. Alonza's son Milford Elliott, though, failed to appreciate the drink's sublime qualities. "God, that was awful stuff," he recollected. "I tasted it, and it just pulled the skin right off as it went down, I thought. I never tasted nothing like it." But Milford's father loved the liquid. While making his nocturnal runs in *Dixie*, he'd stick a piece of white hose in one of the barrels he was hauling and take copious sips en route.

Dixie almost went out in a blaze of glory one night, Milford recalled. Alonza and Milford's brother Rufus were returning with a boatload of southern Maryland's finest when the engine conked. "The motor kept coughing for gas, you know, askin' for gas, and after a while she quit," said Milford. She shouldn't have been out of fuel, and she wasn't; something had gone awry. "The gas line . . . shook loose, and the gas run out on the bottom of her and she caught fire." Rufus sprang into action, "and when he lifted the little hatch up . . . the fire come up and got him, and he jumped over the side of the boat and held on to the side and ducked hisself down and put the fire out and washed him off. And then there's my father, about two-thirds drunk with his boat on fire . . . ."

"They couldn't go any further, so they got a tow—it was between the mouth of the big Choptank and Hoopers Island down there, is where they were, out there in the Bay between. Somebody, some crabber, come out and my father got him to tow him in to the crab house . . . my father knew the crab house man." When Alonza told the crab house man that *Dixie* needed fuel, "The feller said, "Lonzie, you don't have to buy my gas . . . you got plenty of it there!'" The crab house man pointed at the barrels of whiskey. "'It'll burn!'"

It was 1927. Babe Ruth hit his sixtieth single-season home run, a baseball record that would stand for decades. Charles Lindbergh took off from New York in a single-engine monoplane called *Spirit of St. Louis*, flew to France, and became a hero to millions. The first talking motion picture, *The Jazz Singer*, opened. Anarchist immigrants Sacco and Vanzetti, alleged murderers and political *causes célèbres*, were executed. Attempting to capitalize on the Charleston dance mania, Frankie Trumbauer and His Orchestra, featuring the dazzling young cornet hotshot Bix Beiderbecke, recorded an effervescent dance number called "The Baltimore."

And in Baltimore, the wet, reveling town that inspired a Roaring Twenties jazz strut, a rumrunner named Pete Kelly reigned as "King James," underworld royalty until the Coast Guard nailed him red-handed out on the Bay pulling up alongside a boatload of booze. Busting Pete Kelly was just the beginning.

CG-144, out of Fort McHenry, was patrolling the Bay on the night of June 29, 1927, when she sighted a schooner off Fort Carroll, heading for the entrance to Bear Creek. The patrol boat tailed the schooner. The schooner anchored in the creek. The Coast Guard boat pulled up alongside and boarded. Bad sign: no cargo manifest. A guardsman brought cargo samples abovedecks: a case of Gordon's gin and a case of raw alcohol marked triple-X. There was plenty more below. The rumrunner was American, her name was *Ida O. Robinson*, and she was stung hauling seven hundred cases—thirty-one thousand gallons, estimated bootleg street value: two hundred thousand dollars.

Coast Guard Captain William Lacey arrested *Ida O. Robinson*'s crew and ordered the patrol boat to make for Baltimore to fetch *Apache*.

Lacey and others stayed aboard the rumrunner. The capture made good bait. A powerboat showed up, lights doused, circling the schooner, not knowing she was now seized goods. Captain Lacey hailed the powerboat as she neared. No answer. The boat was almost alongside. Captain Lacey hailed her again. A man rose up from the powerboat and gestured at Lacey to shut up. Too late the man realized that this wasn't a fellow smuggler, but a Coast Guard officer. The powerboat threw on running lights and dashed off. Captain Lacey shouted, drew his automatic, and fired across her bow. The men surrendered and pulled alongside. The Coast Guard had three more prisoners. The one who had stood and beckoned for silence now claimed merely to be out for a late-night joy ride. It turned out he was the ringleader himself: Pete "King James" Kelly, brother of Joe Kelly, "wealthy retired saloonkeeper" whose joint had been on Greenmount Avenue and who himself had bumped into the law. King James Kelly was heading up a busy smuggling ring, its ranks filled with black and white participants, active on the Bay in a crime web that reached far beyond the Bay.

Customs inspectors got to work, and in a few months Supervising Agent Frederick Proctor of the Customs Bureau's Third District headquarters at Baltimore reported to the Coast Guard's Intelligence Office, "We have developed other witnesses in this case and other angles and leads which involve a number of persons and vessels that probably have been engaged in the business of smuggling liquor into the Chesapeake Bay for the past year . . . Pete Kelly, and others, have not only been engaged in the business of smuggling liquor in the Chesapeake Bay for sale in Baltimore and vicinity, but have been running rum through here for New York, Philadelphia and Washington interests." The rumrunners had regular landing sites: Cambridge, Crisfield, Fishing Island, Solomon's Island, the Nanticoke River, Nomini Creek, and at various Atlantic coastal points near Ocean City. Below Ocean City, off Wachapreague Inlet, rum ships hovered about 60 miles out to sea. At night they came in 14 miles from shore. Vessels ran out, met them, loaded up, and ran in the goods. At Wachapreague Inlet, the liquor was transferred to barges, then continued the journey up the Chesapeake concealed in fish barrels. Other liquor sacks made it northward camouflaged in oyster barrels in the holds of various types of Bay boats. Once landed, the liquor was transported to New York by truck or by refrigerated railroad car. Some barges continued onward with their "seafood" cargoes—not really seafood, but still really fishy—to the top of the Bay and on through the Chesapeake and Delaware Canal.

Customs investigators got wise too late that there had been some recent major liquor landings in the Chesapeake. One had been at Cambridge: five thousand cases for the thirsty northeast in the summer of 1927. Another had been on the Potomac: three shiploads, at least, for the now-standard waiting truck fleet. Meanwhile, even more offshore stuff, being run in along the North Carolina coast, was making it to Chesapeake Bay by way of railroad transport and by Chesapeake and Albemarle Canal barges.

The number of rum-running vessels involved was legion, but certain craft currently topped the suspect list, the recidivist offender *Dart*, for one. After being seized and released at Norfolk, she went on to make a number of landings up Baltimore way in the vicinity of Sparrows Point. Another was *Anna May*, a New Jersey bunker boat ostensibly involved in the menhaden fishery; her 100-ton cargo hold had housed more spiritous inventory than dead fish lately. *Anna May*'s frequent fellow-traveler was the British two-masted schooner *Maude Thornhill*, likewise nominally a menhaden fisherman, 150 tons, knockabout-rigged, out of Newfoundland, a sleek, lovely vessel making a killing as a Chesapeake rumrunner. *Maude Thornhill* was under the command of the infamous John Campbell, a runner who had done a nine-month jail stint in Jersey on a conspiracy beef that involved some temptable Coast Guard Section Base One personnel. A certain boatswain had been among the Coast Guardsmen tainted by the scandal. Implicated in the conspiracy, he cooperated with investigating officers, thereby avoiding prosecution and getting off with nothing worse than probation stigma. But the boatswain and *Maude Thornhill* were destined to meet again, this time in the Chesapeake, and once again, it was squirm time.

Maude Thornhill had been sighted. The boatswain was command-ing the patrol craft *Forward.* Norfolk Division and, more directly, the commanding officer of the USCG's *Perry* ordered the boatswain to stick to *Maude Thornhill* with tenacity until relieved. The boatswain dis-obeyed the order; worse, he grossly falsified *Maude Thornhill's* position reports, thus allowing the rumrunner to elude the authorities. A board of investigation convened in the lower Bay on the Coast Guard vessel *Manning* in October 1927. Some brass were calling for the boatswain's head. The board spared him the worst, though, ruling that his crimes had been disobedience and navigational ineptitude, but not conspiring with the rumrunner. The Coast Guard Intelligence Office strongly op-posed the ruling. "The Board stated that testimony does not show collu-sion with the *Maude Thornhill,*" argued intelligence officer Charles S. Root, "but this office believes that the Board is mistaken." Comman-dant F. C. Billard stood behind the board's decision, stating that whereas "transmitting false reports constitutes a most serious offense, deserving of condemnation in the strongest terms," it was most likely that the boatswain merely had "made very large errors in navigation, and that his motive was to cover up these errors." The boatswain was "severely censured," but he had dodged a court-martial, and *Maude Thornhill,* meanwhile, lived to run rum another day.

Rampant smuggling translated into a request for more Coast Guard boats in the vicinity. In 1928 new Section Base Eight Commander Lucien J. Ker urged Coast Guard headquarters to grant him four more 75-foot patrol boats for the Norfolk base. "Reports show considerable activity in the vicinity of Great Machipongo, Little Machipongo and Wachapreague Inlets," wrote Ker. "The number of patrol boats at pres-ent attached are barely sufficient to maintain a Chesapeake Bay patrol."

And while the government kept a weather eye offshore, the brisk trade in homemade product continued apace. The picket boat *CG-2314* was patrolling from Craney Island to Fort Wool in the predawn darkness of August 10, 1928. Richard Brim, the boatswain's mate in charge, was scrutinizing foreign vessels at anchor when he came across the Norfolk-based *Ethel May* east of Craney Island Light. Coast Guardsmen boarded her, found 122 jugs of domestic product, impounded the vessel, and arrested the black watermen manning the craft. The Norfolk Police Department and the federal Prohibition authorities had been after the traffickers for a while, and the Coast Guard turned the prisoners over.

Rumors grew of schooners off-loading liquid cargoes at drop-off spots along the Tred Avon River on the Maryland Eastern Shore. *CG-125* combed the Tred Avon from Eastern Bay to Easton Point in 1928, but failed to find the elusive quarry. The six-man crew, anchoring at Easton Point, was patrolling in a hotbed. So out of hand had the bootlegging situation become by 1928 that the Talbot County commissioners, with the prodding of the state's attorney, resorted to hiring a private detective to build cases that, lo and behold, the local police were not interested in pursuing. Soon the detective and his team of operatives were gleaning enough dirt on suspected parties to be filling up the circuit court. Some prominent busts came rolling in. In less than two weeks the detective and his team chalked up some thirty-five arrests. It was a time of increased crackdowns. A state record was set that November in Caroline County, when dry agents destroyed twenty-two stills in one day, mainly in the neighborhood of Henderson and Marydel.

The epic Maryland roundup generated out of Delaware, actually, from the office of George A. Hill, prohibition director for the First State. Five agents—three of them Shore locals, the other two out of Baltimore district headquarters—pulled off numerous seizures. Central to the arrests were eight major moonshine plants in Caroline. Director Hill was on the warpath. In January 1929 he personally led a force of Prohibition agents and local deputy sheriffs in the capture and sacking of a gargantuan liquor factory hidden deep in the woods near Felton, Delaware. Hill and his men charged in with revolvers and dynamite, and found the complex of stills cranking full blast. The three youths running the operation tried to hightail it—unsuccessfully. The officers blew up the 2,500-gallon plant, the largest illegal distilling operation ever found in Delaware.

While the court system dealt with local lawbreakers, rustic jails on the Eastern Shore and in southern Maryland were being filled past capacity with prisoners from elsewhere, federal prisoners who, because there were so many of them, were becoming problematic for the U.S. government. Local jailhouses became the spillover receptacles for the superabundance of Volstead violators. Out-of-area prisoners were thrown into the quickly crowded small-town jails with local petty crooks, creating a dynamic mix, a penitentiary-like melting-pot environment. And the local inmates soon learned one can't always trust the big-city boys. It was such misplaced trust that led to the fizzling of what otherwise would have been a classic jailbreak.

Andrew Davidson went to the Easton jail on the morning of January 31, 1929, to visit his cousin, William Henry, a local citizen awaiting trial for assault and battery. Davidson had brought presents for his incarcerated cousin, a couple of homemade pies. One of the pies had special ingredients: a file and a bunch of hacksaw blades.

Some prisoners kept watch; others went to work on the iron bars in a rear window. They sawed through two of the bars, put them back in place, and sealed the fissures with soap. They hid the tools when guards passed, got to work again when the coast was clear. They had just one bar to go. But they already had erred by confiding in Joseph Sindel, a Baltimore City bootlegger with just two months' jail time left. Sindel told fellow bootlegger Harry Brown, also a short-timer. Brown was working as a trusty, and he ratted. The sheriff rounded up the ringleaders and put them in separate cells. The newspaper fearfully pondered, "One small iron bar is all that kept about twenty-one prisoners from escaping."

Among the prisoners, friction between city and country crooks was rife. Some of the local Easton talent stole $335 from Baltimore bootlegger Lewis E. Berger while he slept. They divvied up the loot and stashed it throughout the cell, a hundred dollars in a ceiling crevice, a couple more C-notes in an old tobacco box hidden by steam pipes. The sheriff managed to recover all but fourteen dollars of the urban bootlegger's money.

Even in the hinterlands, the rum-trade roster included such cosmopolitans as repeat offender Antonio Callusi, arrested for bootlegging on the Eastern Shore on December 11, 1928. The Venice-born Callusi spoke four languages and was once a private detective. Callusi was alleged to have liquor stashes hidden all over the place—in an Oxford shell pile, in an Easton trunk—and he had his own boat for trafficking. The authorities jailed Callusi and tried to get him off the Shore, but he had a way of coming back. After a cakewalk four-month sentence for bootlegging, Callusi returned to action. He liked to boast that no hick lawman could nail him, since he himself had detective credentials and knew how to hoodwink country-bumpkin officers. In July 1929 he was arrested in Easton again, caught with fifty-seven bottles of dubious "bottled in bond." An officer stated that Callusi's hooch was tainted by "a poisonous coloring" that made customers go crazy. It was reported that "a cessation of disturbances about town was noticed by the officers after Callusi was jailed." This go-round, the magistrate hit Callusi with the maximum sentence: three years in the house of correction. After the hearing, as Callusi was being hauled to the jail, the police jeered and teased, rubbing it in that "the country officers finally got him." Callusi seemed peeved and surprised at the severity of the sentence. He needn't have worried. Within days, a Baltimore judge overturned the magistrate's sentence and set Callusi free on a habeas-corpus procedural technicality. By August he was back on the streets of Easton.

Talbot County Sheriff Thomas L. Faulkner, Captain George O. Haddaway, and three federal Prohibition agents boarded a boat and put out from Lowe's Wharf on Sunday afternoon, May 19, 1929. They headed up the Bay and hoped that if spotted, they'd be mistaken for a fishing party. The sheriff had been cooking up this expedition for days; the only thing that had delayed their departure was the arrival of the federal men, who hadn't been told where they were going. Once the boat was north of Poplar Island, the boat changed course. Poplar Island was three islands in those days. One of these, Valliant's Island, was the lawmen's destination. Under cover of the main island's northern point, they arrived at Valliant's. A mean dog barked vicious greetings. The lawmen came on land.

The dog's caterwauling failed to warn the bootleggers. Faulkner's group arrested four men and discovered the mother lode: a giant 1,000-gallon still, several 500-gallon stills, 121,500 gallons of mash, hundreds of cases of glass jars, heaping stores of sugar and rye flour, 42 vats of mash, a 40-horsepower boiler, and scads of paraphernalia indicating impending growth of the operation. Here, on an isolated little chunk of land in the Chesapeake Bay, somebody had set up a factory town.

The sheriff and his men hid their boat in the bushes. They waited. They waited some more. There she was: coming in off the northwest shore, a boat. She docked. The lawmen jumped out, pistols drawn, and arrested the five-man crew.

The boat was decked out with a pair of powerful Palmer engines. From their captives the officers soon confirmed that this was the boat used to move the island product, the boat that reports had pegged for running two hundred gallons of whiskey to Annapolis Friday night and three hundred gallons on Saturday night. Now the boat was used to take the nine prisoners to Baltimore. The officers moored the rumrunner at the Fort McHenry Prohibition Unit. The following day the prisoners were arraigned before U.S. Commissioner J. Frank Supplee. He set bail at two thousand dollars per man. Only Walter Perry was able to furnish the sum. The other eight—Galliano Amando, Maestri Pasquilla, Julian Coats, Marion Coats, Alfred Dasgeth, Herbert Bowig, Joseph Brown, and Sidridge Joyner—went behind bars to await hearings. Joyner, reportedly a Rock Hall man, was said to be the boat's skipper. The rogues' alliance of Chesapeake watermen and Italian racketeers had been a sureshot moneymaker.

The day after the raid, Sheriff Faulkner and another officer returned to the island. They came in a big scow, a roomy vessel for all the evidence they were going to stockpile. They destroyed the still's coil and bashed in the boiler. They loaded the scow with all sorts of parts, gadgets, and moonshine ingredients. They unloaded the haul at Lowe's Wharf and stored it all at the Sherwood Packing Company fish house. One of the prizes they brought off the island was a brand-new rum-running vessel, mightily motored, estimated to be worth about two thousand dollars, ready for launching but not yet used.

It was one of the largest operations of its kind ever found in Maryland. The Poplar Island booze factory was set up to crank out more than fifteen hundred gallons a day. With an estimated street value of three dollars a gallon, it amounted to a five-thousand-dollar-a-day business. And it was only a few weeks old; left unchecked, it would have grown even larger, fast. One of the men arrested on the island reportedly said that if the sheriff had postponed his raid by even a few more days, the operation would have been significantly larger: fifty employees, some of them making a hundred dollars a week. The rumrunners weren't just hauling loads to Annapolis; after just a few weeks' existence, the island factory already was shipping out liquor to all parts of the state. The virgin vessel taken off the island spoke of the business's rapidly growing volume.

Whose business was it? The island was absentee-owned by a gunning club, whose members showed up only during duck season. Months would pass before trails led to those members of the syndicate who were in charge of the liquor operation. The first of these went on trial in Baltimore in November 1929. A number of Italians involved in the venture were deported.

"It was one of the greatest hauls ever made in this section," praised a Shore reporter, "and the plans of the sheriff were well laid."

It was 1929. Herbert Hoover became the thirty-first President of the United States. Declaring crime the number-one problem facing the nation, he appointed the Wickersham Commission to study the Prohibition-criminality connection. Commander Richard E. Byrd planted the U.S. flag on the South Pole. A young, unknown crooner named Bing Crosby toured with the Paul Whiteman Orchestra. *All Quiet on the Western Front* topped the best-seller list. And in October, the almighty stock market fell to pieces, and the great crash heralded the Great Depression. Financial experts tried to assure the public that the economy was fine. Out at sea, the rum ships kept running.

Monday, December 30, 1929, was a perfect night for clandestine off-loading. The fog was thick, the surf conditions ideal for the case-laden Ocean City fishing skiffs making runs from the mystery ship to a deserted stretch of Maryland beach about four and a half miles south of the Ocean City Coast Guard Station. Here, smugglers loaded up trucks that transported the liquor to the inland side of the thin, sandy peninsula. From there, powerboats took over. The ship at sea was disgorging a fortune in whiskey, gin, and champagne from Canada, England, and France (if labels could be believed). The illegality was progressing swimmingly until the Coast Guard showed up and broke up the party.

A local skiff man caught making landings told the Coast Guard what he could about the ship out there in the fog: no name on her bow or stern, but her crew said they were from Halifax, Nova Scotia. The ship maintained her anonymity. The Coast Guard couldn't catch her. "It is, of course, regrettable that the liquor running vessel escaped," said Sixth District Commander James A. Price, "but weather conditions were all in her favor for making a clean escape."

Where were the powerboats on the inland water side going with the stuff? Boatswain's Mate First Class Garwood J. Thomas went to find out. One of the men nabbed on the beach tipped him off. Thomas commandeered a seized boat and headed out singlehanded. He crossed over to the mainland and made a cautious approach to a place known as Coffin's Point. He found a storage building stacked with liquor cases. He found a truck partially loaded with product. He found two men. Garwood Thomas's backup arrived in the form of state police and Coast Guardsmen. They stopped the men trying to make their getaway.

It was a kingly haul, 1,850 cases in all. It took men from the North Beach, Green Run, Fenwick Island, and Isle of Wight Coast Guard stations to transport the cache to Ocean City Station, where it remained under guard pending shipment to the Baltimore Customs House. The handling of the dozens of prisoners and the seized booze hoard was a task that took the cooperation of state police, Ocean City police, and county officials with the Coast Guard.

Pastor Otis P. Jefferson of the Ocean City Methodist Episcopal Church wrote Captain William Purnell of the Ocean City Coast Guard Station on December 31: "As a man who wishes to compliment and honor loyalty for true services rendered, I am glad to write you and your men . . . on your splendid heroism and bravery in making the raid on the liquor smuggling forces Monday morning. . . . *A fine piece of work has been done.* Let the good work continue until our community will be a fit place for parents to rear children in the love and fear of Christ. Surely I feel sorry that persons are willing to participate in lawlessness."

It was the last day of the 1920s. The liquor kept flowing. The syndicates kept profiting from forbidden fruit. And as long as Prohibition continued, it was as if the Twenties kept roaring on into the first few years of the next decade. Prohibition somehow perpetuated, at least partially, the feel of the frenzied decade beyond its calendar finale. The Wall Street crash ushered in an age of gloom, and the early part of the 1930s was a strange overlap of the flapper era and the breadline era. It was the overlap that occurs when cultural currents blend and blur along the cusp between one decade and the next. As long as booze was banned and bootleggers roamed, some of the tenor of the Roaring Twenties echoed on, tinny and wild, like a trumpet solo from a horn man in a speakeasy's band. Except now, a nagging hint of hangover hovered.

Customs took charge of the Ocean City prisoners. In March 1930 the thirty-four men nailed for smuggling went before federal Judge Morris A. Soper at Easton and pled guilty. Awaiting sentencing, they spent a night in Easton's jail, now so crowded that Sheriff Faulkner had to set them up in the lobby with cots. The next night, the Easton Armory was used to handle the spillover. The case was tried twice due to a jury disagreement. The defense tried to have the case moved to Baltimore, to no avail. Ringleaders Sam Hill and George Bolton each were sentenced to two years at Atlanta. The other two key members, Edward S. Murtha and Edward Miller, got eighteen months and fifteen months, respectively. Roland Driscoll, who lined up the men for the job, got six months. Boatowners E. B. Elliott, Spence J. Elliott, and Crawford O. Savage got four months.

The others got sentences ranging from two months to two years' probation.

By May, the people of Ocean City were appealing to Judge Soper for leniency. The jailed men had families to support, and their livelihood, the fishing industry, was getting into full swing this time of year. The court ruled that the judge already had been as lenient as possible in his sentencing. The men would have to do the time. The residents of Ocean City launched a drive to raise funds for the relief of the smugglers' families. "Quite a sum was raised," the *Star-Democrat* reported, ". . . and this is being used to keep the wolf from the door of the wives and children while the fathers and husbands are in jail."

Summer was coming, and before long Sixth District Commander Price was sending forth orders slugged, "Subject: Increased activity, rum runners." Patrol boat *CG-200* was on duty off Parramore Bank on the night of June 1 when the lookout spied a vessel about a half mile away, running north by northwest without lights. *CG-200*'s motors cranked up to full speed. She closed the distance. Her Klaxon horn screamed. Her searchlight beam lit her Coast Guard flag flapping in the night. The dark vessel's response to these warnings was simple: she sped up and ran off. The patrol boat chased her. Crewmen aimed the one-pounder and fired a warning shot at the fleeing craft. The shot shocked the runners into stopping. The patrol boat came alongside starboard and homed the searchlight sternward on the dark vessel's name: *Metmuzel*, out of good old St. Pierre, the island off Newfoundland. She was French, an ex-U.S. Navy subchaser. Boatswain Charles F. Garrison, *CG-200*'s officer in charge, hailed *Metmuzel*'s captain. A man came out of the pilothouse and said that would be he.

The Coast Guard officer asked him what he had on board.

The captain cracked wise: "Eleven men."

The Coast Guard officer asked, more specifically, what cargo he had on board.

The captain was blunt: "Whiskey."

The rough sea was trying to bang the boats together. The patrol boat worked around to *Metmuzel*'s port side, but the collision-damage danger was still there. It took some maneuvering, but they managed to throw a line from the patrol boat's bow to *Metmuzel's* stern. The rum crewmen were ordered aboard *CG-200*. They were searched for weapons as Boatswain Garrison rifled through the canvas sack that held the ship's papers. They were written in French; the closest thing to a cargo manifest was not properly made out to qualify legally as such. There were no documents about where the ship was carrying what for whom, but Coast Guardsmen reported that they had seen one of the *Metmuzel* crew come out of the pilothouse and dump stuff overboard. Garrison radioed for backup.

Metmuzel was loaded with 1,103 bags of various choice whiskies, primarily bourbon. The Coast Guard towed the French runner into Norfolk for adjudication and handed over twelve new prisoners, all either British or French subjects, to the Collector of Customs. It was cut and dried; everything about *Metmuzel* seemed illegal that night: no lights, no flag, no proper papers, a fat cargo of whiskey headed for the Virginia Eastern Shore, an attempted escape when ordered to halt. But Albert Flahaut, *Metmuzel's* captain, and his crew wasted no time in seeking their release from the federal authorities. A New York lawyer came to Norfolk, and all of a sudden the case wasn't so cut and dried.

Metmuzel, the Coast Guard claimed, had been captured 6.6 miles from shore, beyond the 3-mile territorial limit of U.S. law, but well within the 12-mile limit established by the 1924 treaties with Great Britain and France. The treaties, written to give the United States a leg up in fighting the rum war, gave patrol craft an extra 9-mile enforcement zone in which they were permitted to chase, board, and seize rum ships. But the added area was one of murky waters, legally speaking. Between the standard 3-mile limit and the exigency-created 12-mile limit, there was plenty of wiggle room for a rumrunner with a decent attorney. And in the few years the treaties had been in effect, a substantial body of law already had grown up, precedents that snuffed the effectiveness of the 12-mile idea. New York attorney Louis Halle came heavily armed with such precedents, and with a convincing manner of arguing them.

In Norfolk Halle joined forces with local legal talent Ralph Daughton, and the two began to systematically ventilate the airtight case. They made a motion for dismissal on the grounds that the prosecution hadn't shown that any actual crime had been committed within the jurisdiction of the United States or Virginia's eastern district. As for the fact that *Metmuzel* was running booze within the 12-mile limit, Halle argued that the criteria were different at 12 miles out than they were at 3 miles out. Within the 3-mile limit, the seizure would have been legitimate. But beyond that line, it took more to justify the action. "There is no such thing as the National Prohibition Act outside of the United States," Halle said, "and the *Metmuzel* and these men were outside the territorial waters of the United States." Beyond 3 miles, it wasn't enough just to catch a rummy red-handed, loaded down and bound for shore. It was necessary, contended Halle, that "an overt act or a conspiracy" be proven. Halle and Daughton cited several case rulings that buttressed the hair-splitting. They convinced U.S. Commissioner Harry A. Brinkley, and that was all that mattered: Brinkley dismissed the case.

"There is nothing in the treaty from which it could be reasonably in-ferred that it was the intention of the high contracting parties to extend the criminal laws of the United States beyond the three-mile limit." the court ruled. The *Metmuzel* dozen were free.

They were released despite the sworn statements of the Coast Guard officers who had interrogated Captain Flahaut two days after his arrest. According to the officers' testimony, the rum skipper had admit-ted he was bound for Parramore Bank buoy with the liquor; he was sup-posed to hook up with another rumrunner there for a cargo transfer. If the Parramore Bank rendezvous failed to pan out, the skipper was to take *Metmuzel* 65 miles offshore and wait until "a man named Miller" showed up with a boat to run the stuff in. And there was more proof: charts and logbooks aboard *Metmuzel* indicated that she indeed had been bound for Parramore Bank. Nonetheless, the *Metmuzel* dozen went free, and if any of them knew what their ship's name meant, they must have been amused. *Metmuzel* is derived from the Hebrew word meaning "good luck."

Not everyone was amused. "While the so-called 'twelve-mile' treaty allows these craft to be boarded outside the territorial three-mile limit for investigation and hauled into an American port if there is 'reasonable cause for belief' that it is trying to violate the prohibition laws, actually proving that it was trying to violate the law is another matter," complained a Norfolk editorial. "Mere possession of the liquor would have been competent evidence of intended violation if the boat had been caught inside the three-mile limit. Since it was caught outside this limit, it was necessary to prove conspiracy or to show some overt act of intended law violation, and this, it appears, the Government could not do. It is true that it is next to impossible to imagine a legitimate transportation mission for a comparatively small power boat hauling St. Pierre liquor in these waters, but proof arrived at by eliminating what can't be easily imagined is not always valuable in a court of justice. . . . Just when you seem to have the goods you haven't got the evidence. Just when you seem to understand the reason why, you can't find the motive. Life and the law are that way."

An anonymous tip led to a big seizure at Thomas Wharf, Virginia. It was 3:10 P.M., July 1. The phone was ringing at the Wallops Beach Coast Guard Station. Boatswain Ernest Pointer took the call. It was someone near Willis's Wharf, Virginia, dropping a dime about an illegal boatload supposedly about to be off-loaded somewhere in the neighborhood of Red Bank. Pointer headed out via automobile to investigate, accompanied by Machinist's Mate John W. Birch from Assateague Beach Station and Surfman George J. Merritt from Wallops Beach Station. Meanwhile, picket boats from Wallops, Assateague, and Cobb's Island stations were ordered to converge on Willis's Wharf. Pointer and his men got to Red Bank at twilight and started poking around.

The trail was cold, but they did augment their force with Chief Boatswain's Mate Ira Andrews, on leave from Smith Island Station and eager to join the hunt. Casting their net wider, the group gathered more information. The night dragged on. They parked and hid along the seashore road and waited to make their move. At 5:45 on the morning of

July 2, Pointer called Sixth District headquarters from Exmore, Virginia, reporting that he had "found the liquor stored in an old shuckin' house."

He swore out a warrant to search the residence on the property. The search roused four men, who tried in vain to escape. They ended up in the Eastville Jail. The ringleader's name was John Roache. In the meantime, the Virginia State Police had arrested three men, suspected smugglers, in an automobile. They'd had the lack of sense to tell the police they were down here to see . . . John Roache.

The shucking shack was freshly stacked with 541 sacks of assorted liquors. A Coast Guard patrol boat hauled the hoard to the Collector of Customs at Norfolk. "The men engaged in the seizure of the liquor and capture of the men believed implicated in the actual smuggling are worthy and deserving of praise," stated Sixth District Commander Price, who arrived on the scene shortly after the rumrunners were caught. "Not only was the place where the liquor was stored difficult to locate, but some of the men captured bear noteworthy reputations for being extremely dangerous to handle. On this occasion, they did not surrender without it being necessary for the force to resort to firearms to frustrate their escape."

The coastline crews had grown accustomed to such dangerous operators—flagrant, flippant, audacious, with a willingness to openly challenge authority in a taunting manner that was either arrogant, sporting, or somehow both. In August two such men calling themselves Johnson and Darby (aliases probably) approached a crewman of the Lewes, Delaware, Coast Guard Station and offered him a bribe. They said they were from New Jersey. They also said they'd pay the Coast Guardsman a fat sum for the privilege of landing their liquor along his stretch of shoreline. "They indicated . . . even if he refused to consider their proposition, they would get it in where the coast was not so well guarded," reported Commander Price. "From this, it is evident they will continue their operations in the lower end of the district, as a certain section there cannot be thoroughly covered with the boats now assigned."

The two alleged New Jerseyites trying to put the fix in at Lewes were right; there was plenty of porous coastline, impossible for the authorities to patrol with 100 percent thoroughness. Bribe or no bribe, the liquor could find a way through the sparse policing presence. Once the rum ships made it to the vicinity of the coast, success was akin to the 5-yard line rush, just a matter of muscling through to the end zone. If a sportive metaphor is inappropriate when musing on the violation of federal law, it is at least apt in the sense that this was indeed a game, a cat-and-mouse game. And these were frisky rodents. On one side, the rumrunners enjoyed advantages of speed, deception, trickery, local collusion, and an understaffed adversary. On the other side, the authorities had to rely on the timely receipt of information, on being at the right place at the right time, and on the ability to become wise to the smugglers' tricks and to adapt accordingly.

Sometimes the law won, as on November 18, 1930, when Base Eight Coast Guardsmen captured the 34-ton gas screw *I. H. Tawes*, replete with about seventeen hundred cases of liquor, at the entrance to Chesapeake Bay. More often than not, the lawless won; Coast Guard reports were filed prolifically with accounts ending in some variation on the phrase, "The vessel escaped by superior speed."

The old double-team decoy routine was still popular: while one rummy lured a patrol boat away from the Chesapeake entrance in a futile seaward chase, another rummy would dart up between the Capes. At night, at the mouth of the Bay, with rum ships "running dark" to avoid capture and patrol boats running likewise to avoid detection, the situation lent itself to confusion, dangerously so when gunfire was a factor. Two Coast Guard vessels, *CG-199* and *CG-175*, came close to capturing each other on the night of December 21. *CG-175* fired warning blanks at a suspicious vessel. The vessel scurried. *CG-175*'s machine gun drilled the darkness. Now came another vessel, running dark like the first one. *CG-175* made toward it. It was *CG-199*; her masthead light went on just in time to avoid friendly fire.

CG-199 had been up near Fisherman's Light when Boatswain's Mate Glen F. Stevens spied the distant flashes of gunfire. *CG-199* quickly stood down toward the action in order to head off any other rumrunner attempting to enter the Bay during the gunplay. *CG-199* came close to running dark for a minute too long.

Commandant F. C. Billard stressed in subsequent orders that "it is desired to point out the necessities for thoroughly indoctrinating officers-in-charge of patrol boats . . . to the end that one patrol boat shall not fire on another patrol boat or on an innocent craft. With several patrol boats operating in a restricted area such as Chesapeake Bay Entrance, and running without lights at night, great care must be used in the application of force."

If there was one time a suspected rumrunner could be expected to submit to boarding, it was when she was without incriminating cargo. Why run then? The Coast Guard stopped and searched the gas screw *Violet* at the mouth of the Chesapeake on December 20. " Information is at hand that this boat was built for Florida interests, ostensibly for shrimp fishing," read the boarding report. "However, the type of the boat would lead one to believe that she was intended for rum-running. Her speed is known to be at least 17 miles per hour." That night, *Violet* was clean. But the Coast Guard's distrust proved accurate. Less than a month later, Norfolk Division nabbed *Violet* hauling seven hundred sacks of booze.

For smugglers who made it past the Chesapeake entrance gauntlet, the vast, labyrinthine tableau of excellent drop-off sites beckoned. Crisfield, the teeming junction for Bay-country moonshine, had become a popular disembarkation point for international wet wares as well. The Coast Guard was on the lookout for a "Chesapeake Bay workboat, painted black and named *Blanche*," alleged to be landing liquor at Crisfield "on an average of three times a month." *Blanche*, a 45-foot gas screw, had been built as a schooner in 1857, but in recent years she'd had her mast and sails removed and bowsprit sawed off, and had been converted to engine power. She was bringing in sacks of whiskey from a Canadian supplier, the prevailing brand being Golden Wedding. "From Crisfield the contraband is loaded into fast cars and taken north," stated the Coast Guard confidential report.

Blanche wasn't the only runner hovering off Crisfield. Sixth District Commander Price learned from Crisfield Sheriff Luther Daugherty that "the vessels that have been operating, generally lay at anchor five or six miles distant from Crisfield during the day and then unload at various places along the creeks at night. There are many places that can be used for this purpose, good roads lead to most of them, which are in sparsely settled sections, and even if discovered would not be exposed to officers of the law."

Sheriff Daugherty phoned Commander Price on January 22, 1931, and said he needed ten men to help snare a vessel due to make a drop. "The description of the vessel on this occasion was of the sub-chaser type and painted gray." A force was rounded up among the Coast Guardsmen of the Isle of Wight and Ocean City stations; they piled into automobiles and headed to Crisfield. The bust fizzled; Price strongly suspected the runners had been tipped off. It was a frustration to which law enforcers had grown accustomed.

Nocturnal back-creek drop-offs were the name of the game, but sometimes, in a fit of cockiness, Chesapeake rumrunners would take brazen advantage of public boat-landing facilities. On the Wicomico River, "a long, gray boat landed liquor at the Rock Point Steamboat Wharf on February 18 or 19, at midnight," a Coast Guard officer reported. What he wasn't able to report was the name of the vessel, or that the vessel had been captured. She had parked her contraband right at the steamboat landing and had gotten away with it.

By early 1931 Commander Price was pressuring Coast Guard headquarters for reinforcements: "To properly enforce the blockade against rum-runners, it is requested that three additional boats be furnished for use in this district. That number, it is believed, can cover all inlets in the lower part of the district that are now more or less exposed.

"The thirty-six foot cabin type is desirable, but if that type cannot be furnished, seized boats that have been converted for picket duty, if of no greater draft can be used.

". . . It is realized that Headquarters has difficulty in furnishing all the boats requested for this duty, but it is evident that the rum-runners will remain active in this section as long as some of the inlets are left unguarded. With the number of picket boats now in the district, it is impossible to cover all the inlets on the same night. It is also evident that watchers for them promptly report the location of the boats when on patrol and this gives them the greater advantage."

Undermanned, outrun, and thwarted by local citizenry, the Coast Guard was finding the Chesapeake to be an increasingly vexatious patrol area. Ultimately, perhaps, the only effective law-enforcement method would have to involve violence.

"It is confidently expected," Commandant Billard came to declare, "that the liberal use of gunfire will discourage operations of rum-running vessels."

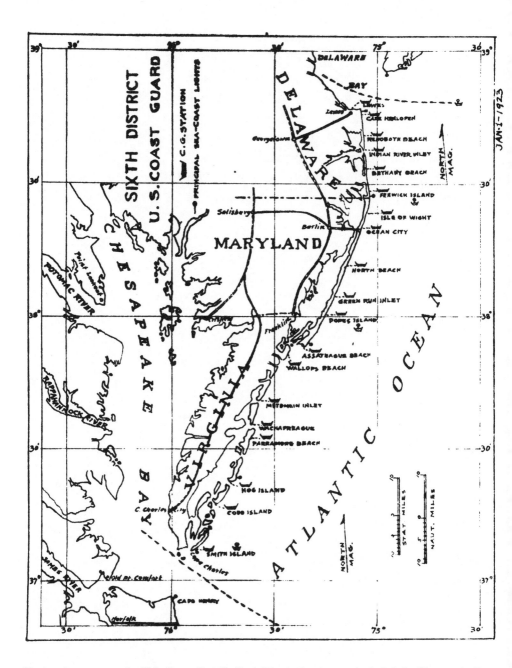

During the rum war, the U.S. Coast Guard's Sixth District battle zone included the Chesapeake Bay and the Delmarva Atlantic coast. Courtesy U.S. Coast Guard.

The fast Hooper Island draketail *Dixie* (shown here at the Chesapeake Workboat Races in 1922) diversified from crabbing into rum-running, making nocturnal deliveries of southern Maryland white lightning to waiting trucks on the Eastern Shore. Courtesy Chesapeake Bay Maritime Museum.

Violet was nabbed for trying to run booze into the Bay. As with many seized rum boats, the Coast Guard appropriated her, turning her into a patrol vessel. Courtesy National Archives.

The Coast Guard had pegged the British rum-running schooner *Tessie Aubrey* as "a very suspicious craft." Courtesy National Archives.

Big Bill McCoy, reputed father of Rum Row, intended to make his first-ever delivery in *Henry L. Marshall* at Chesapeake Bay; the deal fell apart and he headed up the coast.

The rumrunner *Firmore* frequented the Bay. Courtesy Calvert Marine Museum, Solomons, Maryland.

The British steam yacht *Istar* was the "flagship of the rum fleet." Courtesy National Archives.

The Newfoundland-based schooner *Maude Thornhill* was one of the Chesapeake's repeat offenders. Courtesy National Archives.

The American ex-subchaser *Nomad* was caught redhanded with a champagne cargo in the Chesapeake. Courtesy National Archives.

The Nassau-based schooner *Pesaquid* was known to frequent the Chesapeake approaches with product to be off-loaded. Courtesy National Archives.

Three photos of the bourbon-smuggling *Metmuzel,* caught in the waters off the Virginia Eastern Shore and hauled into Norfolk. *Top:* Courtesy National Archives. *Bottom and facing page:* Courtesy The Mariners' Museum, Newport News, Virginia.

Second Mate Maurice Rebmann

Melbourne Mossman

Alphonse Lelorieux

Robi Mossman

Above and facing page: These rumrunners from *Metmuzel* were captured off Chincoteague. Courtesy National Archives.

John Murphy

James Randall Harris

Charles Joseph Maloney

Edouard Fouchard

Master Albert Flahaut

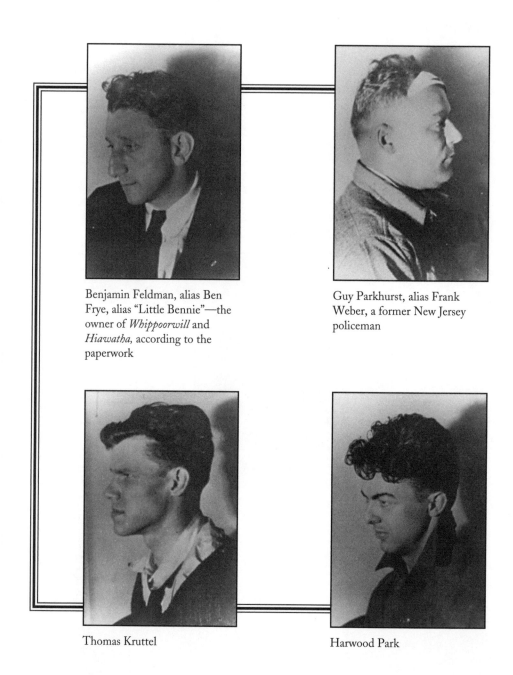

Benjamin Feldman, alias Ben Frye, alias "Little Bennie"—the owner of *Whippoorwill* and *Hiawatha*, according to the paperwork

Guy Parkhurst, alias Frank Weber, a former New Jersey policeman

Thomas Kruttel

Harwood Park

Above and facing page: Many out-of-state lawbreakers were captured at Taylors Island when the authorities finally caught up with *Whippoorwill* and *Hiawatha*, a pair of legendarily swift smuggling speedboats. Courtesy National Archives.

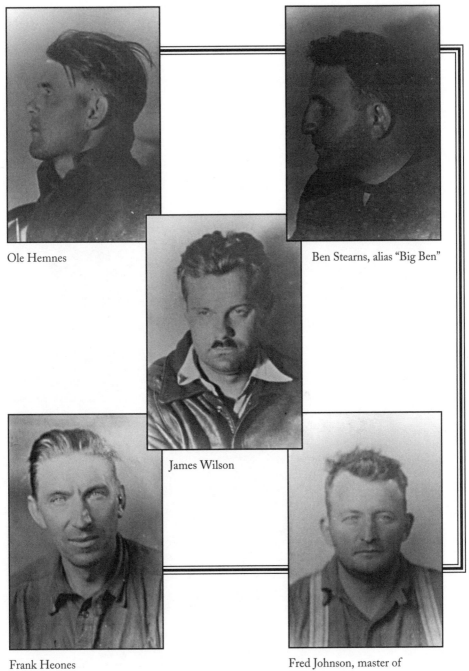

Ole Hemnes

Ben Stearns, alias "Big Ben"

James Wilson

Frank Heones

Fred Johnson, master of *Whippoorwill*

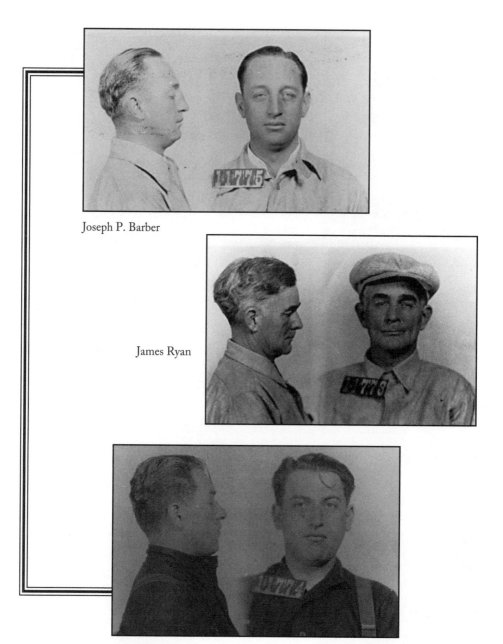

Joseph P. Barber

James Ryan

George Leaming

Crewmen of *Matilda Barry* were arrested after a high-speed chase on the Bay; the captain perished. Courtesy National Archives.

Smoke screens and a zigzag fleeing pattern couldn't keep *Matilda Barry* from being caught. Courtesy National Archives.

Coast Guard gunfire damaged *Matilda Barry*. Courtesy National Archives.

Top and right: Cask, out of Glasgow, delivered bounteous amounts of the Scottish national beverage to the Potomac for the thirsty D.C. market. Courtesy Frederick Tilp Collection, Calvert Marine Museum, Solomons, Maryland.

A Coast Guard boarding crew comes alongside a mid-Atlantic rumrunner. Courtesy National Archives.

A former rumrunner settles into a post-Prohibition existence on the St. Mary's River in 1934. Photograph courtesy of Historic St. Mary's City.

CHAPTER SIX

"THE LURE THAT TAKES US OFF THE BEATEN TRACK"

Captain William T. Bell, a master mariner of the Virginia Eastern Shore, had been going to sea for thirty years. He said he had piloted ships into "almost every port in the world," and it made sense that a man of his seafaring talents would be approached. The approaching was done by an acquaintance named Neal Chandler on February 4, 1931. Chandler asked Captain Bell to pilot a boatload of whiskey to the Broad Creek Club, on the Virginia shore near Machipongo Inlet. The captain said he'd think about it. Chandler hooked him up with Sam Goldberg, alias "Sam the Gas Man," alias "Sam the Ice Man," who waved the cash that convinced the captain. The deal went down in Salisbury: five hundred dollars to run the load, seventy-five dollars up front. Bell pocketed the advance, went to Chincoteague, and went to sea again.

The vessel was *Hammitt L. Robbins,* and Captain Bell and his crew motored out to deep water. Several miles out, with land no longer in sight, the old mariner felt his feet get cold. "I got to thinking what a fool I was, under our Constitution and the laws of the United States," Bell later testified in court, "so I changed my course and pretended I was going to the rum ship, but I was not. It began breezing up and I told the fellows on board it was too rough to go to a rum ship and I put back to port."

Rough sea or no, Bell could have made it to the rum ship, but he misled his mates. "I was scared almost to death," he said, not of the angry ocean, but of the situation he was in and the men he was with. He holed *Hammitt L. Robbins* up in a small bay. By two in the morning the crew was grumbling about putting to sea again. At daylight, Bell got her under way. He didn't head seaward. He headed for the site of their original departure. "One of the fellows grabbed the wheel and asked where I was going," said Bell. "I pushed him back and told him I was going to Chincoteague, but he grabbed the wheel and said I wasn't, that I was going to sea. I told him to go ahead and take the wheel, but he would run on a sand bar and the Coast Guard would be there in a few minutes. Then he let me go. I got off the boat as soon as I could and I told them I was through and would have nothing more to do with it and the plan to bring in the liquor."

Captain Alfred Lewis, another Eastern Shore waterman, took over for Bell. *Hammitt L. Robbins* ran out to the waiting rum ship, loaded up with 434 sacks and 9 kegs, and charted a course for the Broad Creek Club. She ran aground in Machipongo Channel.

Two Hog Island Station Coast Guard crewmen, traveling by mail boat on their return from shore leave, spied the stranded *Hammitt L. Robbins* on the afternoon of February 6. She was a known rumrunner, and they reported the sighting when they arrived at their post. Their commander called headquarters at Lewes and got permission to tap the Parramore Beach and Cobb's Island stations for backup. Picket boats converged on the stranded motorboat at about 5:15 P.M. The crew was gone. Hubbard Frank Nelson, a state Prohibition agent based in Eastville, Virginia, was discovered on board. The deck was covered with oyster shells. Half the forward hatch was off. In the hold was abundant booze. It looked like some had been unloaded. While Coast Guardsmen kept watch on the boat, others searched the shore, paying special attention to known liquor-landing locations. They turned up nothing. They floated the rum boat, towed her, and anchored her in Peters Channel.

From there she was towed by Section Base Eight's *CG-221* to Norfolk for adjudication, and the federal marshal commandeered the contraband.

The *Hammitt L. Robbins* case exposed an elaborate Eastern Shore smuggling ring. Ultimately, thirty-two men were brought up on conspiracy charges, including Prohibition agent Nelson and his son-in-law, U.S. Coast Guard Boatswain Chester D. Robbins. The boatswain had been on the stranded craft with his father-in-law before the Coast Guard arrived in force, and the government accused the two of being in cahoots with Sam Goldberg. John Sutter, Jr., engineer of *Hammitt L. Robbins,* had been left aboard the stuck rummy to keep watch on the goods while the rest of the crew evacuated and made emergency offloading arrangements. Sutter testified that the Prohibition agent and the Coast Guard boatswain came aboard while he was on his lonely sentinel. They let him grab a couple cases of whiskey, and the Coast Guardsman told him to "get goin' while the goin' is good."

The two defendants ardently denied the scenario when they took the stand. The jury failed to reach a decision on their verdict. Captain Alfred Lewis, the waterman who manned the helm of *Hammitt L. Robbins,* fared less fortuitously; he was convicted. Twenty-four others pleaded guilty in the case. Another four simply didn't show up for trial. And as for Captain Bell, the master mariner who had second thoughts about rum-running, the jury let the old man go.

A rumrunner's greatest attribute, naturally, was speed, and one vessel would live on in watermen's lore through the rest of the century. The vessel whose name became synonymous with rum-running on Chesapeake Bay was *Whippoorwill*—72 tons, 53 feet 6 inches long, 11 feet 5 inches wide, New York–owned, juiced by three 450-horsepower Liberty motors—and she had the reputation of being the fastest thing afloat on the Bay.

Agents lay in waiting at the Taylors Island bridge. Two months earlier, a ship-and-truck gang had dodged capture near Cambridge. The officers had come upon forty-five men, some heavily armed, waiting with trucks; the boat or boats got wise somehow and pulled a no-show. This time the law hit the big score: fourteen prisoners, two speedboats, a truck fleet, and six thousand cases of champagne, Benedictine, and whiskey. The *Crisfield Times* dubbed it "the most spectacular seizure the Eastern Shore has witnessed since the enactment of the federal prohibition law."

It was May 12, 1931. Federal and county officers headed by Irving W. Windsor, the Salisbury Prohibition unit chief, jumped out and ambushed the rum caravan. The smugglers were armed with sawed-off shotguns and automatic pistols, but the lawmen had them surrounded. The Taylors Island stakeout had nailed none other than *Whippoorwill* herself, along with her equally fast running mate, *Hiawatha*—56 feet 4 inches long, 14 feet wide, equipped with a triumvirate of powerful 12-cylinder engines.

Whippoorwill had developed a Chesapeake reputation. She had been sighted repeatedly on various Bay tributaries, particularly the Nanticoke. The Taylors Island raid was intended as the first strike in the smashup of a Chesapeake rum-running ring that boasted not only fast boats, but a well-scattered selection of landing sites as well, not to mention a secret wireless station. Taylors Island, according to Prohibition unit chief Windsor, had been a major depot for Canadian and Bahamian liquor imports for more than a year.

Most of the prisoners were New Yorkers; two of them, John Erickson of *Hiawatha* and Frank Heones of *Whippoorwill*, initially scooted but were rounded up the next day in Wingate. *Whippoorwill*'s skipper, Fred Johnson, alias J. F. Tonnenson, had been master and owner of another known rumrunner, *Gloria*. Three other prisoners gave aliases at first, but the masquerade faded fast: Timothy Connolly, alias Tim McCloskey, and Guy Parkhurst, alias Frank Weber, were former New Jersey state policemen who'd gone over to the dark side. And Benjamin Feldman, alias Ben Frye, alias "Little Bennie," would turn out to be central to the *Whippoorwill-Hiawatha* enterprise.

Among others included in the sting were Axel Ohlsen, captain of *Hiawatha;* Harwood Park, the smugglers' radio man; James Wilson, the automobile jockey leading the booze-truck convoy; and Ben Stearns, alias "Big Ben," Little Bennie's right-hand man.

They spent a couple of nights in the Cambridge jail. The U.S. marshal corralled them onto a bus and hauled them to the Baltimore City lockup. They were arraigned before U.S. Commissioner J. Frank Supplee on conspiracy-to-smuggle charges. By July a federal grand jury would indict the fourteen, and three more members of the ring subsequently captured, for possession and transportation as well as conspiracy and smuggling. In the meantime, Commissioner Supplee set their bail at $126,000 total. A captured truck and the two prize rum speedboats were used to transport the six thousand cases of contraband to Baltimore for storage at Customs House.

One of the rumrunners had a big mouth; he came close to implicating himself and his crewmates in a mysterious death. Ulman Owens, lighthouse keeper at the remote Holland Bar near Crisfield, had been found dead on March 15. The coroner ruled it an accidental death, but the Owens family suspected foul play.

Months later, during the Taylors Island arrest, Guy Parkhurst, the ex-cop, was heard to say as he pointed at some revenue men who'd helped set the trap, "There go the rats that turned us in. Well, that lighthouse keeper got in the headlines. We did that. What these guys will get will be worse." Someone told Parkhurst to shut up. Parkhurst said, "If you guys will forget that crack of mine we will be good friends." The accidental-death ruling stuck, but Ulman Owens's family never bought it.

Customs agents info-sharing with Coast Guard Intelligence learned that the crews of *Whippoorwill* and *Hiawatha* were part of a syndicate that had vessels active all up and down Rum Row. Customs had a good snitch—his tumbling had led to the Taylors Island sting in the first place—and he kicked forth with more boat names: *Pronto* and *Mary Yvonne*, working the Cape Cod stretch; *Semeramis*, running down south; and *Rex II*, *Betty and Ida*, *Malbo*, and *Rosalie*, hovering between 20 and 60 miles offshore along the Jersey-to-Virginia coast. The syndicate also was about to put *Gloria* into action again, along with a black two-master called *Ocean Maid*. According to the snitch, the word in

Massachusetts was that the vessels ostensibly were owned by Yarmouth ship's chandler Benny Cann, but that they really were owned by a New York syndicate led by Sam Lee, alias "Sam the Chink."

Whippoorwill and *Hiawatha* were auctioned off at the Arundel Cove Coast Guard depot on July 22. Both went for a song. *Hiawatha,* her value estimated by the feds to be $25,000, went for $2,675. *Whippoorwill,* worth $15,000, went for $2,250. Several of the boats' crewmembers, expensively out on bail, attended the auction. The U.S. District Court declared the sales null and void on the suspicion that the rum syndicate was using the auction process to regain ownership of their confiscated vessels for peanuts. "In many districts the filing of liens has developed into a racket," wrote Commander Frank J. Gorman, Coast Guard intelligence officer, "in order to permit the owners to frustrate the taking over of the boats by the Coast Guard or Customs and to permit them to buy back the boats at a fraction of their worth. . . . I . . . am satisfied, judging from the course of events subsequent to the filing of the liens, that the lienors worked hand in hand with the rum-runners. The vessels were sold for much less than the amount of the liens and were bought back by the rum-running syndicate which owned them, or at least by a rum-running syndicate associated with the former owners." *Hiawatha* and *Whippoorwill* were through as rumrunners; the front men who bought them at auction were reimbursed for their final bids.

The *Whippoorwill-Hiawatha* case was tried in December 1931. Twelve of the seventeen defendants were present for the Baltimore proceedings; all twelve were convicted and found guilty on all counts. Of the five who failed to appear, one was nabbed by a customs agent in New York, another surrendered himself, and the remaining three forfeited an aggregate twenty-six thousand dollars in bail money, a small price for tenuous freedom. For those who showed up and faced the music, sentences, concurrent on all counts, ranged from six months to two years.

And the legendary *Whippoorwill* and *Hiawatha*—capable, it was said, of speeds up to 55 miles per hour—were still afloat. "The boats," reported the *Washington Post,* ". . . will be converted into chasers, as they are declared to be faster than any ship now operating on the Chesapeake Bay." Who had owned them? Regional rumor evolving into regional folklore would associate *Whippoorwill* with a powerful American political figure. Then there were the Benny Cann–Sam Lee factors. But the official government paperwork listed both *Whippoorwill* and *Hiawatha* as being the property of "Bango Shipping & Chartering Corporation, Benjamin J. Feldman, President, Room 712, 305 Broadway, N.Y." Nominally, at least, it was Little Bennie, sentenced to a federal prison stint, who had been the man behind the Chesapeake's fast and notorious lawbreaking boat. She and her rum-running partner would now become law-enforcing boats. The converted *Whippoorwill* joined the Coast Guard ranks as *CG-987*; *Hiawatha* became *CG-834*.

A timely tip from an informant was worth months, years, of work. The American auxiliary yacht *Nomad,* an ex-subchaser out of New York City, had been under Coast Guard suspicion since October 1927. She was boarded in the Chesapeake; her crew had an incriminatingly huge amount of cash, but there was no booze so there was no case. Then Henry De Groot, a steward on *Nomad,* showed up at Section Base Eight headquarters in May 1931 and snitched: *Nomad* was back in the Bay and loaded with good-label liquor. *CG-138* made for Hampton Roads, intercepting *Nomad* a quarter-mile off Sewell's Point. It was a good bust: nine prisoners and a diverse inventory that included Superieur champagne, Lanson champagne, and other brands of bubbly; Cointreau liqueur; Chartreuse wine; Pilsener beer; Bacardi rum; Martini and Rossi and various other vermouths; Hennessey cognac; Johnnie Walker Scotch; Gilbey's gin, and Spanish sherry, hundreds of bottles tightly hidden in the bilges.

Informants were a godsend, providing targeted initiative when every boat entering the Bay was a potential smuggler, foreign or native, yacht or workboat. Virginia trawl fishermen lately were coming under the gun for their practice of smuggling liquor beneath fish and ice. In any conveyance imaginable, the alcohol continued to flow into the Bay country by sea, by land, and now even by air.

Residents of the Eastern Shore hamlet of Trappe reported repeated sightings of a mysterious airplane in early 1931. "The machine flies over the town but a very few feet above the tree tops," the *Star-Democrat* reported. "One man said the wind from the propeller almost blew his hat off, so close was the machine to him." The plane was alighting in fields on the outskirts of town. "One day it will land in one place and the next trip it will seek a landing quite some distance from the other place. It is never known just where it will land, and the residents are kept guessing." Whether it was flying imports in or flying moonshine out, or both, was unknown. But this much could be noted: wild public drunkenness seemed to follow in the wake of the plane landings. "The people are of the opinion that the plane is used to transport liquor. They are satisfied as to this, but just where the contraband is they are unable to tell. The results are very evident on the streets, especially on Saturday nights."

Another mysterious plane was active in southern Maryland, recalled Bruce Scheible of St. Mary's County. The plane was said to make hops to Washington, D.C., and seemed to have an affiliation with the swift rumrunner *Wild Rose*. Throughout the watershed, airborne smuggling was a growing problem. Complaints were already found in Coast Guard correspondence in the lower Chesapeake, where the guardsmen had plenty enough to keep them busy without adding airplane-borne criminals to the mix.

It was 4:40 P.M., July 5, 1931. The phone rang at the Ocean City Coast Guard Station. Boatswain Thomas T. Moore grabbed it. It was Harry Lieberman, special collector, Department of Justice, calling from Salisbury. His request: five men in a hurry. A drop was about to happen at Quantico Creek. The justice and Coast Guard men, with a deputy sheriff and a local snitch, headed out from Salisbury, went about 18 miles, hid their automobiles, and crept down to the landing. There she was: 2 miles distant, anchored downstream, the rumrunner. The lawmen watched and waited. She got underway and came up the Quantico. She breezed right past them as they hid, eager to pounce. The runner was *Norma*, out of Crisfield. She went around the creek bend. The lawmen piled into rowboats and dogged her. They caught up to her, tied up and ready to disgorge, after a mile and a half. They boarded her, examined her, seized her, and arrested the three men aboard: Suthard Woodfield, the skipper; Edward Diggs, the black crewman; and Jack Koler, an agent for the larger rum ship that had just transferred cargo to *Norma*.

The lawmen loosed *Norma*'s lines and brought her back downstream. Some stayed aboard; others went to Salisbury to phone for backup. Men and trucks arrived from the Fenwick Island and Isle of Wight Coast Guard stations and convoyed to the landing. Customs took charge of the prisoners. *Norma* was brought out to the Nanticoke River, where the Coast Guard cutter *Winnisimet* met her and towed her to Pier 2, Pratt Street, Baltimore. *Norma* had been nailed with a prolific cargo: 531 bottles of Campbell's White Heather Scotch, 1,488 bottles of Early Times rye whiskey, 470 bottles of Seagram's Very Old rye whiskey, 2,139 bottles of Guggenheim rye, 913 bottles of Jessie Moore rye, 120 bottles of Perfection Scotch, 300 bottles of Landon champagne, 294 bottles of Mumm's champagne (quarts), 22 bottles of Mumm's champagne (pints), 190 bottles of Cinzano vermouth, 8 bottles of Pikesville rye, 78 kegs of Highland and Islay Malt Scotch, 13 kegs of Sheriff's Scotch, and 9 kegs of unlabeled Scotch. Estimated total value was $67,259.

The tip-off advantage could go either way. Timely information from a man on the inside could spare a rumrunner big trouble. Less than a week after the successful capture of *Norma*, federal agents learned that a liquor load was about to land at Oak Orchard, a popular resort on Indian River in Sussex County, Delaware. The agents went to the Oak Orchard riverside and watched and waited. As expected, the speedboat came in from the Atlantic Ocean through Indian River Inlet, right on time. But the runners turned her about, made distance, and instead unloaded at Sandy Landing, three miles away on the opposite riverbank. After her business was done, the speedboat put to sea, breezing jauntily past the empty-handed federal men, who were unable to give chase because they were boatless and hadn't brought the Coast Guard in on the action. The sting had gone sour because someone had told the rummy.

Someone had tipped off the feds, and then someone had tipped off the rumrunners that the feds had been tipped off. Betwixt the back-and-forth salvo of dueling tips, that which made customers tipsy had snaked through the gauntlet.

More foreign liquor was headed for the Patuxent River, Norfolk Division learned. Two boatloads of offshore contraband were bound from the Patuxent drop-off for Washington, D.C., "where it will be stored in the cellar of a large house on Sixteenth Street," according to a Coast Guard communiqué. "It is understood that operations will be carried out under the direction of a man named White, formerly identified with the rum-running business in the vicinity of Havre de Grace." Closer to the oceangoing ship sources, the stretch of Murderkill River west of Lewes, Delaware, also had become a hot spot for clandestine cargo dispersal. A Coast Guard boatswain's mate combed the waterfront and gleaned that a whole lot of liquor was being landed from Bowers Beach to Frederica. "Jack Higgins, who lives in a house at Jones River, Del., is employed by the Jersey Rum Gang to land some of the liquor," stated the Sixth District report. ". . . He takes his load off steamers and barges. . . . Another man named Gean [sic] E. Morris runs liquor in a white party boat. The liquor is landed at Jones River, then the next time at Webb Landing, then at Old Stone. The runners are careful not to land in the same place twice in succession."

The Sixth District flotilla was stretched thin. "We have only seven picket boats to guard fifteen hundred inlets and some are in need of overhaul," wrote C. J. Sullivan, the new Sixth District chief, to Coast Guard headquarters in late 1931. One of the district's picket boats and personnel had been ordered transferred, and Sullivan futilely entreated the top brass to rethink the move. "It is thought that perhaps Headquarters is not fully cognizant with the conditions as they exist," Sullivan argued, ". . . we are urgently in need of more equipment, especially picket boats, and cannot spare a boat or piece of equipment and efficiently carry on." Each vessel had too large an area to police efficiently. *CG-2389,* based at Hog Island Station, was responsible for patrolling a 40-mile expanse of intricate coastline: Little Machipongo Inlet, Great

Machipongo Inlet, Sandy Island Channel, the Swash Channel, North Channel, Great Machipongo River, Hog Island Bay, the entrance to Willis Wharf, Thomas Wharf, and Red Bank Creek. Cobb's Island Station's *CG-2390* had a 50-mile beat: Ship Shoal Inlet and channel, Myrtle Inlet, New Inlet, Smith Island Inlet, Oyster, Virginia, the entrance to Magotha, Virginia, and all the inside routes from Hog Island to Smith Island. "The places mentioned are important," said Sullivan, "and several boats carrying liquor have been seized there. Liquor is still getting in." The roster of rumrunners currently exploiting the Delmarva coastal beaches included *Heiline Elizabeth, Doris,* and *John Leonard,* out of Philadelphia; *Irene,* out of Holly Beach, New Jersey; *Eleanor May,* out of Nantucket; and *Aline,* out of Norfolk. "The notorious Billie Bell of Nassawadox, Virginia, is one of the crew of the *Aline,*" noted Sullivan. Riding herd on the rumrunners, difficult enough already due to diminishing staff and an expansive patrol zone, was made all the more difficult by the sheer volume of water traffic. "Approximately fifteen hundred boats of various types use these inlets daily," said Sullivan, pointing out "the urgent need of all our boats . . . to enable this district to make a more favorable showing than in the past."

The phone rang for James S. Baker, officer in charge of the Indian River Inlet Coast Guard Station, at 4 P.M. on November 28, 1931. Mr. Anonymous on the other end asked Baker to meet him at the inlet. The officer made the rendezvous and found four men waiting in a Chrysler sedan with New York plates. The only one of the four Baker recognized was Hilary Cathell, alias "Smokey Joe," a rumrunner from Long Island. "They informed me that they had a boat load of liquor laying off shore, which they wished to land at Cotton Patch Hill," Baker reported. ". . . After I refused to have anything to do with them, they left in their car driving toward Bethany Beach, Delaware." Indeed, an informer soon was warning Sixth District headquarters that a drop was about to be made at Cotton Patch or between Indian River and Bethany Beach. If the runners couldn't punch it through either of those places, they would try to get it in via Salisbury, and hopefully in time for Christmas. Five days before Christmas, someone tried yet again to put in the fix with Baker. The fixer was known by a number of different names—Sumner, Summers, and others—all considered fictitious. He offered Baker five hundred dollars a night if the officer would temporarily go blind while a shipload of rum was brought to shore, portaged across the beach, and floated up the inlet on scows. Instead of giving the briber a flat-out no, this time Baker tried to extract more information, but as soon as he started questioning, the fixer hopped into a car with Morris Lippman, "a chicken buyer who lives in Ocean View," and headed off. Two days later, another Coast Guardsman reported that the same Sumner or Summers had approached him with the offer: hear no evil, see no evil, let the rum land at Cotton Patch and have some easy money. Baker theorized "that this Summers is an agent of a man known in New York and Jersey as Hagen, as I have seen Hagen, who also is known as Taylor, in this vicinity in the last few days, and it is my belief that an attempt will be made to land rum somewhere on the coast as soon as the moon darkens."

Delmarva was crawling with shifty individuals. Thomas T. Moore, the guardsman recently instrumental in the *Norma* capture, reported from Ocean City Station that "there were five strange men hanging around Berlin, Maryland. . . . the men had rooms at the Atlantic Hotel . . . they had been looking around in this vicinity for several days claiming to be looking for a site for a gunning club. They have been communicating by telephone several times each day from a certain business place in Berlin . . . to New York and other cities. . . . They are using three automobiles. Two of the automobiles have Delaware tags while the other has New York tags. They have been seen at Bethany Beach several times. . . . a wireless set had been discovered in their room. These men are suspicious of being connected with a rum smuggling gang which may be preparing to work or is already working in this locality." Some cadre or another, through bribes or artful dodging, did manage to push a cargo through along the coast where Sumner had been trying to put Coast Guard personnel on the take for several weeks that winter. But the distribution plans were aborted on January 26, 1932, when a Coast Guard officer discovered the stash: 219 sacks of assorted liquor stacked in a Bethany Beach chicken house. The contraband was intercepted, but the runners got away.

Boatswain's Mate First Class Leonard D. Melvin, Master Machinist's Mate Second Class Harvey Beebe, and Surfman Lee Mason were aboard *CG-2308,* anchored in Chincoteague Channel, on the night of February 9, 1932. Beebe was on watch. It was 9:20 P.M. when he spied them, two boats, coming from the south, running without lights. Beebe hit the searchlight, showed the Coast Guard flag, then aimed the beam at the oncoming craft. The Coast Guard horn blared. One boat complied and came alongside. The other boat ran for the shoal. *CG-2308* couldn't pursue in that shallow direction, so she got underway and hastened up the channel to where she could head the runner off at the pass. At 10:30 P.M. the Coast Guard caught its quarry: *5303-S,* out of Chincoteague. Packaging debris spelled overboard cargo. Boatswain's Mate Melvin notified the feds and the Chincoteague police. The Coast Guardsmen hung along the channel shore and waited for the tide to go out. At 6:40 in the morning they found what they were looking for out on the flats: sixteen intact sacks, a couple of broken sacks, and numerous scattered bottles, an assortment of whiskey, wine, and gin. Henry Leonard, the Chincoteague skipper of *5303-S,* was under arrest.

Chincoteague, ever the smugglers' lair, was getting even more out of hand. A three-man squad of treasury agents was assigned to an undercover investigation at Chincoteague in early 1932, while the region's many inlets swarmed with rumrunners from diverse ports of call. Up the coast, along the Maryland-Delaware beach stretch, cash-brandishing syndicate boys continued their brazen attempts to get Coast Guard personnel on the take. Garwood J. Thomas, instrumental in the big Ocean City beach raid of December 31, 1929, was now working out of Indian River Inlet Station, acting as officer in charge when he got a phone call at 11 P.M. on April 28, 1932. It was John R. Massey, a Lewes man, calling from Dover. He had something to discuss with the Coast Guardsman. Thomas agreed to meet him. "He asked me if I wanted to make a little money and if I was open to a business proposition," Thomas reported. "When I asked him the nature of the business he replied, to land

As Prohibition limped through its final year, the rum vessels kept on coming up the Bay. Throughout 1933, Coast Guard Commander William J. Wheeler, Norfolk Division's final dry era chief, issued missives about the proliferation of the rum traffic and the increasing difficulty of the shrinking Coast Guard's ability to thwart it. "There is a great deal of activity on the Eastern Shore of Virginia, Maryland, and in the vicinity of Chesapeake Bay entrance. Coast Guard Base Eight . . . is very poorly equipped with boats," Wheeler wrote at the beginning of the year. Toward the end of the year he was sounding familiar: "The width of Chesapeake Bay entrance makes it almost impossible for less than three or four boats to actually close the entrance against a rum runner of speed greatly exceeding that of the swiftest picket boat attached to Base Eight." The sense of futility manifested itself in a number of chase-and-shoots similar to that of the *Matilda Barry* capture. "On Sunday, 24 Sept., a 75-footer and a picket boat were sent to try to cover Chesapeake Bay entrance, a task that is manifestly beyond the capacity of two such boats, each of limited speed for her class. At about 8:00 P.M., they sighted an incoming rum boat at a distance and fired 10 rounds of 1-pounder and 60 rounds of machine gun ammunition in an endeavor to stop her but the rum runner escaped," reported Wheeler. "On 25 Sept., *CG-2321* sighted another speed boat coming in and fired at her without being able to stop her."

The chasers and the chased were enmeshed in a ghost dance. It was Prohibition's twilight. U.S. Coast Guard Sixth District headquarters had been moved from Lewes to Chincoteague that summer. Base stations were closing, consolidating. It was all part of a general scaling-down of the Coast Guard, a reduction of funding. It was all over soon.

On February 20, 1933, Congress adopted a resolution to repeal Prohibition. Repeal, in the form of the proposed Twenty-first Amendment to the Constitution, went to the states for ratification. Two-thirds, or thirty-six states, were required to ratify, and the magic number was hit in less than a year.

On December 5, 1933, the dry era was dead. Throughout the land, at watering holes once again legal, patrons stood twelve deep outside the door waiting to buy their first federally permitted libation in twelve years, ten months, and nineteen days. As Virginia braced itself for assumption of state liquor control, Attorney General John R. Saunders expected no great flood from neighboring states. "There is so much liquor in Virginia already that outsiders hardly can hope to transport liquor into the state with any great profit," he pointed out. He did acknowledge the likelihood that some "Baltimore liquor" would make its way down, but expressed doubts that "it would be able to compete for long with the Virginia product."

In Baltimore, the fifty-third annual meeting and dinner of the city's Bar Association opened with a toast. Judge Calvin Chesnut of the U.S. District Court and U.S. Attorney Simon E. Sobeloff were among the dignitaries present. They stood, raised their martinis, and drank to liberty. Throughout Baltimore City, the night's festivities began slowly, unlike the spontaneous exuberance that had marked the legalization of beer. But as the reality sank in, the streets grew more crowded, the bars filled up, and liquor supplies ran out. By 11 P.M. the nightclubs were filled to capacity. A customer chided a speakeasy proprietor for still referring to it as a speakeasy. "Well, I guess that's right," the proprietor responded. "I reckon the old speak's a 'taproom' now." A *Baltimore Sun* reporter noted that bar demographics had changed since the long-ago days of the pre-Prohibition saloon: "There was a large sprinkling of women in the barroom crowds, not only sitting at tables but propped against the bars, elbow to elbow with the men." The revelry was centered in the downtown section. There were traffic jams on every corner. Nightclubs had been turning people away for hours. The bars of the Belvedere, Southern, Emerson, and Rennert hotels were packed. At the Rennert, the first glass was handed to H. L. Mencken. Crammed in on all sides at the bar, the cynical sage of the age lifted his glass and quaffed amid shouts and cheers. Earlier in the day, he had pontificated joyfully on the repeal of the Eighteenth Amendment: "It is not often that anything to the public good issues out of American politicians; this time they have been forced to be decent for once in their lives. The repeal of the Eighteenth Amendment

means vastly more than the return of the immemorial beverages of civilized man.

"It means, above all, a restoration of one of the common liberties of
the people. It was as absurd and oppressive for fanatics and politicians to
tell them what they could drink and not drink as it would have been for
the same mephitic shapes to tell them what to eat or wear. I am in hopes
that we'll now be free for a space from such preposterous legislation, but
I am not too sure.

"The Messianic delusion still rages. It is, indeed, the characteristic
American disease. We must be prepared for the next onslaught, and
meet it with an unyielding resistance. Nor must we forget our late op-
pressors."

Thus did the Noble Experiment sputter, fizzle, and die. It was easy
to forget amid the repeal revelry that the experiment had been born of a
movement with worthy intentions, a movement that had arisen in reaction to the wild excesses and day-to-day tragedies of an alcoholic America. Read an editorial in the *Easton Star-Democrat:*

Prohibition is gone. Legalized liquor and the licensed saloon are back.
Now is the time for the temperance advocates and societies to pick up
again and carry on the good work they were doing when the bone-dry fanatics interrupted them in their progress towards making this a temperate
nation. . . . Temperance was making giant strides in this country when its
march was halted by the foolish move of a few dumb zealots, who believed
the day of complete teetotalism could be hastened by Prohibition. The
movement was gaining ground every year. More and more and bigger and
bigger dry spots were appearing on our map with every turn around the
sun. The army of voluntary drys was being augmented with new recruits
every month, every week, every day. The battle against the demon rum was
progressing with telling effect. We were rapidly approaching the top of the
hard hill. Then came the blow of Prohibition, and all that the temperance
promoters had built up was torn down; the battle stopped; the march up
the hill was not only halted, but forced back to the bottom of the grade.
And now the forces must be reassembled; the parade must be formed

again; a new start must be made, and the climb up the hill undertaken once more. The time has arrived to begin the new climb; and our best wishes go with those courageous souls who will take the lead.

With Prohibition's demise, many began predicting that the criminal infrastructure it had created would continue apace nonetheless. "The men who keep watch over the Chesapeake Bay have always had a hard and thankless task with some 4,612 miles of shore line, made up of the Bay itself and the countless navigable indentations which afford perfect shelter for swift smuggling craft," noted the *Baltimore Sun* in an end-to-Prohibition think piece. "Once inside the bottle neck at the Virginia Capes . . . the smuggler had things pretty much his own way, with only bad luck to prevent him from making a landing." With the profit taken out of rumrunning, the *Sun* predicted, the smuggling system would maintain itself by changing to some other outlaw cargo.

"The trade has grown to such large proportions that it could be switched profitably to any of a number of other commodities. . . . There are narcotics, always in demand, and evidence gathered by officials indicates that the organized gangsters already have invaded this field."

"Little enough has been said in praise of rum runners," opined Big Bill McCoy, "and perhaps they deserve no more approval than they have received, yet they were not the completely depraved folk the moralists said they were. If they had been, they would have quit handling bulky cases of liquor and turned to narcotics.

"Some of them did, a good many, perhaps, but the bulk of the rum fleet left that dirty game alone. . . . The rats that went into that racket made, and are still making, fortunes and taking not one tenth the risk we liquor carriers ran.

"The activity of the drys has been almost humorously lopsided. Hundreds of millions of dollars have been spent to parch an increasingly wet nation. Only the smallest fraction of that amount has been used to fight a far more deadly menace.

". . . It is easy to see why the narcotic trade is increasing . . . Rum is bulky stuff. You must have a big ship. You must have a loading organization and an unloading organization. You must have clearance papers from the port you leave. You cannot sail without them.

"Drugs are compact. Cocaine or heroin or morphine to the value of a schooner load of Scotch can be carried in a suitcase or so. Where tons of liquor can be loaded and discharged, drugs can be put ashore with not one tenth the difficulty. The liquor runner is not the worst and most unscrupulous of his breed, by a long jump."

Illegal stills continued to produce moonshine even though good bonded liquor was available on store shelves once more. Moonshining continued for various reasons: the untaxed quality of the enterprise, the inimitable mule-kick purity of the drink itself, the backroad bonds of community and kinship, and the spirit of defying the government. In 1953 the Maryland legislature created a special tax unit, operating under the Alcoholic Beverages Division of the Comptroller's Office, to crack down on the flourishing moonshine industry. The unit had five agents. One covered Garrett, Allegany, Washington, Frederick, and Montgomery counties. Another had his hands full in St. Mary's, Charles, Calvert, and southern Prince George's counties. Another worked Cecil, Harford, Baltimore County, Baltimore City, Howard, Anne Arundel, and northern Prince George's. The other two, headquartered in Salisbury, covered the Eastern Shore. Working with twenty federal agents assigned to Maryland and with state and local police, they busted 326 Maryland stills in 1954 and admitted they had just barely scratched the surface. Lost tax revenues on the product of those 326 stills alone were estimated to be nearly ninety-three thousand dollars. In 1955 it was estimated that the manufacture and sale of moonshine whiskey in Maryland was a $5 million annual business. In West Virginia and Virginia, it continued to flourish as well, and the stills kept cooking well past the 1920s, past the 1950s and into the ensuing decades, evolving from the days of carloads and workboat-loads smuggled along remote coastlines to an age of semi-truckloads carried on interstate highways—an ongoing big business that had cut its teeth in the heady days of Prohibition.

The men who profited from rumrunning on the Chesapeake went their separate ways. Some parlayed their ill-gotten gains into long-term prosperity. Brothers who peddled Canadian whiskey along the Wicomico River became a dominant force in the lower Eastern Shore business community and a major influence in the development of the region. One of the wealthiest men in southern Maryland would admit years later that he had made his money running moonshine in a barge to Baltimore. Some looked back fondly on the dangerous years. "The mystery of tomorrow is gone, the lure that takes us off the beaten track," reminisced Scottish rumrunner Alastair Moray. ". . . Even if I haven't made my fortune, it has been well worth while. . . . Naked nature though it was, it was good. So, when I am again sailing a wee motor-boat on the Clyde, or a lug-sail in the West Highlands of Scotland, I'll think of the days when I had something to do with the adventure of 'what tomorrow will bring.'"

Alonza Elliott, the Dorchester County rumrunner, eventually got caught. He cut a deal with the prosecutor and gave evidence against the bootleggers with whom he had trafficked. When they got out of jail, Alonza Elliott grew fearful for his safety. "They were gonna whip him, and I don't blame 'em much," recalled Alonza's son Milford Elliott, who became renowned as a Bay boatbuilder. The bootleggers never did hurt Milford's father, partly because Milford acted as his father's bodyguard. "They didn't bother him when I was around," Milford said. "I was younger, like 25, 26, 27 years old, bigger than I am now and a street brawler. I could take care of him and me both, and they didn't bother him when I was around."

After Alonza Elliott died, *Dixie*—his rum-running draketail workboat—went to Milford's brother Rufus, who as a boy had helped his father haul southern Maryland moonshine across the Chesapeake. It was the ultimate fate of *Dixie* to perish, perhaps fittingly, in a rush of nocturnal criminality. "She was about as out of date as the Model T would be now by time all that was over, you know," said Milford. Patrol boats on the Chesapeake were getting faster by the 1940s, but Rufus Elliott continued to use *Dixie* for the occasional illegal oystering activity. In the early 1950s, returning from a midnight handscrape run, "the law got after him with a few oysters in her," said Milford. "You know, it didn't take many for a little boat like that to weight her down too much . . . so they were chasing him, they were gaining on him, so he was taking a short cut across the bar, Stony Bar. Run her on it with them few oysters in her and she laid there, and he left her . . . he got home and he run up and got in the bed with his boots and clothes on—that's what they told me, he said it weren't so—but they went in and got him with his wet stuff on. They didn't do anything to him. They couldn't prove nothin'."

As for *Dixie*—twenty-five dollars to run a load of moonshine, four 55-gallon barrels a run—she died aground with too many oysters in her, right where Rufus ditched her. "She laid there, and he left her, and she broke in two. She broke, and that was the end of that boat . . . that was the end of that boat."

Others outgrew their delinquency. *Anna D.*, a 93-foot British schooner active in the Chesapeake rum-running trade at the end of the era, had been built in Meteghan, Nova Scotia, and was named after Anna Deveau, daughter of the owners of the Meteghan Shipbuilding Company. The schooner's registered top speed was 9 knots, but Coast Guardsmen who had tailed her knew that to be a deceptively conservative figure. A rum syndicate acquired *Anna D.* in 1932, giving the Meteghan Shipbuilding Company a vessel valued at five thousand dollars plus an additional thirty thousand dollars cash. According to the U.S. Intelligence Office, it was the same syndicate that owned *Aristocrat*, *Tatamagouche* (another Chesapeake supplier), and *Bear Cat*. The syndicate operated under the orders of B. B. Cann of Yarmouth, no doubt the same Benny Cann whose name was linked to the notorious Bay runner *Whippoorwill.*

Anna D. could haul up to thirty-five hundred cases of liquor. Prohibition wound down. The mob sold *Anna D.* to a seafood outfit.

She had left her criminal past behind.

She had gone legitimate, and she lived out her days in peace, carrying lobsters and swordfish instead of booze.

Years went by. Times grew tough, then calamitous, then good. The Bay country grew crowded. Memories of a debauched decade became the stuff of back-creek legend and secret oral tradition. Defilers of federal statutes went back to their seine nets. Smuggling vessels became pleasure craft or rejoined the work fleet; ones that didn't succumb to time's rot became floating antiques. Throughout the marshland, citizens who had engaged in wrongful deeds emerged unscathed, uncaught, unidentified. They got away with it. They remained anonymous. They were taciturn to outsiders and adhered to a code of silence about lawless endeavors undertaken in the golden crime spree of youth. They got on with their lives. They kept their mouths shut and grew old. For erstwhile rum boat and reformed rum smuggler alike, the scandalous moment had ended, and the wild night was over.

NOTES

CHAPTER 1
"I Love to Hate You"

The appearance of so nationally prominent a personage as **Billy Sunday in Norfolk** to fete Prohibition's inception naturally garnered nationwide attention. See the *Norfolk Virginian-Pilot*, January 17, 1920, and *Baltimore Sun*, January 17, 1920. See also Kobler, p. 12; Fleming, p. 81; and Sann, p. 21.

The overview of **drinking in early America** was derived from Carson, pp. 1–10; Fleming, pp. 47–60; Hammett, pp. 371–372; Miller, pp. 182–188; and Tilp, pp. 325–326. Rorabaugh's insightful study, buttressed by revelatory statistics, is especially worthwhile; see pp. 5–57. See also Sinclair, pp. 10–22; Taussig, pp. 1–114; and Semmes, pp. 145–161.

For **the birth and rise of the Temperance movement**, see Fleming, pp. 61–80; Sinclair, pp. 36–128; Kobler, pp. 23–75; Sann, pp. 21–26; Carson, pp. 62–68; Brugger, pp. 431–32 and pp. 448–49; Hammett, p. 372; Preston, pp. 122–124; and William Williams, pp. 151–155. For Carry Nation-Anne Royall anecdotes, see Carson, p. 62; Tilp, p. 3; and Preston, p. 124. For the 1886 Maryland Temperance Alliance extracts, see Higgins, MHS file #MP 3 .H634P. For the definitive study of the 1914 Virginia referendum, see Hohner, pp. 473–488.

Wartime laws and encroaching dryness by geographic increments spawned **Chesapeake pre-Prohibition criminality.** The information on whiskey-running by automobile between Baltimore and Washington is from the *Baltimore Sun*, January 19–20, 1919. For Chesapeake steamboat smuggling from Baltimore to Norfolk, see the *Baltimore Sun*, January 30, 1919, and January 13, 1920.

Once Prohibition was a reality, the **dry debate** raged. The anti-Prohibition diatribe by "F.A.R." is from the *Baltimore Sun*, January 29, 1919. William Washam's letter decrying the "Puritanical fanatics" is from the *Baltimore Sun*, January 10, 1920. All Billy Sunday quotes are from his aforementioned Norfolk speech, transcribed in the *Norfolk Virginian-Pilot*, January 17, 1920. For the victory meeting of the Baltimore chapter of the Woman's Christian Temperance

Union, see the *Baltimore Sun,* January 17, 1920. For background on the Anti-Saloon League's victory rally at Baltimore's Lyric Theatre, and for Crabbe and Kramer quotes, see the *Baltimore Sun,* January 26, 1920. For Kramer's April speech to the East Baltimore Federation of Men's Bible Classes, see the *Baltimore Sun,* April 7, 1920.

Activities on the **eve of Prohibition,** including the loading of cargo ships in Baltimore Harbor and the stockpiling of liquor in bonded warehouses, are described in the *Baltimore Sun,* January 1–3, 10, and 15–17, 1920. For the Maryland Club cellar-liquidation ceremony, see the *Sun,* January 12, 1920.

One of the first results of Prohibition enactment was the **crime wave of 1920.** The Monument Street garage heist is reported in the *Sun,* January 14, 1920. The raid on Henry Hulseman's bungalow is in the *Sun,* January 17–18, 1920. The thwarted Gwynnbrook Distilling Company job is chronicled in the *Sun,* January 18, 1920. The Wineke-Arey warehouse theft is in the *Sun,* February 3, 1920. The Stone House Cove railroad-car caper is in the *Sun,* February 20, 1920. The McGuire booze-stash burglary is in the *Sun,* March 15, 1920. The botched robbery of the sacramental wine at Grace and St. Peter's Church is in the *Sun,* February 23, 1920. For tidewater brandy thieves, see the *Norfolk Virginian-Pilot,* September 3, 1920. For the Eastern Shore whiskey larceny at Readbourne, see the *Centreville Record,* January 3, 1920. The repeated Fairchance distillery robberies and the Dr. Joseph Gilder murder case are in the *Sun,* February 18–19, 1920. The Harvest Moon Shore case and subsequent legal-issues brouhaha are detailed in the *Sun,* February 22–25 and March 5–6, 1920. The arrest sweep related to the Legum Company St. Patrick's Day heist is in the *Sun,* April 15, 1920. The case of whiskey-trafficking storekeeper John Maggid is in the *Sun,* February 22, 1920. The Monticello Distilling Company robbery-shootout is in the *Sun,* April 29, 1920. The raid on a truck delivery of whiskey at Madson's reborn saloon is in the *Sun,* April 12, 1920. The raid on the bulldog-guarded party house is in the *Sun,* March 6, 1920. The Mount Vernon Distillery holdup is found in the *Sun,* March 11–12 and 14, 1920. For the Hotel Kernan champagne-party roust, see the *Sun,* March 27, 1920. The Carozza robbery, attempted by soldiers from Fort McHenry, is described in the *Sun,* April 7, 1920. For background on the scandalous, far-reaching Triaca plot, see the *Sun,* February 20, March 17–18 and 23, 1920.

For examples of **early shipboard smuggling,** see the *Sun,* January 18, February 11, March 14 and 18, and April 19, 1920. The saloon funeral for John Barleycorn was noted in the *Sun,* July 5, 1919.

CHAPTER 2
"One Hundred Illegal Stills Where There Was Only One"
The efforts of Dodson to combat those taking advantage of the **medicinal-alcohol loophole** were covered in the *Baltimore Sun* on February 14, 21, 22, 25, and 27; March 2, 13, 19, and 27; April 30; and May 2 and 6, 1920. Reports also appeared in the *Easton Star-Democrat* on February 14 and 21, April 3 and 24, July 17, August 14, and November 20, 1920, and on January 8 and March 12, 1921. The *Centreville Record* carried an article on February 21, 1920. For pharmacist Jeppi's reminiscences, see the *Sun,* July 28, 1968.

The era quickly saw a proliferation of illegal stills and the **rise of moonshining**. The first Davidson letter is from the *Baltimore Sun*, quoted in the *Easton Star-Democrat* on February 4, 1922. The second Davidson letter is from the *Star-Democrat*, March 4, 1922. The raid on moonshiners' stills in the Great Dismal Swamp was reported in the *Norfolk Virginian-Pilot*, January 17, 1920. For details of still construction and the distilling process, see Adams, pp. 53–72. The Powhatan still made with a railway milk can was described in the *Virginian-Pilot*, January 22, 1920. The Suffolk moonshiner's gun-barrel still was reported in the *Virginian-Pilot*, September 26, 1920. The information on aging whiskey in attics and aboard oystering vessels is from Hall, interview with the author; see also Tilp, p. 329. The anecdote about courtroom audience members taking "recipe" notes during a moonshiner's trial is from the *Easton Star-Democrat*, December 3, 1921. The Powell farm bust was reported in the *Norfolk Virginian-Pilot*, January 25 and 27, 1920. The ambitious Ocean View Boulevard moonshine operation was described in the *Virginian-Pilot*, December 14, 1922. For the Butts Station raid, see the *Virginian-Pilot*, January 26, 1923. A busy month of raids was summed up in the *Virginian-Pilot* February 3, 1923. For the prolific nature of southern Maryland moonshine activity, see Tilp, pp. 326–331; Hammett, p. 373; Pogue, pp. 286–295; and Brugger, p. 468. The Bruce Scheible quote is from Scheible, interview with the author. For examples chronicling the rapid growth of moonshining in Baltimore, see the *Baltimore Sun*, February 3, 1920, and January 8, 1924. The Mencken comment about Charm City brewing is from *Heathen Days*, pp. 200–201. For the synergy between moonshining and pig-farming, see the *Virginian-Pilot*, June 9, 1923, and Tilp, p. 328. Still-busting sweeps by federal agents on the Eastern Shore can be found in the reportage of the *Centreville Record*, June 30, 1923, and the *Star-Democrat*, December 9, 1922. The account of agents disguising themselves as waterfowl hunters is from the *Virginian-Pilot*, December 13, 1922. The John Raisin manhunt, leading to a still discovery, was described in the *Record*, February 10, 1923. The Delaware cemetery still was in the *Record*, July 28, 1923. The biggest still busted to date in Maryland was reported in the *Sun*, May 27, 1923. For celebrated "brands" of southern Maryland moonshine, see Tilp, p. 333.

Poison liquor was an early by-product of alcohol illegality. For the surgeon general's wood-alcohol admonishments, see the *Baltimore Sun*, January 3, 1920. The Park Heights Avenue housemaid and other victims of alcohol poisoning were mentioned in the *Sun*, January 24 and 26, 1920. The Eastern Shoreman's gasoline-based hooch was described in the *Easton Star-Democrat*, September 25, 1920. The mash-killed turkey report appeared in the *Centreville Record*, June 30, 1923. The health risk posed by metal-still "monkey rum" was warned about in the *Norfolk Virginian-Pilot*, January 27, 1920. The corroded-zinc jar-lid poisonings were in the *Star-Democrat*, July 29, 1922. Bad-batch death-rate stats appeared in the *Star-Democrat*, January 13, 1923. The *Hwah Jah* rotgut-importation incident was recorded in the *Virginian-Pilot*, August 27, 1920. For details on the Layman Senate Prohibition Bill, see the *Virginian-Pilot*, March 6, 1924. The "vast tidal wave" of booze-related deaths was reported in the *Star-Democrat*, December 8, 1923. The Davidson quotes are from the *Star-Democrat*, March 4, 1922, and February 4, 1922. Information on the rise of insanity cases on the Eastern Shore is from the *Star-Democrat*, March 22, 1924.

After Prohibition became law, the political war continued to rage between **Maryland wets and drys**. The Eastern Shore gathering of Woman's Christian Temperance Union delegates was chronicled in the *Easton Star-Democrat,* May 6, 1922. For background on Governor Ritchie, see Essary, pp. 295–328. The Ritchie speech quote is from Essary, pp. 306–307. See also Harold Williams, p. 216, and Brugger, pp. 453 and 456–457. Baltimore Police Department statistics charting the crime-rate increase concomitant with Prohibition were cited in the *Baltimore Sun,* January 8, 1924. The Davidson quote about the unenforceability of the Volstead Act is from the *Star-Democrat,* February 4, 1922.

Illicit booze fueled **Jazz Age licentiousness.** The Virginia educator's lament about flappers overrunning college campuses is from the *Baltimore Sun,* January 10, 1924. The local box-office success of the scandalous floozy epic "Flaming Youth" was noted in the *Norfolk Virginian-Pilot,* February 27, 1924. Mencken's Puritan-skewering comment is from *Prejudices: Second Series,* p. 220.

Regional rum-running escalated rapidly. The customs search of the dead sailor's coffin was reported in the *Baltimore Sun,* April 23, 1920. For the symbiosis that existed between oystering and booze-smuggling, and for mention of Bay boatyards creating custom-built rum-running vessels (with hidden cargo space), see Tilp, pp. 330–331. The information on the Dorchester County watermen/rumrunners and the Milford Elliott quotes are from Elliott, interview with the author. For more on the Elliotts' Hooper Island draketail *Dixie,* see Lesher, p. 19.

Examples of criminal inventiveness were taken from the following: the chauffeur/bootlegger busted en route to Bowie race track—*Sun,* April 17, 1920; the chauffeur/bootlegger outrunning the law near Royal Oak—*Easton Star-Democrat,* April 1, 1921; the Norfolk Police nabbing the Studebaker and Ford gangs—*Norfolk Virginian-Pilot,* January 13, 1923; the Delaware bootleggers bailing out before crashing into a train—*Centreville Record,* September 22, 1923; the high-speed 50-mile chase through Washington, D.C., and Ellicott City—*Sun,* March 17, 1931; the stealing of confiscated liquor from the lawmen's car—*Star-Democrat,* March 17, 1923; Jacob Cohen's scam at the pharmacist's house—*Sun,* March 24, 1920; James Wray's elaborate concealment devices—*Sun,* April 8, 1920; Burwell Jones's craftily customized automobile—*Virginian-Pilot,* June 9, 1923; the fishing-pier booze off-loading scheme: *Virginian-Pilot,* January 2, 1923; the oldest illegal trafficker—*Virginian-Pilot,* January 2, 1923; the youngest illegal trafficker—*Sun,* January 15, 1924. The Davidson quote about corrupted youth and bootlegger blatancy is from the *Star-Democrat,* August 19, 1922.

Enforcement difficulties led to **police corruption.** For police department shakeups and cases of individual cops going bad, see *Norfolk Virginian-Pilot,* August 21, 1920, and December 14, 1922; see also the *Easton Star-Democrat,* February 4, 1922. The incident of the bottle of evidence that nobody wanted to remove from the courtroom was reported in the *Baltimore Sun,* February 4, 1920. The Davenport case was in the *Virginian-Pilot,* February 22, 1924.

Thanks largely to popular lore, **temperance crusaders** too often have been characterized as wild-eyed zealots, but legions of dry crusaders were well-meaning and devoted to an ideal that was rooted in hopeful intentions. The Shaner WCTU oration is from the *Easton Star-Democrat,* October 28, 1922. The saga of the Reverend Bicking vs. the Pocomoke booze mob was reported in the *Crisfield Times* on August 13, 23, and 25, September 22, and October 13 and 20, 1923; and in the *Centreville Record,* on July 28, August 25, September 22, and October 13 and 20, 1923.

The "Where do they get the whiskey?" query is from the *Easton Star-Democrat,* December 18, 1920. The quote about the increased use of motorboats in liquor-trafficking is from the *Star-Democrat,* April 30, 1921. The "Captain Kidd" quote is from the *Norfolk Virginian-Pilot,* May 27, 1923.

CHAPTER 3
Scotch and Water
The arrival of *Istar* and her consort vessels off the Chesapeake—and the subsequent hotel roust of her land agents—received detailed reportage in the *Norfolk Virginian-Pilot,* May 26–29 and June 1 and 3, 1923. See also the *Baltimore Sun,* May 27 and 29, 1923, and the *Washington Post,* June 2, 1923. How the rumrunners took advantage of the Chesapeake and Albemarle Canal was reported in the *Sun,* June 1, 1923. Correspondent Tompkins's observations from the Coast Guard cutter *Apache* appeared in the *Sun* on May 26 and 30, and June 1, 1923. See also Willoughby, p. 46.

For general background on the mid-Atlantic **rum war,** see Behr, pp. 129–145; Waters, pp. 49–63; and especially Willoughby, pp. 22–74. The quotes about McCoy's maiden smuggling voyage, and how Chesapeake almost became the birthplace of Rum Row, are from Van de Water, pp. 26–27. For the *Glen Beulah* incident, see the *Norfolk Virginian-Pilot,* June 4 and 5, 1923. Ship-name aliases were one of many ruses employed by rumrunners. The *Julito (Leader)* incident is recounted in Everett Allen, pp. 88–89. The bizarre case of *Mary Beatrice* was reported in the *Virginian-Pilot,* June 14–16 and 18, 1923.

For the elevation to boom-town status of Nassau, Bahamas, and St. Pierre, see Van de Water, pp. 42–44, 68–72, and 89–91. Did Alastair Moray smuggle scotch to Chesapeake Bay in *Cask?* Tilp, p. 330, suggests so, with intriguingly precise (yet unsourced) details; Moray's own account doesn't specify. Quotes from the Scotsman's *Diary* are from pp. xiii, 4, 187–188, 195, and 229. The action involving the Norfolk City Police gunboat is described in the *Virginian-Pilot,* April 28, 1923.

Coast Guard crews were kept busy as **Chesapeake Bay rum chasers.** Henderson's orders to Coast Guard stations along the Atlantic coast from the Delaware Breakwater to the Virginia Capes are found in U.S. Coast Guard Records, Record Group (RG) 26, Entry 283A, Box 1244. For background on the 1924 federal appropriation for beefing up the Coast Guard, and the resultant increase in business for the region's boatyards, see Entry 283A, Box 1265; the *Norfolk Virginian-Pilot,* February 3 and November 7, 1924; the *Centreville Record,* June 14, 1924; and Willoughby, pp. 46–47. Billard's pro-Henderson comments are in Entry 283A, Box 1265. Henderson's instructions to the men of the newly formed Section Base Eight are likewise in Entry 283A, Box 1265. Government statistics on the growth of the rumrunners' fleet were publicized in the *Virginian-Pilot,* February 22 and March 9, 1924. The Treasury Department report citing the Chesapeake region as one of the "troublesome spots" regarding smuggling was presented in the *Virginian-Pilot,* November 12, 1924. Steele's warning to Coast Guardsmen to check all vessels is in Entry 283A, Box 1244, as is the official report on the *X 10 US–Tessie Aubrey* incident that inspired Steele's remarks. Vipond's report on Chesapeake rumrunners is found in the same USCGR file. Information on *Tessie Aubrey* is in Entry 291, Seized Vessel Files (alphabetical by vessel name), *Tessie Aubrey* folder.

Baltimore was an oasis for the imbibement-minded. The case of the liquor-laden motor launch at the Baltimore pier was chronicled in the *Baltimore Daily Post*, June 15, 1925. For information on the many transportation routes and conveyances servicing Baltimore's demand for supply, see the *Baltimore Sun*, January 14, 1962, and December 10, 1967; Brugger, pp. 468–70; Hammett, p. 375; and Tilp, p. 329. The unrest surrounding the bust-up of Jacob Miller's still was reported in the *Sun*, May 30, 1922. For the botched raid on Shalitsky's, see the *Sun*, October 7, 1922. For the incident of the dry agent mauled by the street mob, see the *Daily Post*, May 29, 1925. For names of some noted speakeasies, see the *Sun*, January 14, 1962. The "chain saloon" was described in the *Daily Post*, June 2, 1925. The cat-and-mouse game between feds and barmen at the Dolphin Street watering hole was detailed in the *Daily Post*, May 28, 1925. The major crackdown on saloons, and the resultant increase in private-residence, private-club style speakeasies, was reported in the *Sun*, January 4, 1924. For a litany of Baltimore drinking joints prospering around the time of the aforementioned crackdown, see the *Sun*, January 3, 5, 6, 8, 9, and 12, 1924. For the USIA industrial-alcohol skim racket, see the *Sun*, January 14, 1962.

Norfolk nightlife rivaled the ribaldry of the sin city to the north. Baltimore's role in supplying booze to Norfolk received coverage in the *Norfolk Virginian-Pilot* on February 26 and March 23, 1924, and in the *Daily Post* on February 17, 1925. The inside scoop on the Black Belt speakeasy appeared in the *Virginian-Pilot*, November 28, 1920. See also the *Virginian-Pilot*, November 21, 1920; and February 12, 13, and 27, and November 11, 1924.

Regarding the **return of *Istar***, Sir Broderick's investors' prospectus was heavily quoted in the *Norfolk Virginian-Pilot* on February 10, 1924. The reappearance of the rum fleet in general, and *Istar* in particular, was covered in the *Virginian-Pilot* on March 2, 6, 7, and 8, 1924. The "wicked old sinner" quote about *Istar* is from a confidential telephone transcript in U.S. Coast Guard Records, RG 26, Entry 291, Seized Vessel Files, *Istar* folder. The capture of *Istar* was recorded in the *New York Herald*, April 27, 1924.

Coast Guard statistics showing the increasing numbers, and increasing internationalism, of the **rapidly growing rum fleet** were given in the *Virginian-Pilot* on March 9, 1924. Walker's quotes about an Englishman's prerogative to smuggle are from Barbican, pp. 308–309. The Phillips report about flagrant rumrunners hovering off the Chesapeake is in U.S. Coast Guard Records, RG 26, Entry 283A, Box 1244. Steele's report containing the *"catch them we must"* quote also is filed there.

CHAPTER 4
Wading in Whiskey

The text of Senator Bruce's **"Federal Invasions of State Rights"** speech is in Maryland Historical Society file #PAM 4138; see also the *Baltimore Sun*, August 30, 1925.

In the wake of the first wave of the rum war, the federal crime-busting initiative segued **from sea to land**. For background on the 1925 Coast Guard scale-down, see the *Baltimore Daily Post*, May 18, 1925. Haynes's boastful pronouncements of rum-war success were quoted in the *Daily Post*, May 26, 1925. Skepticism about the rum war, voiced by Wheeler et al., was aired in the *Daily Post,* May 19, 1925. The McCoy quote is from Van de Water, p. 209; see also pp. 193–212. The reporting about the offshore floating moonshine factories appeared in the *Sun,* January 1, 1924. See also the *Norfolk Virginian-Pilot,* March 16, 1924. The "Old Smuggler" dilution comment is from Moray, p. 147. The crackdown on booze-smuggling aboard commercial shipping lines was reported in the *Daily Post,* May 18, 1925. For the *Beaufort* incident, involving the courts-martial of naval personnel for liquor smuggling, see the *Daily Post,* May 27 and June 2, 1925. Lone Wolf Asher's undercover exploits were featured in the *Virginian-Pilot,* November 11, 21, and 23, 1924; see also the *Daily Post,* February 17, 1925. The Annapolis "rum ring" exposé, replete with corrupt women dry agents, was outlined in the *Daily Post,* February 17, 1925. The Norfolk wiretap trap is described in Carse, pp. 232–233. The "traveling school" for dry agents was visited by the *Sun,* May 30, 1929. The nabbing of "society bootlegger" Conley was noted in the *Virginian-Pilot,* February 25, 1924. For the Alligator Swamp moonshine "city," see Parramore, pp. 306–307. The overall improvement in the quality and chemistry of moonshine was reported in the *Virginian-Pilot,* November 11, 1924.

The **mid-decade land-based initiative** was up against **elaborate moonshining methods.** The raid on the mighty Larchmont still was covered by the *Norfolk Virginian-Pilot,* November 30, 1924. The Anne Arundel County still served by its own railroad track was described in the *Baltimore Daily Post,* May 22, 1925. The big moonshine-manufacturing operation at the abandoned municipal piggery was described in the *Baltimore Sun,* May 3, 1924.

Eastern Shore moonshining was rampant. The George Williams information is from Hall, interview with author. The observation on Cambridge cop indifference vis-a-vis citizens drinking is from Elliott, interview with author. The litany of moonshining operations throughout the Eastern Shore is gathered from the *Easton Star-Democrat,* January 8, 1921, and May 2, 1925; and the *Centreville Record,* February 2, April 12, July 26, and August 30, 1924. For the federal initiative to wipe out Eastern Shore distilling, see the *Star-Democrat,* August 22 and September 19, 1925. The story of waterman Gotman's foray into moonshining appeared in the *Star-Democrat,* February 13, 1926. The oysters-and-whiskey-bottle anecdotes were culled from the *Star-Democrat,* January 13 and February 3, 1923, and September 20, 1924; see also March 17, 1928. Booze-fueled racial tension manifested itself in the small-town life of the era: Graham's Alley, Easton—*Star-Democrat,* April 10, 1926, and September 20, 1930; Skinner Street, St. Michaels—*Star-Democrat,* January 24, 1931; Trappe—*Star-Democrat,* February 15, 1930.

The **fizzling of the land campaign** in the war against alcohol was explained in the *Easton Star-Democrat,* May 8, 1926. The prediction of a "renewed attempt" among offshore rumrunners ran in the *Baltimore Daily Post,* May 18, 1925. McCoy's remark about the futility of trying to win the rum war is from Van De Water, pp. 278–288. Johnson's Easton speech was quoted in the *Star-Democrat,* February 23, 1924. How the police court judge came to be standing up to his ankles in whiskey was recounted in the *Norfolk Virginian-Pilot,* February 26, 1924.

CHAPTER 5
"Subject: Increased Activity, Rum Runners"
More rum-running occurred on the Bay from mid-decade on. Reports relating to the rumrunners *Sabalo* and *Eugie,* and Henderson's memorandum about Crisfield and other drop-off

spots, are in U.S. Coast Guard Records, RG 26, Entry 291, Seized Vessel Files, *Sabalo* folder. For the development of the "sack" as a standard packaging method, see Willoughby, p. 18. Information on the legendary southern Maryland runner *Wild Rose* is from Scheible, interview with author; see also Hammett, p. 376. The Alonza Elliott anecdotes are from Elliott, interview with author. The nabbing of "King James" Kelly is logged in Entry 291, Seized Vessel Files, *Ida O. Robinson* folder; see also the *Baltimore Sun,* June 30, 1927. The Robinson folder also is repository for the Proctor report quoted herein. The movements of *Maude Thornhill* and *Anna May* are charted in Entry 291, Seized Vessel Files, *Maude Thornhill* folder, which also includes material on the case of the semi-exonerated boatswain. The Ker request for more patrolling vessels, and information on the runner *Ethel May,* are in Entry 283A, Box 1265.

Enforcement attempts continued. *CG-125*'s patrolling of Talbot County waters was reported in the *Easton Star-Democrat,* March 4, 1928; for Talbot's hiring of a private detective to handle alcohol cases, see the *Star-Democrat,* August 18, 1928. Hill's crackdown on Shore stills was covered in the *Centreville Record,* November 8, 1928; the busting-up of the largest still ever found in Delaware was described in the *Record,* January 17, 1929. Jail overcrowding was a late-Prohibition story in the hinterlands; see the *Star-Democrat,* December 1, 1928. The thwarted mass breakout from the Easton Jail was written about in the *Star-Democrat,* February 2, 1929. The comings and goings of recidivist bootlegger Callusi were chronicled in the *Star-Democrat* on December 15, 1928, and on July 6 and August 3 and 31, 1929. The raid on the surprisingly elaborate Poplar Island booze factory was reported in the *Star-Democrat,* May 25 and November 23, 1929, and in the *Baltimore Sun,* June 3, 1929. Official dispatches on the huge end-of-decade beach bust near Ocean City are in U.S. Coast Guard Records, RG 26, Entry 283A, Box 1244; Pastor Jefferson's letter of gratitude also is filed therein. The imprisonment and judgment of the Ocean City rumrunners received coverage in the *Star-Democrat,* March 29 and May 3, 1930. Price's communique on "increased activity: rum runners" is in U.S. Coast Guard Records, RG 26, Entry 283A, Box 1265. The saga of *Metmuzel* is contained in Entry 291, Seized Vessel Files, *Metmuzel* folder; see also Entry 283A, Box 1265. Papers relating to the Coast Guard's Thomas Wharf raid, involving booze stashed in a shucking shack, is in Entry 283A, Box 1244. The bribe attempt at Lewes is noted in Entry 283A, Box 1243. For the capture of *I. H. Tawes,* see Entry 283A, Box 1265, where information also can be found on the near-collision of patrol vessels at the entrance to the Chesapeake. The capture of *Violet* is recorded in Entry 283A, Boxes 1265 and 1288. For data on *Blanche,* see Entry 291, Seized Vessel Files, *Blanche* folder; see also Entry 283A, Box 1288. Price's information on Crisfield miscreance is filed in Entry 283A, Box 1243, as is his request for more patrol vessels. The audacious rum crew off-loading right at the Rock Point steamboat wharf is mentioned in Entry 283A, Boxes 1265 and 1288. Billard's suggestion on employing "the liberal use of gunfire" is in Entry 283A, Box 1288.

CHAPTER 6
"The Lure That Takes Us Off the Beaten Track"

The case of *Hammitt L. Robbins* is preserved in U.S. Coast Guard Records, RG 26, Entry 291, Seized Vessel Files, *Hammitt L. Robbins* folder; see also Entry 283A, Boxes 1243 and 1244. Papers detailing the legendary *Whippoorwill* and her sister runner *Hiawatha* are in Entry 291,

Seized Vessel Files, *Whippoorwill* folder. See also the *Washington Post,* May 16, 1931; the *Crisfield Times,* May 16 and 30, 1931; and the *Baltimore Sun,* July 23, 1931. For the theory connecting the *Whippoorwill-Hiawatha* crews to the Owens murder, see the *Sun,* March 16, 17, 18, 20, 22, 24, 29, and 31, 1931; and Vojtech, pp. 111–117. The conversion of the fast rum boats into Coast Guard vessels is charted in Willoughby, pp. 167, 170.

The Chesapeake rumrunners kept it up straight through to the **end of the era**. The liquor-smuggling airplane in the skies over Trappe was reported in the *Easton Star-Democrat,* February 2, 1931; information on the southern Maryland aero-smuggler is from Scheible, interview with the author. The plump *Norma* capture is in U.S. Coast Guard Records, RG 26, Entry 283A, Box 1244; see also the *Crisfield Times,* July 11, 1931. The Coast Guard tip on a pending Patuxent River drop-off is in Entry 283A, Box 1288. The Murderkill information is in Entry 283A, Box 1243, as is Sullivan's report on rum-running activity and his request for reinforcements. The November 1931 bribe attempt is noted in Entry 283A, Box 1244, as is the report on suspicious characters lurking about in Berlin's Atlantic Hotel. The report on the Bethany Beach bust, uncovering a liquor-filled chicken house, likewise is filed in Entry 283A, Box 1244. Also therein: the February 1932 Chincoteague bust and the April 1932 bribe attempt. Background on *Bertha Maie* is in Entry 291, Seized Vessel Files, *Bertha Maie* folder. Sightings and searches of *Anna D., Emmahelene,* and a host of other rumrunners are reported in Entry 283A, Boxes 1265 and 1288. Proceedings of the Coast Guard officers' meeting are in Entry 283A, Box 1288. The capture of the radio expert and his henchmen is in Entry 283A, Box 1243. The incident involving duck-hunter Mears being waylaid by smugglers is noted in Entry 283A, Box 1244.

The chase of *Matilda Barry* and the death of her captain are chronicled in U.S. Coast Guard Records, RG 26, Entry 291, Seized Vessel Files, *Matilda Barry* folder; see also the *Norfolk Virginian-Pilot,* December 12, 1932, and the *Norfolk Ledger-Dispatch,* December 12, 1932.

Wheeler's request for reinforcements and his filings on Chesapeake rum-running activity during **Prohibition's final year** are in Entry 283A, Box 1288. Scenes of revelry at Prohibition's end were gathered from the *Baltimore Sun,* December 5 and 6, 1933. Mencken's remarks are from the *Sun,* December 6, 1933. The Temperance editorial is from the *Easton Star-Democrat,* December 15, 1933. The predictions about future drug-smuggling on the Chesapeake are from the *Sun,* September 24, 1933. McCoy's comments on drug-smugglers are from Van de Water, pp. 130–131. The continuation of moonshining was a multimillion-dollar industry; see the *Sun,* August 3, 4, and 5, 1955. The names of individuals who made it big in Prohibition-era bootlegging and rum-running and who later became prosperous pillars of the community were given off-the-record in interviews with the author. Moray's wistful farewell to the rum-running life is from Moray, pp. 271–272. The recounting of the demise of *Dixie* is from Elliott, interview with the author. The background on *Anna D.* is from Entry 291, Seized Vessel Files, *Anna D.* folder.

BIBLIOGRAPHY

Principal source material on rum-running vessels is from the Records of the United States Coast Guard, Record Group 26, in the National Archives.

Newspapers:
Baltimore Daily Post
Baltimore Sun
Cambridge Daily Banner
Centreville Record
Crisfield Times
Easton Star-Democrat
New York Herald
Norfolk Star-Ledger
Norfolk Virginian-Pilot
Washington Post

Interviews by the author:
Milford Elliott
Geneva Hall
Joseph Norris
Warren Parker
Ty Pruitt
Bruce Scheible
. . . and others who preferred to remain off the record.

Additional reading:

Adams, John F. *An Essay on Brewing, Vintage and Distillation, Together With Selected Remedies for Hangover Melancholia; or How to Make Booze*. Garden City, N.Y.: Doubleday & Company, 1966.

Allen, Everett S. *The Black Ships: Rumrunners of Prohibition*. Boston: Little, Brown and Company, 1965, 1979.

Allen, Frederick Lewis. *Only Yesterday*. New York: Harper & Brothers, 1931.

Barbican, James [Eric Sherbrooke Walker]. *The Confessions of a Rum-Runner*. New York: Ives Washburn, 1928.

Behr, Edward. *Prohibition: Thirteen Years That Changed America*. New York: Arcade Publishing, 1996.

Bruce, William Cabell. "Federal Invasions of State Rights." Maryland Historical Society file #PAM 4138. Text of address delivered at the Atlantic Hotel, Ocean City, Maryland, August 29, 1925.

Brugger, Robert J. *Maryland: A Middle Temperament, 1634–1980*. Baltimore: Johns Hopkins University Press, 1988.

Carse, Robert. *Rum Row*. New York: Rinehart & Company, 1959.

Carson, Gerald. *The Social History of Bourbon*. New York: Dodd, Mead & Company, 1963.

Essary, Jesse Frederick. *Maryland in National Politics: From Charles Carroll to Albert C. Ritchie,* 2nd ed. Baltimore: John Murphy Company, 1932.

Fleming, Alice. *Alcohol: The Delightful Poison*. New York: Dell, 1979.

Grossman, Harold J. *Grossman's Guide to Wines, Spirits, and Beers,* 4th rev. ed. New York: Charles Scribner's Sons, 1964.

Halley, Ned. *The Wordsworth Dictionary of Drink*. Hertfordshire, England: Wordsworth Editions, 1996.

Hammett, Regina Combs. *History of St. Mary's County, Maryland*. Ridge, Md.: published by author, 1977.

Higgins, Edwin. "Prohibition for Maryland." Maryland Historical Society file #MP 3 .H634P. Baltimore: Maryland State Temperance Alliance, 1886.

Hohner, Robert A. "Prohibition Comes to Virginia: The Referendum of 1914." *The Virginia Magazine of History and Biography,* 75 (1914).

Kobler, John. *Ardent Spirits: The Rise and Fall of Prohibition*. New York: G. P. Putnam's Sons, 1973.

Lesher, Ronald E. "The Hooper Island Draketail." *The Weather Gauge* XXIV, no. 1.

Mencken, H. L. *Prejudices: Second Series*. New York: Alfred A. Knopf, 1920.

Mencken, H. L. *Heathen Days: 1890–1936*. New York: Alfred A. Knopf, 1943.

Miller, John C. *The First Frontier: Life in Early Colonial America*. New York: Dell, 1966.

Moray, Alastair. *The Diary of a Rum-Runner*. London: Phillip Allan & Company, 1929.

Parramore, Thomas C., with Peter C. Stewart and Tommy L. Bogger. *Norfolk: The First Four Centuries*. Charlottesville, Va.: University Press of Virginia, 1994.

Pogue, Robert E.T. *Yesterday in Old St. Mary's County*. New York: Carlton Press, 1968.

Preston, Dickson J. *Newspapers of Maryland's Eastern Shore.* Centreville, Md.: Tidewater
    Publishers, 1986.
Rorabaugh, W. J. *The Alcoholic Republic: An American Tradition.* New York: Oxford Univer-
    sity Press, 1979.
Sann, Paul. *The Lawless Decade.* New York: Crown Publishers, 1957.
Semmes, Raphael. *Crime and Punishment in Early Maryland.* Baltimore: Johns Hopkins
    Press, 1938.
Sinclair, Andrew. *Prohibition: The Era of Excess.* Boston: Little, Brown and Company, 1962.
Taussig, Charles William. *Rum, Romance & Rebellion.* New York: Minton, Balch & Com-
    pany, 1928.
Tilp, Frederick. "Drinking on the Potomac River," *Chronicles of St. Mary's* 22, nos. 1 and 2
    (January and February 1974).
Van de Water, Frederick F. *The Real McCoy.* Garden City, New York: Doubleday, Doran &
    Company, 1931.
Vojtech, Pat. *Lighting the Bay: Tales of Chesapeake Lighthouses.* Centreville, Md.: Tidewater
    Publishers, 1996.
Waters, Harold. *Smugglers of Spirits: Prohibition and the Coast Guard Patrol.* New York:
    Hastings House, 1971.
Williams, Harold A. *The Baltimore Sun: 1837–1987.* Baltimore: Johns Hopkins University
    Press, 1987.
Williams, William H. *The Garden of American Methodism: The Delmarva Peninsula,
    1769–1820.* Wilmington, Del.: Scholarly Resources, 1984.
Willoughby, Malcolm F. *Rum War at Sea.* Washington, D.C.: U.S. Government Printing
    Office, 1964.

INDEX

Bicking, Paul, 61
Bicking, Willard, 61
Biddle Street Saloon, Baltimore, 90
Bie & Schott, 97–8
Bienemann, Walter J., 32–3
Billard, F. C., 85, 129, 143, 145
Birch, John W., 140
Blanche, 143
Blue, Rupert, 44–5
Bodkin Creek, 112
Bolton, George, 136
Booker's beer hall, Baltimore, 90
Boston, Mass., 159
Bow, Clara, 122
Bowers Beach, Del., 155
Bowie, Md., 55
Bowig, Herbert, 133
Braumeister's saloon, Baltimore, 89
Brim, Richard, 129
Brinkley, Harry A., 139
Bristol's brothel, Norfolk County, 92
Broad Creek Club, Virginia Eastern Shore, 146–7
Brown, Andrew, 37
Brown, Angus, 37
Brown, Harry, 131
Brown, Joseph, 133
Bruce, Howard, 28
Bruce, William Cabell, 99–101, 104–5, 118
Bruckner, Fred, 57–8
Bryantown, Md., 43
Buccaneer, The, 75
Budnitz, Edgar, 115, 118
Buffalo, N.Y., 159
Burger, Carl, 89
Butta's speakeasy, Baltimore, 89
Butts Crossing, Va., 39
Butts Station, Va., 40
Bye, Adolph, 62
Byrd, Colmore E., 62
Byrd, Richard E., 134
Byrd, William II, 8

Callusi, Antonio, 131–2
Calvert County, Md., 12, 167
Cambridge, Md., 48, 54, 114, 127, 128, 148, 150
Campbell, John, 128
Campbell, Leroy, 57
Camp Holabird, Md., 28
Campostella, Va., 55
Cann, Benny, 151, 152, 169
Cannon, James M., Jr., 14

Cape Charles, Va., 42–3, 69, 71, 74, 159, 161
Cape Hatteras, N.C., 83
Cape Henry, Va., 71, 82, 83, 95
Caroline County, Md., 12, 113, 114–5, 130
Carozza, Antonio T., 28
Cartona, 67
Cask, 80–1
Cathell, Hilary, 156
Cecil County, Md., 12, 114, 167
Centreville, Md., 43
CG-8, 160
CG-125, 130
CG-138, 152
CG-144, 126
CG-163, 161–2
CG-175, 142
CG-185, 123
CG-193, 85
CG-196, 85
CG-199, 142–3
CG-200, 137–8
CG-221, 148
CG-834, 152
CG-987, 152
CG-2308, 158, 160
CG-2314, 129
CG-2321, 163
CG-2389, 155–6
CG-2390, 156
Chandler, Neal, 146
Charles County, Md., 43–4, 167
Chase's Tavern, Baltimore, 11
Chesapeake and Albemarle Canal, 71, 128
Chesapeake and Delaware Canal, 87, 128
Chesapeake Bay, 3, 16, 19–20, 24, 30, 36, 40, 43, 44, 46, 53–4, 63, 64–75, 77–84, 86–7, 98, 104, 116, 123–9, 132–3, 142–3, 145, 148, 149, 151–2, 153, 160, 161, 163, 166
Chesnut, Calvin, 164
Chestertown, Md., 43
Chincoteague, Va., 65, 87, 95, 98, 146–7, 158, 159, 160, 163
Chincoteague Channel, 158
Choptank River, 53, 115, 117, 125
Christiana Creek, Del., 55
Church Creek, Md., 54
Clark, John, 21
Coan River, 53
Coats, Julian, 133
Coats, Marion, 133
Cobb's Island, Va., 71

something. I then asked him if he was out of his head and why he came to me? He said some New York men asked him to come to me (it is supposed he was paid for this) and find out."

Sixth District supplied the intelligence; Norfolk Division Command issued the confidential orders to all units: watch *Bertha Maie* like a hawk. Operating out of Cape Charles, she was 46½ feet long by 13½ feet wide, owned and captained by Charles S. Reynolds. "This boat is at present in the vicinity of the Hog Island Station," declared Norfolk orders. "A strict watch should be kept for this boat and [she] should be boarded and thoroughly examined wherever found. . . . Joe Jester, one of the crew, has been known to operate on rum boats in the southern part of the district." Hog Island Station crewmen had tried to bust *Bertha Maie*, but the most they were able to do was slap Reynolds with a not-enough-life-preservers fine. *Bertha Maie* was local talent, a small fish swimming with big fish from afar. In August 1932 the black ships *Anna D., Emmahelene,* and *Tatamagouche* were sighted 30 miles east of Chesapeake Lightship. The Coast Guard beefed up the patrol thereabouts, while information arrived that the speedboat *Detroit* and a companion craft were about to move fifteen hundred cases through the Chesapeake Capes. Meanwhile, the speedboat *Helen,* a known rumrunner out of Providence, Rhode Island, was sighted at Harborton, Virginia. At Chincoteague, more rum boats were converging: *Oblay,* out of Providence; *Huilzilopocetli,* out of Boston; *Suspalstchic,* out of Buffalo, New York; and *Oysninaniskak,* out of Philadelphia. The Coast Guard strengthened its Chesapeake Capes cordon as best it could, and at a subsequent officers' meeting at Norfolk Division headquarters, the rumrunners' elusive stratagems were dissected, including the gambit of using local officials as disinformation-spewing decoy men. "Past information submitted by Chief of Police and Sheriff of Crisfield was discussed and the reliability of same appeared to be questionable," it was reported in the meeting's minutes. "There was a discussion as to the possibility of this information being designed to lead patrol boat or boats from a location where unloading of cargo by a black was contemplated. . . . There was a discussion and description of creeks of Eastern Shore of Chesapeake Bay, demonstrating the fact that they are navigable and are being used by rum runners."

Boatswain's Mate First Class Leonard D. Melvin was on patrol again aboard *CG-2308* in Chincoteague Inlet when the speed skiff *N-12867*, a suspected troublemaker, appeared on the night of December 2, 1932. Melvin halted her and took her crew in for questioning. The skiff was towed to Assateague Beach Station. The skiff's occupants— owner Raymond F. Klaess, skipper Joe Miles, and crewmen Alfred Marshall and Charles Johnson—were all Baltimoreans. Commander Sullivan and others flew in Coast Guard plane *CG-8* from Lewes to Assateague to be in on the questioning. The skiff's skipper said they were on a cruise from Baltimore to Atlantic City. But, said Sullivan, "we were of the opinion that Marshall was going to be put aboard a British rum vessel operating off the Chesapeake Light Vessel for the purpose of testing and repairing the vessel's radio." Skiff crewman Marshall finally admitted to a knowledge of electricity; in fact, it turned out that he used to sell and install radios. Among the paraphernalia found aboard the skiff was a Weston 566 radio-testing outfit. Charts found aboard the skiff had interesting pencil delineations: approaches to New York, Nantucket, Cape May, Chesapeake Bay, and Cape Hatteras; routes from 100-fathom deepwater locations to Parramore Bank and Chincoteague Inlet; a highlighted spot 50 miles out from the Chesapeake Bay entrance; and numerous other intriguing points and lines. The Coast Guard contacted Customs in Baltimore and learned that an agent had been tracking the crew by land for days; they had been driving a car with stolen Virginia plates. After the largely fruitless Coast Guard questioning, the skiff crew cooled heels in the Accomac County Jail until they were tried, fined, and sprung, their fines paid. They left Chincoteague fast in a Buick sedan with New York plates. "It is my opinion that this crew should be regarded as suspicious characters wherever found," said Sullivan, "especially Charles Johnson, who was rough both in his talk and appearance."

Oscar Mears, citizen of Accomac, went duck-hunting on the Chesapeake between Thanksgiving and Christmas 1932. As he motorboated home in the chilly evening, he stumbled upon rumrunners making a boat-to-truck drop-off near Onancock. The rumrunners held Mears prisoner until the trucks were all loaded and on their way. Afterwards, they let him go, no harm done. Mears noted that absolutely none of the rumrunners, on the boat or in the trucks, were local people. They were all strangers to him.

Waves were kicking up, and cold rain was drilling down in the thick, dark mist on Saturday night, December 10, 1932. *CG-163* was on patrol in the lower Chesapeake, 2 miles southwest of Old Plantation Light. Boatswain's Mate First Class Charles Thaler was on watch. It was about 7:30 P.M. when he spotted a speedboat "of the usual rum runner type" coming up the Bay. The speedboat likewise spotted the patrol boat. A Pennsylvania passenger steamer was making for nearby Cape Charles City. The speedboat veered off and sped up, trying to get the passenger steamer between herself and the Coast Guard patrol. Boatswain Thaler rang full speed. The crew swarmed. Thaler manned the machine gun. Chief Boatswain's Mate Robert H. Wilson, the officer in charge, grabbed the one-pounder. Everyone took their stations. They torched a flare, blasted the horn, and popped off three warning blanks. The runner failed to get around to the other side of the passenger steamer. The chase was on. Her blanks ignored, the patrol boat started firing hot shot now. The speedboat was showing stern, her 2,000-horsepower triple-engine giving her three times the speed of the Coast Guard chaser. All *CG-163* could do was try not to lose her—and keep firing. As she bounced and pitched in the heavy swell, Thaler and Wilson spat forth a relentless barrage; a dozen solid shot and a whole pan of machine-gun lead plowed into the fleeing rumrunner. A lucky shot snapped the rumrunner's wheel rope. Her rudder went lame. The speedster started zigzagging on the Bay, careening, still zooming full-tilt. As she got erratic, the patrol boat gained on her. *CG-163* was close now. The rumrunner was on the windward side. *CG-163* got closer. The rumrunner vomited a huge black cloud. The Coast Guardsmen hacked and gagged, eyes burning in the cloying chemical miasma of the smoke screen. The runner was getting away again.

CG-163 kept up her fire and kept on coming. Machine-gun bullets peppered the air. The speedboat's captain panicked. He got the dory over the side and tried to clamber over the rail. Machine-gun fire kept raining down. The speedboat captain slipped. The dory flipped. Their skipper overboard, the rumrunners gave up. *CG-163* had ceased firing. The speedboat slowed to a stop and the patrol boat came alongside. Armed Guardsmen boarded. She was *Matilda Barry*, out of Philadelphia. The captain overboard was wailing for help. In the rain, the darkness, the residual smoke-screen cloud, and the rough seas, it was hard to find him.

The patrol-boat searchlight pinpointed him. They brought him aboard. Coast Guardsmen tried mouth-to-mouth resuscitation for three hours. But it was no good. The rum captain was dead.

The shot-riddled *Matilda Barry* was hauled into Section Base Eight. Her cargo consisted of 419 sacks of various liquor imports, brought in from an unidentified rum ship below the Chesapeake Capes. Her crewmembers—New Jerseyites George Leaming, Joseph P. Barber, and James Ryan—were turned over to the U.S. marshal at Norfolk. They identified their dead captain as William Bauers, forty-four, of Philadelphia, but subsequent Coast Guard correspondence tagged him as Carl Peterson of Wildwood, New Jersey. He was survived by his wife. *Matilda Barry*, stated the Coast Guard, had been one of the fastest rumrunners on the coast, her two Wright motors and one Liberty engine giving her a top speed of 40 knots. The chase that curtailed her final run had covered more than 5 miles.

Fishermen took up a collection for the rumrunner's widow.

Campaigning on a platform that included a call for the eventual repeal of Prohibition and the immediate legalization of beer, reform-minded Democrat Franklin D. Roosevelt was elected president in 1932. On March 22, 1933, he signed into law the measure, effective April 17, that legalized beer and wine with a maximum 3.2-percent alcohol content. Those opposed to the measure had predicted widespread beer-fueled lawlessness, but civilization survived past April 17. Beer was legal again, and liquor wasn't far behind.